CROSS-CULTURAL ESSENTIALS 8

RESOURCING THE CHURCH

BIBLE TRANSLATION, LITERACY AND CURRICULUM DEVELOPMENT

23 TUTORIALS WITH DISCUSSION
POINTS AND ACTIVITIES

Resourcing the Church
Bible Translation, Literacy Development and Curriculum Development
Church Foundations, Module 8 of the Cross-Cultural Essentials Curriculum

Copyright © 2019, 2016 AccessTruth

Version 1.2

ISBN: 978-0-9944270-1-4

All Rights Reserved. Except as may be permitted by the Copyright Act, no part of this publication may be reproduced in any form or by any means without prior permission from the publisher. Requests for permission should be made to info@accesstruth.com

Scripture quotations marked NASB are from the NEW AMERICAN STANDARD BIBLE®, Copyright © 1960, 1962, 1963, 1968, 1971, 1972, 1973, 1975, 1977, 1995, The Lockman Foundation. Used by permission.

Scripture quotations marked NKJV are from the New King James Version®. Copyright © 1982 by Thomas Nelson. Used by permission. All rights reserved.

Scripture quotations marked NIV are taken from the Holy Bible, New International Version®, NIV®. Copyright © 1973, 1978, 1984, 2011 by Biblica, Inc.™ Used by permission of Zondervan. All rights reserved worldwide. www.zondervan.com The "NIV" and "New International Version" are trademarks registered in the United States Patent and Trademark Office by Biblica, Inc.™

Scripture quotations marked NLT are taken from the Holy Bible, New Living Translation, copyright ©1996, 2004, 2007, 2013, 2015 by Tyndale House Foundation. Used by permission of Tyndale House Publishers, Inc., Carol Stream, Illinois 60188. All rights reserved.

Published by AccessTruth
PO Box 8087
Baulkham Hills NSW 2153
Australia

Email: info@accesstruth.com
Web: accesstruth.com

Cover and interior design by Matthew Hillier
Edited by Simon Glover

Table of Contents

About the Cross-Cultural Essentials Curriculum — 5

TUTORIAL 8.1 — 7
Form and meaning in Bible translation

TUTORIAL 8.2 — 9
Bible translation introduction

TUTORIAL 8.3 — 11
Bible translation introduction 2

TUTORIAL 8.4 — 13
Bible translation in church planting

TUTORIAL 8.5 — 19
Text analysis in Bible translation

TUTORIAL 8.6 — 35
Groupings: Cohesion and Boundaries

TUTORIAL 8.7 — 59
The semantic structure of language

TUTORIAL 8.8 — 73
Propositional structure 1

TUTORIAL 8.9 — 85
Propositional structure 2

TUTORIAL 8.10 — 95
Concept relations within propositions

TUTORIAL 8.11 — 103
Communication relations

TUTORIAL 8.12 — 119
The translation process

TUTORIAL 8.13 127
Assessing the translation

TUTORIAL 8.14 133
What is literacy? Is it important?

TUTORIAL 8.15 141
Assessing literacy needs

TUTORIAL 8.16 181
Developing an orthography

TUTORIAL 8.17 189
Developing literacy materials

TUTORIAL 8.18 207
Teaching literacy and getting community involvement

TUTORIAL 8.19 229
Bible resources for the church

TUTORIAL 8.20 259
Developing Bible resources

TUTORIAL 8.21 269
Ata Bible resources 1

TUTORIAL 8.22 275
Ata Bible resources 2

TUTORIAL 8.23 285
Ata Bible resources 3

About the Cross-Cultural Essentials Curriculum

It's no secret that there are still millions of people in the world living in "unreached" or "least-reached" areas. If you look at the maps, the stats, and the lists of people group names, it's almost overwhelming. The people represented by those numbers can't find out about God, or who Jesus Christ is, or what He did for them because there's no Bible in their language or church in their area – they have *no access* to Truth.

So you could pack a suitcase and jump on a plane, but then what? How would you spend your first day? How would you start learning language? When would you tell them about Jesus? Where would you start? The truth is that a mature, grounded fellowship of God's children doesn't just "happen" in an unreached area or even in your neighborhood. When we speak the Truth, we need to have the confidence that it is still the same Truth when it gets through our hearer's language, culture and worldview grid.

The *Cross-Cultural Essentials* curriculum, made up of 10 individual modules, forms a comprehensive cross-cultural training course. Its main goal is to help equip believers to be effective in providing people access to God's Truth through evangelism and discipleship. The *Cross-Cultural Essentials* curriculum makes it easy to be better equipped for teaching the whole narrative of the Bible, for learning about culture and worldview and for planting a church and seeing it grow.

More information on the curriculum can be found at *accesstruth.com*

Introduction to Module 8: Resourcing the Church

The first part of Module 8 provides readers with a comprehensive guide to the foundational principles of communicating meaning in another language and culture. Bible translation principles and many practical examples with exercises are given to help equip anyone intending to teach or translate God's Word in another context. Later in Module 8, a series of tutorials explore the area of literacy; what it is, how it affects the church in particular, and how to develop and nurture a community literacy project. Finally, is the area of developing Bible teaching curriculum and resources for the church. Helping to present the principles of teamwork and a careful, collaborative approach for curriculum development.

ABOUT THE CROSS-CULTURAL ESSENTIALS CURRICULUM

How to use this module

 Read / watch / listen: Read through the tutorial. If you have an online account at *accesstruth.com*, or the DVD associated with this module you can watch the video or listen to the audio of the tutorial.

 Discussion Points: At the end of some tutorials there are discussion points. It may be helpful to write down your answers so you can process your thoughts. If you are doing the tutorials in a group, these points should prove helpful in guiding the discussion.

 Activities: Some tutorials have activities that involve practical tasks, worksheets that need to be completed, or may just ask for a written answer.

Primary Contributors

Dave Brunn spent over 20 years in Papua New Guinea where he served the Lamogai people through church planting, literacy training and Bible translation and consultation. Among his works is a complete translation of the New Testament into the Lamogai language. Dave is the author of *One Bible Many Versions: Are All Translations Created Equal?*

Linda Mac and her husband, Paul, spent 11 years in Papua New Guinea doing pioneering church planting work among the Ata people group. With no written language Linda worked to see the first Ata literacy program developed. Linda now provides consultancy to others around the world in the areas of language, literacy and culture.

Other Contributors

Paul Mac, John Sharpe, Trevor McIlwain, Mike Griffis, Kaikou Maisu

8.1 Form and meaning in Bible translation

 OBJECTIVES OF THIS TUTORIAL

Learners will recognize the appropriate relationship between form and meaning in Bible translation:
- Demonstrating the impracticality of aiming for total word-for-word correspondence between any two languages.
- Validating meaning-based translation principles as employed to varying degrees by the translators of every version.
- Embracing the primacy of meaning over form in Bible translation.

The next three tutorials require having a copy of the book *One Bible Many Versions: Are All Translations Created Equal? By Dave Brunn* (Downers Grove, IL: InterVarsity Press, 2013). If you don't already have a copy you can purchase a printed copy at most Christian Bookstores or get it on Kindle through Amazon.

ACTIVITIES

1. Watch the "Form and Meaning" video[1] (30 minutes) available on accesstruth.com.

2. Read *One Bible Many Versions: Are All Translations Created Equal?* Chapters 1 and 2.

DISCUSSION POINTS

1. Describe "faithfulness" and "accuracy" in translation.

2. Explain two or three ways in which your understanding of Bible translation was broadened, challenged, or transformed through this tutorial.

3. Explain the axiom "Meaning has priority over Form" – use at least two examples from Scripture.

---

1. Video by InterVarsity Press

8.2 Bible translation introduction 1

✓ OBJECTIVES OF THIS TUTORIAL

The learners will be exposed to some fundamental principles of Bible translation:
- Recognizing the tension between philosophical ideals and real translation practice.
- Understanding that truly consistent "word-for-word" translation is not possible to achieve.
- Learning four basic reasons translators set aside the ideal of reflecting the original form.

This tutorial requires having a copy of the book *One Bible Many Versions: Are All Translations Created Equal? By Dave Brunn.*

BIBLE TRANSLATION INTRODUCTION 1

➡ ACTIVITIES

1. Read *One Bible Many Versions: Are All Translations Created Equal?* Chapters 3, 4 and 5.

2. Give three examples where a literal Bible version chose a rendering outside of its "ideal" range.

3. Using a concordance, an inter-linear translation and/or a lexicon (or the Hebrew and Greek texts if you can read them), find examples where a Hebrew or Greek word is translated differently in various contexts. Give a brief explanation for each context. Here is an example:

logos (Greek)	
Acts 1:1 (ESV)	*logos* is translated *"book"* since it refers to the entire book of Acts
Gal 5:14 (HCSB)	*logos* is translated *"statement"* since it refers to a phrase instead of a word
1 Cor 14:19 (NASB)	*logos* is translated *"words"* since it refers to single words

Make charts patterned after the logos chart above for at least three different Hebrew or Greek words, giving three contexts where those words are translated differently.

4. See Figure 5.1 ("Adjustment Flowchart") in chapter 5 of *One Bible, Many Versions*:

- Find five footnotes in a literal English version where the translators acknowledge making an "adjustment." (Do NOT use footnotes which mark differences between manuscripts.)

- For each footnote, state the reason(s) for the adjustment: 1) grammar, 2) correct meaning, 3) clarity, 4) naturalness. In some cases, it could be more than one of these reasons. Here is an example:

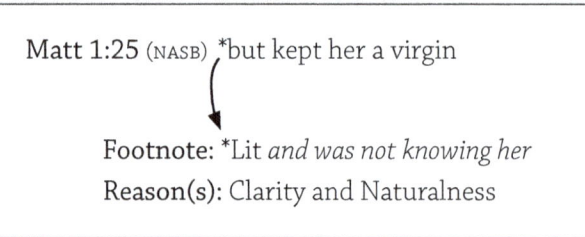

8.3 Bible translation introduction 2

 OBJECTIVES OF THIS TUTORIAL

Learners will be exposed to some additional principles of Bible translation:
- To understand the relation between the doctrine of inspiration of and the practice of translation.
- To perceive more fully the challenge of translation within the worldwide linguistic context.
- To recognize the value of using an assortment of Bible versions.

This tutorial requires having a copy of the book *One Bible Many Versions: Are All Translations Created Equal? By Dave Brunn.*

BIBLE TRANSLATION INTRODUCTION 2

➡ ACTIVITIES

1. Read *One Bible Many Versions: Are All Translations Created Equal?* Chapters 6, 7 and 10 (chapters 8 and 9 are also recommended, but not required).

❓ DISCUSSION POINTS

1. Look through the footnotes in a literal English version of the Bible and do the following:

Find three places where the translators chose to omit a Hebrew or Greek word, and not reflect it in their translation. Briefly explain why they left the word untranslated. Consider the four criteria for adjustment in *One Bible, Many Versions*, chapter 5, figure 5.1.

Find three places where the translators chose to add a word (or words) not in the original. Briefly explain why. Consider the four criteria for adjustment.

Find one place where the translators substituted a modern equivalent term (a word or a phrase) in place of a biblical term.

2. Discuss why it is important to look, not only at English, but also at other languages when determining what is acceptable translation practice.

3. In chapter 10 of *One Bible, Many Versions*, there is a list of twenty-six bullet points that itemizes translation practices used in every English Bible version. Choose two of these points that were particularly eye opening or impactful to you personally. Reflect on and interact with these two points, explaining their significance.

8.4 Bible translation in church planting

✓ OBJECTIVES OF THIS TUTORIAL

Learners will gain a sense of the level of commitment necessary for doing Bible translation and correlate the importance of translated vernacular Scriptures with effective church planting.

Translation: is it worth the time, effort and sacrifice?

Translating God's Word into a previously unwritten language requires a serious commitment of painstakingly careful effort over a period of several years.

The Old Testament has over 23,000 verses. The recommended Old Testament portions for a foundational Bible teaching program total about 4,000 verses. The New Testament consists of about 8,000 verses. That means when we are all finished, we could end up translating about 12,000 verses—about one and a half times the volume of the New Testament.

No sacrifice too great

In the sixteenth century, William Tyndale devoted his time and effort to translating God's Word into the English language. Since translating the Bible into English was outlawed in England, Tyndale went to Germany to work on his translation.

In 1526, the first copies of the newly translated New Testament were smuggled into England. Tyndale then pressed ahead with Old Testament translation, completing the Pentateuch in 1530. In 1535, William Tyndale was betrayed into the hands of the authorities and thrown into prison. In 1536, he was burned at the stake as a heretic.

William Tyndale gave a lot more than just "time" and "effort." He gave his life to see God's Word translated into the English language. Many generations of English speakers have benefited greatly from his sacrifice.

It is unlikely that we will be asked to die for the sake of Bible translation. But we should have the same unwavering commitment to making the written Word of God available to people who have never had access to it in their own language.

Do we appreciate what it means to have the "written Word"?

We who are English speakers have the written Word of God so readily available that we may tend to take it for granted. There are many good translations in English and more are being produced all the time. But for much of the world, it is not that way.

There are about 7,000 *living languages* in the world today.[1] About 22% have translation work in progress. About 13% have at least one BOOK of Scripture. Another 15% have just the New Testament. Another 6% (including English) have entire Bible. And about 44% have a probable translation need—more survey work needs to be done.

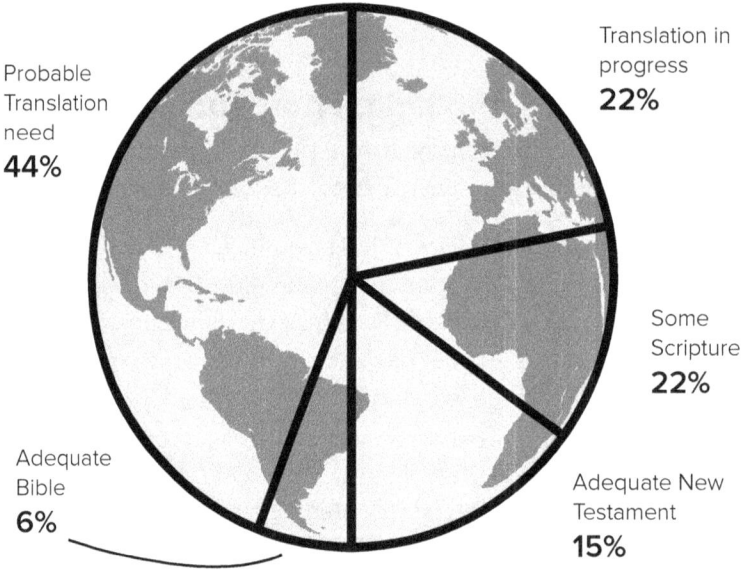

Only 1/3 of the world's languages have some or all of the Bible. That means 66% (2/3) of the world's language groups still have little or no Scripture.

If we consider the minimum amount of translated Scripture for any given language group to be a complete New Testament, with some Old Testament portions, there is still an urgent need for a translation in about 80% (4/5) of the languages of the world.

---

1. M. Paul Lewis, ed., Ethnologue: Languages of the World, 16th ed. (Dallas: SIL International, 2009), www.ethnologue.com

Geographic breakdown of the world's languages

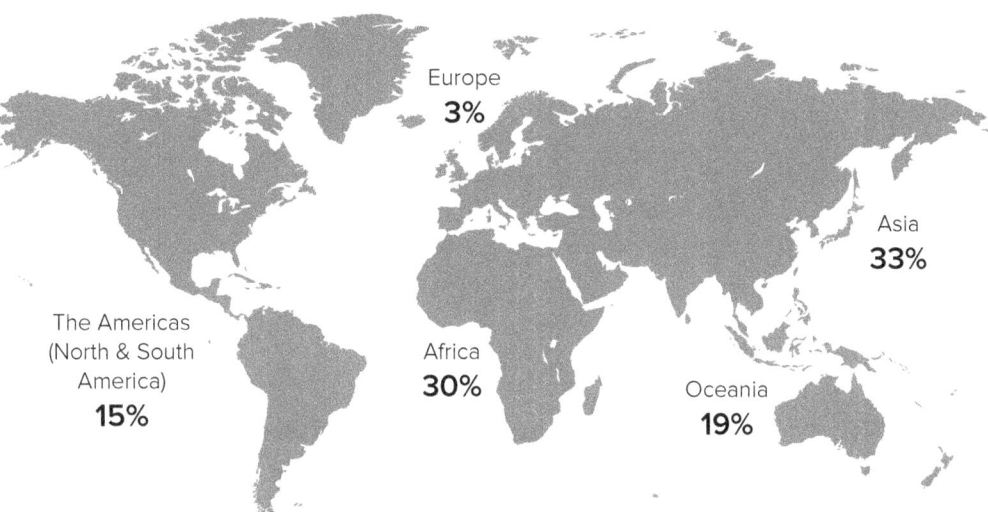

Asia and Oceania are often combined and considered as one geographical region. These two regions together account for more than half of the world's languages—about 52%. That's not half of the world's population—it's half of the world's languages. It actually accounts well over half of the population because about 60% of the world lives in Asia.

The "written Word" is God's chosen means of communication

In ancient times, God communicated His Word orally. Sometimes He spoke directly to individuals; sometimes He communicated through the prophets, giving His message directly to a prophet who would communicate that message to the rest of the people.

Today, however, everything we know about God and His truth comes from His written Word. That is the means God chose for communicating His truth to us, so it makes sense that we should use this same means to pass it on to others.

The basis of a foundational teaching program

In order for a Bible teaching program to be effective, it must be based on a clear translation of God's Word. The first thing we do in a foundational Bible teaching program is establish the fact that God's written Word is the underlying authority for everything we teach. It is a trustworthy benchmark that we can always go back to. It contains the eyewitness accounts.

When we did foundational teaching among the Lamogai people of Papua New Guinea, we continually emphasized the fact that God's Word is the ultimate standard. We reminded them that we were not telling them "our" thinking or someone else's thinking; we were telling them God's truth.

We said, "If someone tells you something that lines up with God's Word, it is true. But if someone tries to tell you something that does *not* line up with God's Word, it is false."

The emphasis the Lamogai believers received on the authority of God's written Word would make it difficult for anyone to come into their area and turn aside any significant number of the believers to false teachings. Obviously, there will always be some on the fringe who could be turned aside, but it is unlikely that would happen to the church as a whole.

God's Word in written form assures preserved accuracy

If we do not give the target audience God's Word in written form, what assurance do we have that the message will remain pure after we are gone? Without God's written Word, the message can drift. God's written Word needs to be the core of future teaching and outreaches by the churches we plant.

It must be our goal, not just to plant churches, but to plant strong, lasting churches that will perpetuate the Gospel to succeeding generations. If we do not give them God's Word in a written form in their own language it is less likely that the churches we plant will be "lasting" churches.

Believers feeding themselves

A strong church is made up of strong Christians. We will never have a strong church if the church members are not able to feed themselves spiritually. Bible teaching meetings are important for giving spiritual nourishment to every believer, but it is also important that each believer have the opportunity to feed himself or herself outside of the teaching sessions.

When we taught the Lamogai believers, we continually emphasized to them that the Bible is not just another book—it is the living and powerful Word of God. "*Faith comes by hearing and hearing by the Word of God.*" (Romans 10:17 NKJV) We told them that God's Word is our "spiritual food." It helps us to grow spiritually.

I think we all understand this principle, but sometimes we give priority to other things in our lives. Relating this to our physical food, when is the last time you forgot to eat? Have you ever said something like this? "*I don't have time to eat this week. There are too many things going on. Next week, I'll make up for it and take double-sized portions at every meal.*"

Or maybe you have said: *"Hey, I have been so busy that I hadn't thought about it, but I just realized I haven't had a bite to eat in three days."* For me that only happens when I'm sick. That's when I can easily forget about eating. I don't want any food.

A person who is healthy and physically active will get hungry. In the same way, a person who is spiritually healthy and spiritually active will have an increased hunger for God's Word.

Another thing that can cause me to have no appetite at mealtime is if I am already full of something else—junk food, for example. If we are full of spiritual junk food, then we won't have much of an appetite for God's Word.

We are abundantly blessed! In the home countries where most of us come from, we have an abundance of food compared to much of the rest of the world. Sometimes we can be very wasteful with our food. Also, in our home countries, God's Word is more available than in many other parts of the world. Let's not waste this precious resource.

We can't expect the individual new believers to feed themselves spiritually if we don't give them God's Word in written form. It must be the conviction of every church planter that we cannot plant lasting, indigenous churches without the written Word of God in the heart language of the target people.

❓ DISCUSSION POINTS

1. Visualize writing out a *Church Planting Strategy Statement*. Realizing that translation involves a lot of hard work, and there may be pressures to try to do church planting without doing translation, consider this question:

"Why is Bible translation a necessary part of the overall church planting effort?"

As you answer this question, make a list of reasons to be recorded in your written *Strategy Statement*. This list is for you to go back to in the event you consider omitting translation from your church planting effort.

8.5 Text analysis in Bible translation

OBJECTIVES OF THIS TUTORIAL

Learners will be exposed to some fundamental principles of text analysis including:
- Communication Situation
- Discourse Genre
- Embedded Discourses
- Thematic and Non-thematic Material in Narrative Discourse

In translation we work with texts - not just words

Translation consists of transferring the meaning of the Source Language (SL) text into a text in the Receptor Language (RL). The receptor language is also called the Target Language. In Bible translation, the SL text is the portion of Scripture you will be translating. The RL text is the same Scripture portion in the language you will have learned before you begin to translate.

Discourse Analysis of Receptor Language Text

Prior to beginning translation, you, or someone else working in the receptor language, will have done text analysis (also called "discourse analysis") of the receptor language to determine the grammatical forms used to express meaning on every level.

Exegesis of Source Language Text

The first step in the actual process of translating is exegesis, which is "text analysis" to discover the meaning of the source language text or passage to be translated. In the model illustrated in *figure 1*, the downward arrow represents *exegesis*. The upward arrow represents the actual *translation*.[1]

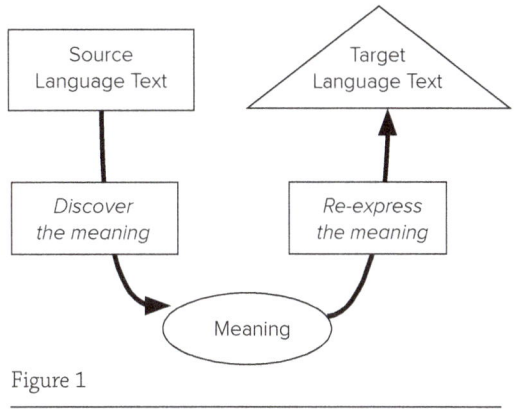

Figure 1

---

1. Mildred L. Larson, Meaning Based Translation: a guide to cross-language equivalence, revised edition, (Lanham, MD: University Press of America, 1998), p. 4 display 1.1; see also Katharine Barnwell, Introduction to Semantics and Translation (Horsleys Green, UK: Summer Institute of Linguistics, 1974, 1980), p.14.

The Communication Situation[2]

In Bible translation, as in Bible teaching, it is dangerous to take a word, phrase, or verse out of context. However, it is important that we consider more than just the grammatical context. The Communication Situation includes the entire *life context*. Below are some features of the Communication Situation:

The Author
Who was the author? What was the attitude of the author toward the information he communicated? What was his attitude toward his target audience?

Purpose of Author
What is the discourse genre? (We will discuss this in a moment.) The particular discourse type chosen by the author will depend on his purpose for writing.

Audience/recipients
Who was the original audience? Where did they live? What was the relationship between the author and his audience? Who is your target audience? How much information is shared by the audience who originally read the source text and the audience who will read your translation? What was the educational level of the original audience? What is the educational level of your target audience?

Setting
What historical situation occasioned the original writing? What was the location of the writing? What was the time of the writing?

Culture
Culture is a complex set of beliefs, attitudes, values, and rules which a group of people share. The writer of the source document understood the culture of the audience for which he wrote. This mutual understanding affects the writing. As a translator, you will need to have a basic understanding of the cultural assumptions made by the author in order to accurately understand the meaning of the source text, and adequately translate it for a people who have a different set of beliefs, attitudes, values, and rules.

Discourse Genre[3]

One of the first things a translator needs to do is identify the discourse genre (discourse type) of the document or passage to be translated. Various discourse types are appropriate for writing about different kinds of subjects. There are many kinds of discourse genres in English, both written and spoken. For example the *Business Letter Genre*:

---

2. Larson, Meaning Based Translation, pp. 34-36.
3. Ibid., pp. 399-423.

certain features of business letters make them distinct from other written discourse. Also, the *Fairy Tale Genre*: What is the opening line of a Fairy Tale? And what is the closing line?[4]

In our discussion about Bible translation, we will limit our focus to three main types of discourse: *narrative*, *explanatory* and *hortatory*. These main types include sub-types which we will mention briefly, but not highlight.

Narrative Discourse
The normal purpose of narrative discourse is to relate a series of events—usually in the past—which is either real or imaginary (mythological). Narratives tell a story. Much of what is written in the four Gospels and the book of Acts is narrative discourse. Also most of the Old Testament portions recommended for a foundational teaching program are narrative. A sub-type of narrative discourse is "dialogue," which incorporates direct speech exchange along with a series of "narrative" events recounted by a narrator.

Explanatory Discourse
The normal purpose of explanatory (also called expository) discourse is to instruct or inform about a certain topic. A sub-type of explanatory discourse is "descriptive" which gives information about an item or event.

Hortatory Discourse
The purpose of hortatory discourse is to exhort, command, suggest, recommend, convince, deride, correct, warn, etc. A sub-type of hortatory discourse is "procedural," which imparts a step-by-step process.

Each language has its own way of constructing various discourse genres. It is important that every translator and cross-cultural communicator have a good understanding of how the target language constructs various kinds of discourses. The discourse structure of our translated materials needs to come through in a way that is clear and natural to the hearers.

Embedded Discourses
It is very common for a text to have one primary genre with several smaller embedded discourses of other genres. Direct speech within quotation marks is often embedded discourse material of another genre. In a *narrative* discourse, for example, a direct quote could be an embedded *explanatory* or *hortatory* discourse.

---

[4]. Answers: a) "Once upon a time…" b) "…and they lived happily ever after."

Here is an example from Mark chapter 1 (NASB):

- **Verse 4** tells us that John the Baptist was preaching in the wilderness. The text is narrative at this point.
- **Verse 5** continues the narrative telling about *all the people listening to John* and *being baptized by him*.
- Then **verses 7 and 8** contain a direct quote: "*After me One is coming who is mightier than I, and I am not fit to stoop down and untie the thong of His sandals. I baptized you with water; but He will baptize you with the Holy Spirit.*"

What genre is this direct quote? It is an embedded explanatory discourse. It gives an explanation about the coming Messiah. After the quote of verses 7 and 8, the narrative series of events is resumed in verse 9 with the statement, "*In those days Jesus came…*"

Later, in verse 15, we see another quote: Jesus said, "*…repent and believe in the gospel.*" What genre is this direct quote? This is an embedded *hortatory* discourse. Jesus was giving an exhortation, instructing the listeners to follow a particular course of action.

Non-Thematic (Background) Material[5]

Another kind of embedded discourse is *non-thematic material* (also called background material) within a text. Non-thematic material is generally a short discourse of another genre, which reflects the perspective of the narrator.

There is an example of non-thematic material in the first part of Mark chapter 1.

- In **verses 4 and 5** we see a series of events taking place: John preached, people came, people were baptized, and people confessed their sins.
- Then in **verse 6** the narrator steps outside of the chronological series of events to give a description of John's clothing and food: "*John was clothed with camel's hair and wore a leather belt around his waist, and his diet was locusts and wild honey.*"
- After that, **verse 7** resumes the series of events with "John preaching…"

The narrator's comment in verse 6 is an *embedded explanatory discourse*. It is non-thematic (background) material. It is *not* part of the theme line; it is not included in the actual series of events.

---

5. Larson, Meaning Based Translation, pp. 441-57.

Thematic and Non-thematic Information Defined[6]

Thematic information (foreground) in narrative discourse is:

- The main event line.
- It is the plot; what actually happened.

Non-thematic information (background) is:

- ... added to make the main series of events easier to understand.
- It is not really crucial to the plot.
- It identifies characters.
- Describes settings.
- Speaks of alternative possibilities that do not actually happen.
- Gives the narrator's personal ideas or experiences.

Two Common Tests of Non-thematic Information:[7]

- It can usually be left out without disturbing the rest of the narrative.
- It may be expressed at one of a number of points without affecting the theme line.

For example, in Mark 1, if we left out the non-thematic information of verse 6, or moved it to another place in the narrative, the rest of the passage would still make sense from a purely grammatical perspective.

Of course, I am *not* suggesting that any translator leave out non-thematic material (or any other material) from a passage of Scripture! I am merely using this as an example of how the "tests" for non-thematic information work. These tests can help us identify non-thematic material within narrative discourse.

Examples from Genesis and Acts

Look at the examples below of thematic and non-thematic information. Compare each occurrence of non-thematic information with the *definition* of non-thematic information as explained above. Also notice how each occurrence meets the two "tests" of

---

6. Joseph Grimes, The Thread of Discourse, (The Hague: Mouton, 1975); Stout, M. and R. Thomson. "Kayapo narrative," in International Journal of American Linguistics, 37:250-256 (1971); Grimes, J. and N. Glock, "A Saramacan narrative pattern," in Language 46:408-425 (1970).
7. Grimes, The Thread of Discourse.

non-thematic information. Read through the left-hand column (*thematic* material) by itself, leaving out the right-hand column (*non-thematic* material). Notice that the theme line flows smoothly without the non-thematic information. Again, I am not suggesting anyone leave out non-thematic material when translating Scripture; I am merely using these examples for illustrative purposes.

Next, try moving some of the sections of non-thematic information, inserting them into different places in their respective texts.

It is not always possible to move every piece of non-thematic information. Just because you cannot move it, does not mean it is not non-thematic information. These "tests" are often helpful for identifying non-thematic material, but they are not foolproof.

Genesis 13:1-2

Thematic	Non-thematic
So Abram went up from Egypt to the Negev, with his wife and everything he had and Lot went with him.	
	Abram had become very wealthy in livestock and in silver and gold.
From the Negev he went from place to place until he came to Bethel…	

Genesis 12:4-5

Thematic	Non-thematic
So Abram left	
	as the Lord had told him:
and Lot went with him.	
	Abram was seventy-five years old when he set out from Haran.
He took his wife Sarai, his nephew Lot, and all the possessions they had accumulated and the people they had acquired in Haran, and they set out for the land of Canaan…	

Acts 12: 2-4

Thematic	Non-thematic
[Herod] had James, the brother of John, put to death with the sword. When he saw that this pleased the Jews, he proceeded to seize Peter also.	
	This happened during the Feast of Unleavened Bread.
After arresting him, he put him in prison…	

Non-Thematic Does NOT Mean "Unimportant"

Calling a portion of text "non-thematic" information does not mean it is not important. It may be a very important piece of information. It is called "non-thematic" simply because it does not cause the plot or main series of events to advance forward. Non-thematic information is a part of a discourse in the same way that a prefix or suffix is part of a word. Prefixes and suffixes are less prominent than the central part of the word, but that does not mean they are not important.

On the word level, *nouns* and *verbs* usually have the greatest prominence. But that does not mean that *adjectives* or *connectors* are insignificant. They also play a very important role, even though they function in a "non-thematic" way. So it is in discourse. Thematic information has the most prominence, but non-thematic information is also important.

Grammatical Marking of Non-thematic Information

In Lamogai narratives, recapitulation (restatement) is a common way of marking non-thematic material. Normally there would be no recapitulation before the non-thematic information. Then after the non-thematic information, there would be recapitulation of the most recent clause of the event line—the clause that immediately preceded the non-thematic information. Look at the following example from a Lamogai text:

Thematic	Non-thematic
We went with them and went and went and _arrived_ at their village.	
	The name of their village is Tapulpu.
We _arrived_ at their village and then we went to the men's house.	

Notice the recapitulation of the word "arrived," which picks up the theme line after the insertion of the non-thematic information.

Another Lamogai Example:

Thematic	Non-thematic
As we were going, my wife and I _went on ahead_.	
	I was really sick. I was so sick I could hardly walk.
We _went on ahead_ and we slept at Arar.	

In both of the above-mentioned Lamogai examples, the recapitulation picks up the event line and flows on naturally just as if the non-thematic information was not there.

Recapitulation in Lamogai narratives preserves the continuity of the event line when non-thematic information is inserted.

English Does the Same Thing

In the example of Genesis 13:1-2, the word "Negev" acts as a link, picking up the theme line after the non-thematic material has been introduced within the series of events.

Genesis 13:1-2

Thematic	Non-thematic
So Abram went up from Egypt to the _Negev_, with his wife and everything he had and Lot went with him.	
	Abram had become very wealthy in livestock and in silver and gold.
From the _Negev_ he went from place to place until he came to Bethel…	

An Example from Mark 1

We already noted that Mark 1:6 is background (non-thematic) information. In verse 7, the theme line is picked up again by recapitulating the verb "preaching" from verse 4.

Mark 1:4-7

Thematic	Non-thematic
⁴John the Baptist appeared in the wilderness _preaching_… ⁵And all the country of Judea was going out to him…and they were being baptized by him in the Jordan River…	
	⁶John was clothed with camel's hair and wore a leather belt around his waist, and his diet was locusts and wild honey.
⁷And he was _preaching_ and saying…	

Avoiding Mismatch

Every language has its own way of handling _thematic_ and _non-thematic_ material. When a translator does not handle the _thematic_ and _non-thematic_ material correctly, it can be confusing to the reader. As a translation consultant, working with translators, this is an area that often requires special attention.

One time I was working through Mark 1:4-7 with an expatriate translator. The translator read the verses aloud in the target language, and then I asked one of the mother-tongue speakers to explain the meaning in Melanesian Pidgin (the trade language of Papua New Guinea). When he did, it was apparent that the non-thematic information was not handled correctly. This is how the native speaker explained the passage to me in Melanesian Pidgin:

- John was preaching (people came, were baptized, etc.)…
- _Then John put on some clothes made of camel hair…_
- _Then he put a leather belt around his waist…_
- _Then he ate some locusts…_
- _And he ate some wild honey…_
- After John finished eating, he started preaching again…

The translator unintentionally translated the *non-thematic* material of verse 6 in such a way that it sounded like *thematic* material to the mother-tongue speakers.

Alternate Purposes of Discourse Genre (Skewing)[8]

In most cases, the discourse genre of each passage reflects the purpose of the author: *narrative* genre tells a story, *explanatory* genre instructs or explains, and *hortatory* genre exhorts. But sometimes authors use the various kinds of discourses to accomplish something other than their normal purposes. This is called "skewing."

For example, a *parable* is a "narrative" discourse, but the underlying purpose is not just to tell a story. It is usually intended to either exhort (hortatory), or to give an explanation (explanatory). We will talk more about "skewing" in later tutorials.

 ACTIVITIES

1. Research and Compile Communication Situation Information for the Gospel of Mark.

- Reread the notes at the beginning of this tutorial as a reminder of the kinds of information included in the "Communication Situation."
- When you research the Communication Situation, read through the book introduction at the beginning of the Gospel of Mark in a Study Bible. Also read through the introductory material in a commentary on the Gospel of Mark.

2. Read Mark chapters 1 and 2 in several different versions.

- Use both literal and nonliteral versions.
- Include other-language versions if you know another language.

3. Locate and Identify Embedded Discourses in Mark 1 and 2 – Use the *Tutorial 8.5 Activity Sheet - page 30*.

Mark each Quote, identifying its discourse type: Explanatory, Hortatory or Narrative.

- Mark each instance of *Non-Thematic Material*, identifying its discourse type: Explanatory, Hortatory or Narrative.
- See *Sample Activity Sheet* on the following page for an example.

---

8. Larson, Meaning Based Translation, pp. 419-20.

TUTORIAL 8.5

Sample Activity Sheet

Mark 1 (NASB)

¹The beginning of the gospel of Jesus Christ, the Son of God.

²As it is written in Isaiah the prophet: "BEHOLD, I SEND MY MESSENGER AHEAD OF YOU, WHO WILL PREPARE YOUR WAY; — *Quote: Explanatory discourse*

³THE VOICE OF ONE CRYING IN THE WILDERNESS, 'MAKE READY THE WAY OF THE LORD, MAKE HIS PATHS STRAIGHT.'"

⁴John the Baptist appeared in the wilderness preaching a baptism of repentance for the forgiveness of sins.

⁵And all the country of Judea was going out to him, and all the people of Jerusalem; and they were being baptized by him in the Jordan River, confessing their sins.

⁶John was clothed with camel's hair and wore a leather belt around his waist, and his diet was locusts and wild honey. — *Non-thematic: Explanatory discourse*

⁷And he was preaching, and saying, "After me One is coming who is mightier than I, and I am not fit to stoop down and untie the thong of His sandals. — *Quote: Explanatory discourse*

⁸I baptized you with water; but He will baptize you with the Holy Spirit."

⁹In those days Jesus came from Nazareth in Galilee and was baptized by John in the Jordan.

¹⁰Immediately coming up out of the water, He saw the heavens opening, and the Spirit like a dove descending upon Him;

¹¹and a voice came out of the heavens: "You are My beloved Son, in You I am well-pleased." — *Quote: Explanatory discourse*

¹²Immediately the Spirit impelled Him to go out into the wilderness.

¹³And He was in the wilderness forty days being tempted by Satan; and He was with the wild beasts, and the angels were ministering to Him.

¹⁴Now after John had been taken into custody, Jesus came into Galilee, preaching the gospel of God,

¹⁵and saying, "The time is fulfilled, and the kingdom of God is at hand; repent and believe in the gospel." — *Quote: Explanatory & Hortatory discourse*

¹⁶As He was going along by the Sea of Galilee, He saw Simon and Andrew, the brother of Simon, casting a net in the sea; for they were fishermen. — *Non-thematic: Explanatory discourse*

¹⁷And Jesus said to them, "Follow Me, and I will make you become fishers of men." — *Quote: Hortatory discourse*

29

Tutorial 8.5 Activity Sheet

LOCATE and MARK Embedded Discourse Material in Mark 1 and 2.

- Quotes
- Non-thematic Material
- Determine the genre of each embedded discourse

Mark 1 (NASB)

[1]The beginning of the gospel of Jesus Christ, the Son of God.

[2]As it is written in Isaiah the prophet: "BEHOLD, I SEND MY MESSENGER AHEAD OF YOU, WHO WILL PREPARE YOUR WAY;

[3]THE VOICE OF ONE CRYING IN THE WILDERNESS, 'MAKE READY THE WAY OF THE LORD, MAKE HIS PATHS STRAIGHT.'"

[4]John the Baptist appeared in the wilderness preaching a baptism of repentance for the forgiveness of sins.

[5]And all the country of Judea was going out to him, and all the people of Jerusalem; and they were being baptized by him in the Jordan River, confessing their sins.

[6]John was clothed with camel's hair and wore a leather belt around his waist, and his diet was locusts and wild honey.

[7]And he was preaching, and saying, "After me One is coming who is mightier than I, and I am not fit to stoop down and untie the thong of His sandals.

[8]I baptized you with water; but He will baptize you with the Holy Spirit."

[9]In those days Jesus came from Nazareth in Galilee and was baptized by John in the Jordan.

[10]Immediately coming up out of the water, He saw the heavens opening, and the Spirit like a dove descending upon Him;

[11]and a voice came out of the heavens: "You are My beloved Son, in You I am well-pleased."

[12]Immediately the Spirit impelled Him to go out into the wilderness.

[13]And He was in the wilderness forty days being tempted by Satan; and He was with the wild beasts, and the angels were ministering to Him.

[14]Now after John had been taken into custody, Jesus came into Galilee, preaching the gospel of God,

[15]and saying, "The time is fulfilled, and the kingdom of God is at hand; repent and believe in the gospel."

[16]As He was going along by the Sea of Galilee, He saw Simon and Andrew, the

brother of Simon, casting a net in the sea; for they were fishermen.

17 And Jesus said to them, "Follow Me, and I will make you become fishers of men."

18 Immediately they left their nets and followed Him.

19 Going on a little farther, He saw James the son of Zebedee, and John his brother, who were also in the boat mending the nets.

20 Immediately He called them; and they left their father Zebedee in the boat with the hired servants, and went away to follow Him.

21 They went into Capernaum; and immediately on the Sabbath He entered the synagogue and began to teach.

22 They were amazed at His teaching; for He was teaching them as one having authority, and not as the scribes.

23 Just then there was a man in their synagogue with an unclean spirit; and he cried out,

24 saying, "What business do we have with each other, Jesus of Nazareth? Have You come to destroy us? I know who You are—the Holy One of God!"

25 And Jesus rebuked him, saying, "Be quiet, and come out of him!"

26 Throwing him into convulsions, the unclean spirit cried out with a loud voice and came out of him.

27 They were all amazed, so that they debated among themselves, saying, What is this? A new teaching with authority!

He commands even the unclean spirits, and they obey Him.

28 Immediately the news about Him spread everywhere into all the surrounding district of Galilee.

29 And immediately after they came out of the synagogue, they came into the house of Simon and Andrew, with James and John.

30 Now Simon's mother-in-law was lying sick with a fever; and immediately they spoke to Jesus about her.

31 And He came to her and raised her up, taking her by the hand, and the fever left her, and she waited on them.

32 When evening came, after the sun had set, they began bringing to Him all who were ill and those who were demon-possessed.

33 And the whole city had gathered at the door.

34 And He healed many who were ill with various diseases, and cast out many demons; and He was not permitting the demons to speak, because they knew who He was.

35 In the early morning, while it was still dark, Jesus got up, left the house, and went away to a secluded place, and was praying there.

36 Simon and his companions searched for Him;

37 they found Him, and said to Him, "Everyone is looking for You."

38 He said to them, "Let us go somewhere else to the towns nearby, so that

I may preach there also; for that is what I came for."

³⁹And He went into their synagogues throughout all Galilee, preaching and casting out the demons.

⁴⁰And a leper came to Jesus, beseeching Him and falling on his knees before Him, and saying, "If You are willing, You can make me clean."

⁴¹Moved with compassion, Jesus stretched out His hand and touched him, and said to him, "I am willing; be cleansed."

⁴²Immediately the leprosy left him and he was cleansed.

⁴³And He sternly warned him and immediately sent him away,

⁴⁴and He said to him, "See that you say nothing to anyone; but go, show yourself to the priest and offer for your cleansing what Moses commanded, as a testimony to them."

⁴⁵But he went out and began to proclaim it freely and to spread the news around, to such an extent that Jesus could no longer publicly enter a city, but stayed out in unpopulated areas; and they were coming to Him from everywhere.

Mark 2 (NASB)

¹When He had come back to Capernaum several days afterward, it was heard that He was at home.

²And many were gathered together, so that there was no longer room, not even near the door; and He was speaking the word to them.

³And they came, bringing to Him a paralytic, carried by four men.

⁴Being unable to get to Him because of the crowd, they removed the roof above Him; and when they had dug an opening, they let down the pallet on which the paralytic was lying.

⁵And Jesus seeing their faith said to the paralytic, "Son, your sins are forgiven."

⁶But some of the scribes were sitting there and reasoning in their hearts,

⁷"Why does this man speak that way? He is blaspheming; who can forgive sins but God alone?"

⁸Immediately Jesus, aware in His spirit that they were reasoning that way within themselves, said to them, "Why are you reasoning about these things in your hearts?

⁹Which is easier, to say to the paralytic, 'Your sins are forgiven'; or to say, 'Get up, and pick up your pallet and walk'?

¹⁰But so that you may know that the Son of Man has authority on earth to forgive sins"—He said to the paralytic,

¹¹"I say to you, get up, pick up your pallet and go home."

¹²And he got up and immediately picked up the pallet and went out in the sight of everyone, so that they were all amazed and were glorifying God, saying, "We have never seen anything like this."

¹³And He went out again by the seashore; and all the people were coming to Him, and He was teaching them.

¹⁴As He passed by, He saw Levi the son of Alphaeus sitting in the tax booth, and He said to him, "Follow Me!" And he got up and followed Him.

¹⁵And it happened that He was reclining at the table in his house, and many tax collectors and sinners were dining with Jesus and His disciples; for there were many of them, and they were following Him.

¹⁶When the scribes of the Pharisees saw that He was eating with the sinners and tax collectors, they said to His disciples, "Why is He eating and drinking with tax collectors and sinners?"

¹⁷And hearing this, Jesus said to them, "It is not those who are healthy who need a physician, but those who are sick; I did not come to call the righteous, but sinners."

¹⁸John's disciples and the Pharisees were fasting; and they came and said to Him, "Why do John's disciples and the disciples of the Pharisees fast, but Your disciples do not fast?"

¹⁹And Jesus said to them, "While the bridegroom is with them, the attendants of the bridegroom cannot fast, can they? So long as they have the bridegroom with them, they cannot fast.

²⁰But the days will come when the bridegroom is taken away from them, and then they will fast in that day.

²¹"No one sews a patch of unshrunk cloth on an old garment; otherwise the patch pulls away from it, the new from the old, and a worse tear results.

²²No one puts new wine into old wineskins; otherwise the wine will burst the skins, and the wine is lost and the skins as well; but one puts new wine into fresh wineskins."

²³And it happened that He was passing through the grainfields on the Sabbath, and His disciples began to make their way along while picking the heads of grain.

²⁴The Pharisees were saying to Him, "Look, why are they doing what is not lawful on the Sabbath?"

²⁵And He said to them, "Have you never read what David did when he was in need and he and his companions became hungry;

²⁶how he entered the house of God in the time of Abiathar the high priest, and ate the consecrated bread, which is not lawful for anyone to eat except the priests, and he also gave it to those who were with him?"

²⁷Jesus said to them, "The Sabbath was made for man, and not man for the Sabbath.

²⁸So the Son of Man is Lord even of the Sabbath."

8.6 Groupings: Cohesion and Boundaries

 OBJECTIVES OF THIS TUTORIAL

Learners will gain an understanding of how smaller language units, such as words, phrases, and sentences, group together to form larger units on the paragraph level and above. They will be able to recognize and describe cohesion and boundaries in both the grammatical and semantic realms.

Form and Meaning

In doing text analysis it is essential that we have a clear understanding of the distinction between the *form* of the message and the *meaning* of the message. Sometimes the "form" is called the *grammatical and lexical*[1] features or the *surface structure*. And the "meaning" is described as the *semantics*, or the *deep structure*. See chart below.

Form	Meaning
Grammatical (and Lexical) Features	Semantics
Surface Structure	Deep Structure

- The *form* includes the actual language units such as words, phrases, clauses, sentences.
- The *form* also includes the way the language units are structured together.

- The *meaning* includes the concepts and inferences conveyed by language units.
- The *meaning* also includes the significant (meaningful) relationships between the units.

As we discuss the contrast between *form* and *meaning* in today's tutorial, we will use the term "*grammatical features*" (for form), and "*semantics*" (for meaning) to describe these two elements of communication and the contrast between them.

---

1. "Lexical" (or "lexicon") primarily refers to words, but it is a broader term that also includes units smaller than words such as prefixes and suffixes (morphemes).

GROUPINGS: COHESION AND BOUNDARIES

In every language on earth, the essence of communication is wrapped up in the relationship between the *grammatical features* and the *semantics*. These two elements of communication function together on all levels of language - from the morpheme and word levels all the way up to the highest discourse levels. It will be important to keep these principles in mind as we consider *groupings* in today's lesson.

Groupings[2]

In language there are *groupings* on many levels. Words group together to form sentences, sentences group together to form paragraphs, and paragraphs group together to form larger discourse units.

Every morpheme, word, phrase, clause, sentence, and paragraph is a single unit both semantically and grammatically. (We'll discuss the difference in a few minutes.) On every level, with every kind of language unit (word, phrase, sentence, etc.) we must ask the question, "What causes this word or phrase or sentence to be considered a single unit?" That question may be fairly easy to answer on the lower levels, such as words, and phrases. But what about the higher levels such as paragraphs? When we indent to mark a new paragraph, we are indicating that this new paragraph is a single language unit.

- How do we know where we should indent?
- How do we know what constitutes a paragraph?
- And how do we know when one paragraph ends and another begins?

The answers to these questions are the focus of today's tutorial. The three key essentials of communication that will give us the answers are *groupings*, *cohesion* and *boundaries*.

Cohesion and Boundaries[3]

The two primary elements that signal paragraph *groupings* (and groupings above the paragraph level) are *cohesion* and *boundaries*. For now we will just focus on the paragraph level.

- *Cohesion* includes all the criteria that produce internal interconnectedness within each unit. Cohesion is the "glue" that joins smaller languages units together to form larger units.
- *Boundaries* are the criteria that indicate a shift from one unit to another unit. With paragraphs, for example, *boundaries* let us know where one paragraph ends and the next paragraph begins.

---

2. Mildred L. Larson, Meaning Based Translation: a guide to cross-language equivalence, revised edition, (Lanham, MD: University Press of America, 1998), pp. 381-97; 425-40.
3. Ibid.

When we identify a *paragraph* within a text, there should be some kind of internal *cohesion* acting like *glue* to unite the information within that paragraph as a single unit. Also the paragraph should be bordered by *boundaries*, indicating a transition to the next paragraph. Then, of course, the following paragraph would have its own internal cohesion.

- *Cohesion* exists in both the *semantic* and the *grammatical* structure.
- *Boundaries* also exist in both the *semantic* and the *grammatical* structure.

Four Key Elements of Communication

We're going to consider these four elements of communication:

- Semantic Cohesion
- Grammatical Cohesion
- Semantic Boundaries
- Grammatical Boundaries

Semantic Cohesion[4]

Remember: *cohesion* is the "glue" that cements thoughts together within a paragraph. It unites smaller units into a larger unit. Cohesion causes words, phrases, clauses, and sentences to function together as a single paragraph. Two common forms of semantic cohesion are *Span* and *Sequencing*.

"Span" as a Cohesive Element[5]

One of the most common features providing cohesion within a semantic paragraph is "Span." There are various kinds of spans:

- Participant Span
- Setting Span
- Event Span
- Time Span
- Location Span
- Etc.

---

4. Ibid., pp. 426-30.
5. Ibid., pp. 156, 401, 426-31, 439, 453, 456.

"Span" Defined and Illustrated

Span is the continued focus given to a particular participant, setting, event, time, location, etc. through a portion of text. For example, if a major *participant* is named Peter, as long as Peter continues to be the primary participant in focus, there would be a *participant span* related to Peter. When the participant span associated with Peter is finished, there could be another participant span focusing on a different participant—John, for example.

With *location span*, there could be one episode which takes place inside the house, followed by another episode that takes place outside.

With *setting span*, there may be one setting followed by a second setting—like two scenes in a play.

Spans can function at various levels—not only the paragraph level. For example, a participant span focusing on Peter could be on a higher level and include more than just a single paragraph.

Sequencing: Logical and Chronological[6]

Span is the most common kind of semantic cohesion, but it is not the only kind. Another feature that provides semantic cohesion within a paragraph is *Sequencing*. With *sequencing*, the thoughts within a semantic paragraph are clearly tied together by virtue of the fact that they must occur in a specific order—either logically or chronologically.

Logical Sequencing[7]

Sometimes a sequence of events has a "domino" effect, like a cascading series of chemical reactions. Logical sequencing often involves a cause-and-effect relationship between clauses or sentences within a paragraph.

- Event "A" caused event "B"
- Event "B" caused event "C"
- Event "C" caused event "D"
- ...and so on

This kind of *logical sequencing* "glues" these events together as a single semantic unit.

---

6. Ibid., pp. 30, 210, 305-10, 312, 348, 353-57, 400, 404, 429.
7. Ibid., p. 439.

Chronological Sequencing

It is often necessary in narrative accounts for the stated series of events to occur in a particular sequence in order to make sense. Here is an example:

> *John woke up.*
> *Immediately he got out of bed.*
> *Then he went to the lake.*
> *And he caught a fish.*

As with *logical sequencing*, the *chronological sequencing* in this example "glues" these events together as a single cohesive, semantic unit.

Grammatical Cohesion[8]

Every *semantic paragraph* has some kind of *semantic cohesion*, which "glues" the thoughts together within that paragraph. For every type of *semantic cohesion*, there will be grammatical features that correspond to the semantic cohesion. These grammatical features are called *grammatical cohesion*.

The semantic cohesion within any given paragraph is universal; it is the same in every language. But the grammatical features marking cohesion within the paragraph may be very different from one language to another. For example, if a paragraph has a *participant span* focusing on "Peter," then "Peter" will be the focus no matter what language that paragraph is translated into.

- The actual participant span (a semantic feature) would be the same in every language: "Peter" is in focus.
- But the way it is handled on the surface (grammatical features) could be vastly different in each language: the way each language lets the hearer know that "Peter" is still in focus.

This is the same principle that we see at work on every level. On the word level, for example, English the word "dog" is basically equivalent to the word "perro" in Spanish. The meaning (semantics) for both words is the same: a canine animal. The form, however, is very different: "dog," "perro."

In the same way when we analyze paragraph structure, the *semantic cohesion* within a paragraph (i.e., the *meaning*), will be the same in every language. But the *grammatical cohesion* (i.e., the *form*), will likely be different.

---

8. Ibid., pp. 430-40.

Grammatical Features which Encode "Spans"[9]

Participant Spans are often marked grammatically by the use of pronouns, generic substitution words, prefixes and suffixes on verbs, etc. For example, in a participant span focused on "Peter," he would initially be mentioned by name, and after that, mostly by pronouns as long as he remains in focus. Pronouns like "he," "him," and "his" referring to Peter could indicate that the narrator assumes Peter is still at the forefront of the hearers' thinking. These pronouns help maintain cohesiveness throughout the participant span.

Time Spans may be marked on the surface by special time words, verb affixes, or the lack of a new time indication as long as it is still the same time span.

Location spans are often indicated by location words (here & there) or simply by not mentioning anything about the location again until there is a change. When there is a specific, explicit reference to a change in time and/or location, that is often an indication of the beginning of a new paragraph.

Grammatical Cohesion for Logical and Chronological Sequencing[10]

Discourses connected through logical sequencing tend to use connectors such as "and," "but," "therefore," "then," etc. to tie thoughts together within a paragraph. In a series of logically connected clauses which uses a lot of connectors, the lack of a connector at the beginning of a sentence or clause may be especially significant. It could signal a break in the cohesion, indicating that there is a boundary (new paragraph).

Recapitulation as Grammatical Cohesion[11]

A common form of grammatical cohesion in narrative paragraphs is recapitulation. We looked at some examples of recapitulation in the previous tutorial when we were talking about thematic and non-thematic material. In recapitulation, some part of the information from the preceding unit is repeated at the beginning of the new unit. Here is an example of recapitulation (The recapitulation is in italics):

We went and arrived at the village.
Having arrived at the village,
we went to the men's house and sat down.
While we were sitting at the men's house,
they brought us some food to eat.

---

9. Ibid., pp. 433-34.
10. Ibid., pp. 435-37.
11. Ibid., p. 485.

TUTORIAL 8.6

Recapitulation can take several different forms:
- A word-for-word repetition of what was said
- A partial repetition of what was said:
  - Repeating only the last part
  - Repeating only the most important or central part
- A summary of what was said (not in the same words)
- A single word or short phrase which refers back to what was just said:
  - "...*with that, they left*"
  - "...*having done that, they came*"

Recapitulation "glues" together the thoughts within a paragraph as a single, cohesive grammatical unit. In a portion of text that uses a lot of recapitulation, it is often the absence of a recapitulation clause that deserves special attention. The lack of recapitulation in this kind of context may signal a boundary (new paragraph).

Example of Recapitulation as Cohesive "Glue"

In the Lamogai language of Papua New Guinea, recapitulation is often used to tie statements together within paragraphs in narrative discourse. Here is an example. The recapitulation is in italic print:

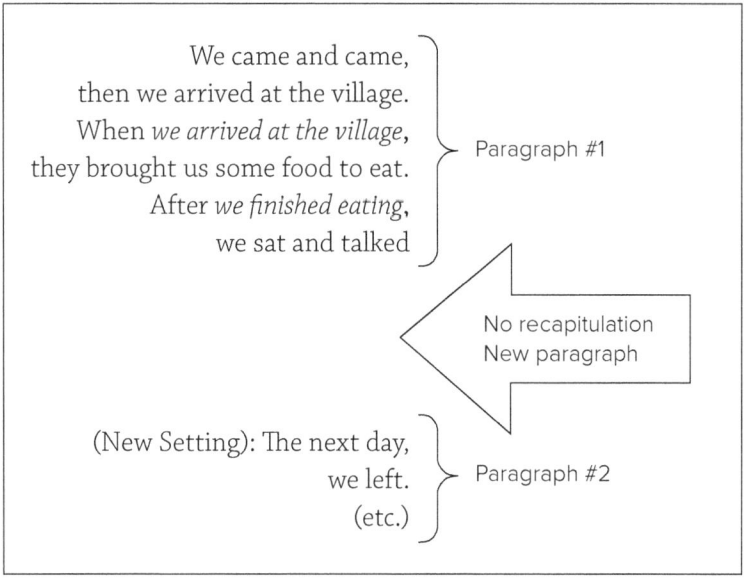

Cohesion and Boundaries Marked by Recapitulation

The recapitulation in this sequence creates grammatical cohesion, gluing the thoughts together within each semantic paragraph. The absence of recapitulation at the end of the first paragraph marks a semantic boundary. It is the start of a new semantic paragraph.

Each of the paragraphs in this example is a single semantic unit. Why? Because they each deal with distinct settings: the first paragraph takes place one day, and the second paragraph takes place the next day. These paragraphs are like separate scenes in a drama.

Along with being single semantic units, each of these paragraphs is also a single grammatical unit. Why? Because the clauses within each paragraph are tied together by the grammatical feature known as recapitulation.

Proper Alignment

When we speak or translate into any language, it is essential that our semantic units and grammatical units line up correctly. If the semantic paragraphs are not marked with the appropriate grammatical signals, our speech and translated materials could be confusing or unnatural—or possibly even unintelligible.

If, for example, I told a narrative story in Lamogai, and failed to include recapitulation in the appropriate places, or if I inserted it where it did not belong, my hearers could be confused—not knowing for sure when there was a semantic change of focus or setting.

The grammatical element of recapitulation helps the hearers pinpoint the semantic boundaries between the paragraphs. If the grammatical signals are wrong, the semantic units will be difficult to recognize.

Sending Conflicting Signals

Sometimes my wife I have been in the middle of a conversation and all of a sudden, in her mind, she changed to a different subject, but she forgot to let me know. So I assumed she was still talking about the same subject she had been talking about a moment earlier. In her mind, she imagined a semantic boundary. But she failed to include the appropriate grammatical signals to mark a grammatical boundary. This is what happens when our *grammatical boundaries* and *semantic boundaries* do not line up.

We have probably all experienced this kind of situation. If this happens when we are speaking our own language, how much more likely is it to happen when we speak another language not our own? The potential for misunderstanding is compounded by the fact that other languages have their own ways of marking grammatical cohesion and boundaries.

Every time there is a semantic shift to a different participant, time, location, event, etc., we need to mark it appropriately with the right kind of grammatical boundary markers.

More about Boundaries

Semantic Boundaries

Semantically, a new narrative paragraph often starts with the introduction of a new incident, place, time, participant, or group of participants—just as cohesion within a paragraph often focuses on the *same* incident, place, time, participant, or group of participants.

Grammatical Boundaries

Grammatically, there may be a connector or some other device used to signal the beginning of a new paragraph. However, there may not be an identifiable grammatical signal for every semantic boundary.

English: "Now..."

One grammatical signal commonly used in English to mark semantic boundaries is the word "now." Consider the way "now" is used in the following verses to introduce a new paragraph (or larger discourse unit):

Genesis 6:11 (NIV)
Now the earth was corrupt in God's sight and was full of violence.

Genesis 11:1 (NIV)
Now the whole world had one language and a common speech.

Genesis 12:10 (NIV)
Now there was a famine in the land, and Abram went down to Egypt to live there for a while...

Genesis 27:5 (NIV)
Now Rebekah was listening as Isaac spoke to his son Esau.

In reading these verses, it is clear that the word "now" is not functioning in its usual role as a present-tense time word. In these examples, the word "now" is functioning on the discourse level, marking a boundary—the beginning of a new paragraph or larger unit.

GROUPINGS: COHESION AND BOUNDARIES

If you study the surrounding contexts, you will find that each of these new grammatical paragraphs correspond to a semantic shift of some kind. The grammatical marker "now" is informing the reader that this is the beginning of a new semantic paragraph or larger semantic unit.

Discourse markers are easy to miss because they often function on more than one level. They tend to hide. If you were studying the discourse structure of one of these Genesis passages, you might be tempted to say, "*There don't appear to be any discourse boundary markers here.*" It would be easy to skip over a simple word like "now" because you already know what it means on the word level and it doesn't occur to you that the same word could carry a different function on higher levels.

➡ ACTIVITIES

1. Determine the Paragraph Breaks for Mark 1 and 2 – Use the *Tutorial 8.6 Activity Sheet - page 47*.

    - Don't just open a Bible to find the indentations.
    - Be prepared to defend your decisions regarding where to break the paragraphs, giving specific examples of cohesion within the paragraphs and boundaries between them.

2. Mark Cohesion and Boundaries in Mark 1 and 2 – Use the *Tutorial 8.6 Activity Sheet*.

    - What cohesive elements can you identify that are acting as "glue" to bond these language forms together as a single unit (semantically and grammatically)?
    - Can you identify anything at the beginning and/or end of each paragraph that may be signaling a semantic or grammatical boundary?

Further Explanation about the Activities

In a real translation project, you won't necessarily do all the work "in writing" as you are doing for these activities. You will learn to do much of it "in your head"—intuitively recognizing language features such as embedded discourses, groupings, cohesion and boundaries. However for this tutorial, we want you to work through these processes on paper, "showing your work," so to speak—as you would in a mathematics problem—since this will help you gain a more complete understanding of each step of the process.

Translation is mostly learned "on the job." The purpose of these Bible translation tutorials with their associated activities is exposure, not mastery. When it comes time to start translating, you should review these principles by attending translation workshops.

This tutorial focuses largely on the paragraph level and above. On these higher levels of discourse, there is much ambiguity and room for interpretation. This is borne out in the fact that the various English versions of the Bible do not all "indent" for a new paragraph at the same places. With this in mind, please note that there will not always be one, exactly correct answer for each part of this activity.

The goal of this lesson is that you understand the principles of cohesion (semantic and grammatical) and boundaries (semantic and grammatical)—not that you get every answer precisely correct, because that will probably not be possible.

GROUPINGS: COHESION AND BOUNDARIES

Sample Activity Sheet

Mark 1	Cohesion		Boundaries	
V. 4	Semantic	Grammatical	Semantic	Grammatical
	Participant span (John) Location span ++ (Jordan River)	and, and… him, him… he and, and…		**
V. 9	Participant span (Jesus) Chronological Sequencing	Passive*: "was baptized" he, him… and	New participant (Jesus) New Time	Explicit mention of Time: "In those days"
V. 12	Participant Span (Jesus) Location Span (desert)	and, and… him, he…	New Location (into the desert)	Explicit mention of Time: "Immediately"

++ The "LOCATION" span may encompass several paragraphs on a higher discourse level.

★ The "PASSIVE" voice is often used to maintain focus. (In this case Jesus is made the subject of the sentence even though he is not the one doing the action.) Other languages may have other devices that do the same thing. If you focus on form, you may literally reflect the Passive, but fail to reflect Semantic Focus. Some languages do not have a passive construction and those that do, may use it differently or less frequently.

** The semantic boundaries will definitely be there, but there may not always be an identifiable grammatical signal for each semantic boundary.

TUTORIAL 8.6

Tutorial 8.6 Activity Sheet

LOCATE and MARK the Paragraph Breaks and Cohesion and Boundaries in Mark 1 & 2.

	Cohesion		Boundaries	
	Semantic	Grammatical	Semantic	Grammatical
Mark 1 (NASB) ¹The beginning of the gospel of Jesus Christ, the Son of God. ²As it is written in Isaiah the prophet: "BEHOLD, I SEND MY MESSENGER AHEAD OF YOU, WHO WILL PREPARE YOUR WAY; ³THE VOICE OF ONE CRYING IN THE WILDERNESS, 'MAKE READY THE WAY OF THE LORD, MAKE HIS PATHS STRAIGHT.'" ⁴John the Baptist appeared in the wilderness preaching a baptism of repentance for the forgiveness of sins. ⁵And all the country of Judea was going out to him, and all the people of Jerusalem; and they were being baptized by him in the Jordan River, confessing their sins. ⁶John was clothed with camel's hair and wore a leather belt around his waist, and his diet was locusts and wild honey.				

47

GROUPINGS: COHESION AND BOUNDARIES

| | Cohesion || Boundaries ||
	Semantic	Grammatical	Semantic	Grammatical
⁷And he was preaching, and saying, "After me One is coming who is mightier than I, and I am not fit to stoop down and untie the thong of His sandals. ⁸I baptized you with water; but He will baptize you with the Holy Spirit." ⁹In those days Jesus came from Nazareth in Galilee and was baptized by John in the Jordan. ¹⁰Immediately coming up out of the water, He saw the heavens opening, and the Spirit like a dove descending upon Him; ¹¹and a voice came out of the heavens: "You are My beloved Son, in You I am well-pleased." ¹²Immediately the Spirit impelled Him to go out into the wilderness. ¹³And He was in the wilderness forty days being tempted by Satan; and He was with the wild beasts, and the angels were ministering to Him. ¹⁴Now after John had been taken into custody, Jesus came into Galilee, preaching the gospel of God,				

TUTORIAL 8.6

	Cohesion		Boundaries	
	Semantic	Grammatical	Semantic	Grammatical
¹⁵and saying, "The time is fulfilled, and the kingdom of God is at hand; repent and believe in the gospel."				
¹⁶As He was going along by the Sea of Galilee, He saw Simon and Andrew, the brother of Simon, casting a net in the sea; for they were fishermen.				
¹⁷And Jesus said to them, "Follow Me, and I will make you become fishers of men."				
¹⁸Immediately they left their nets and followed Him.				
¹⁹Going on a little farther, He saw James the son of Zebedee, and John his brother, who were also in the boat mending the nets.				
²⁰Immediately He called them; and they left their father Zebedee in the boat with the hired servants, and went away to follow Him.				
²¹They went into Capernaum; and immediately on the Sabbath He entered the synagogue and began to teach.				

GROUPINGS: COHESION AND BOUNDARIES

| | Cohesion || Boundaries ||
	Semantic	Grammatical	Semantic	Grammatical
²²They were amazed at His teaching; for He was teaching them as one having authority, and not as the scribes. ²³Just then there was a man in their synagogue with an unclean spirit; and he cried out, ²⁴saying, "What business do we have with each other, Jesus of Nazareth? Have You come to destroy us? I know who You are—the Holy One of God!" ²⁵And Jesus rebuked him, saying, "Be quiet, and come out of him!" ²⁶Throwing him into convulsions, the unclean spirit cried out with a loud voice and came out of him. ²⁷They were all amazed, so that they debated among themselves, saying, What is this? A new teaching with authority! He commands even the unclean spirits, and they obey Him. ²⁸Immediately the news about Him spread everywhere into all the surrounding district of Galilee.				

TUTORIAL 8.6

	Cohesion		Boundaries	
	Semantic	Grammatical	Semantic	Grammatical
²⁹And immediately after they came out of the synagogue, they came into the house of Simon and Andrew, with James and John.				
³⁰Now Simon's mother-in-law was lying sick with a fever; and immediately they spoke to Jesus about her.				
³¹And He came to her and raised her up, taking her by the hand, and the fever left her, and she waited on them.				
³²When evening came, after the sun had set, they began bringing to Him all who were ill and those who were demon-possessed.				
³³And the whole city had gathered at the door.				
³⁴And He healed many who were ill with various diseases, and cast out many demons; and He was not permitting the demons to speak, because they knew who He was.				
³⁵In the early morning, while it was still dark, Jesus got up, left the house, and went away to a secluded place, and was praying there.				

GROUPINGS: COHESION AND BOUNDARIES

| | Cohesion || Boundaries ||
	Semantic	Grammatical	Semantic	Grammatical
³⁶Simon and his companions searched for Him;				
³⁷they found Him, and said to Him, "Everyone is looking for You."				
³⁸He said to them, "Let us go somewhere else to the towns nearby, so that I may preach there also; for that is what I came for."				
³⁹And He went into their synagogues throughout all Galilee, preaching and casting out the demons.				
⁴⁰And a leper came to Jesus, beseeching Him and falling on his knees before Him, and saying, "If You are willing, You can make me clean."				
⁴¹Moved with compassion, Jesus stretched out His hand and touched him, and said to him, "I am willing; be cleansed."				
⁴²Immediately the leprosy left him and he was cleansed.				
⁴³And He sternly warned him and immediately sent him away,				
⁴⁴and He said to him, "See that you say nothing to anyone; but go, show yourself to the priest and offer for your cleansing what Moses commanded, as a testimony to them."				

TUTORIAL 8.6

	Cohesion		Boundaries	
	Semantic	Grammatical	Semantic	Grammatical
⁴⁵But he went out and began to proclaim it freely and to spread the news around, to such an extent that Jesus could no longer publicly enter a city, but stayed out in unpopulated areas; and they were coming to Him from everywhere.				
Mark 2 (NASB) ¹When He had come back to Capernaum several days afterward, it was heard that He was at home.				
²And many were gathered together, so that there was no longer room, not even near the door; and He was speaking the word to them.				
³And they came, bringing to Him a paralytic, carried by four men.				
⁴Being unable to get to Him because of the crowd, they removed the roof above Him; and when they had dug an opening, they let down the pallet on which the paralytic was lying.				
⁵And Jesus seeing their faith said to the paralytic, "Son, your sins are forgiven."				

GROUPINGS: COHESION AND BOUNDARIES

	Cohesion		Boundaries	
	Semantic	Grammatical	Semantic	Grammatical
⁶But some of the scribes were sitting there and reasoning in their hearts,				
⁷"Why does this man speak that way? He is blaspheming; who can forgive sins but God alone?"				
⁸Immediately Jesus, aware in His spirit that they were reasoning that way within themselves, said to them, "Why are you reasoning about these things in your hearts?				
⁹Which is easier, to say to the paralytic, 'Your sins are forgiven'; or to say, 'Get up, and pick up your pallet and walk'?				
¹⁰But so that you may know that the Son of Man has authority on earth to forgive sins"—He said to the paralytic,				
¹¹"I say to you, get up, pick up your pallet and go home."				
¹²And he got up and immediately picked up the pallet and went out in the sight of everyone, so that they were all amazed and were glorifying God, saying, "We have never seen anything like this."				

	Cohesion		Boundaries	
	Semantic	Grammatical	Semantic	Grammatical
¹³And He went out again by the seashore; and all the people were coming to Him, and He was teaching them.				
¹⁴As He passed by, He saw Levi the son of Alphaeus sitting in the tax booth, and He said to him, "Follow Me!" And he got up and followed Him.				
¹⁵And it happened that He was reclining at the table in his house, and many tax collectors and sinners were dining with Jesus and His disciples; for there were many of them, and they were following Him.				
¹⁶When the scribes of the Pharisees saw that He was eating with the sinners and tax collectors, they said to His disciples, "Why is He eating and drinking with tax collectors and sinners?"				
¹⁷And hearing this, Jesus said to them, "It is not those who are healthy who need a physician, but those who are sick; I did not come to call the righteous, but sinners."				

GROUPINGS: COHESION AND BOUNDARIES

	Cohesion		Boundaries	
	Semantic	Grammatical	Semantic	Grammatical
¹⁸John's disciples and the Pharisees were fasting; and they came and said to Him, "Why do John's disciples and the disciples of the Pharisees fast, but Your disciples do not fast?" ¹⁹And Jesus said to them, "While the bridegroom is with them, the attendants of the bridegroom cannot fast, can they? So long as they have the bridegroom with them, they cannot fast. ²⁰But the days will come when the bridegroom is taken away from them, and then they will fast in that day. ²¹"No one sews a patch of unshrunk cloth on an old garment; otherwise the patch pulls away from it, the new from the old, and a worse tear results. ²²No one puts new wine into old wineskins; otherwise the wine will burst the skins, and the wine is lost and the skins as well; but one puts new wine into fresh wineskins."				

TUTORIAL 8.6

	Cohesion		Boundaries	
	Semantic	Grammatical	Semantic	Grammatical
²³And it happened that He was passing through the grainfields on the Sabbath, and His disciples began to make their way along while picking the heads of grain. ²⁴The Pharisees were saying to Him, "Look, why are they doing what is not lawful on the Sabbath?" ²⁵And He said to them, "Have you never read what David did when he was in need and he and his companions became hungry; ²⁶how he entered the house of God in the time of Abiathar the high priest, and ate the consecrated bread, which is not lawful for anyone to eat except the priests, and he also gave it to those who were with him?" ²⁷Jesus said to them, "The Sabbath was made for man, and not man for the Sabbath. ²⁸So the Son of Man is Lord even of the Sabbath."				

8.7 The semantic structure of language

✓ OBJECTIVES OF THIS TUTORIAL

Learners will differentiate *Semantic Structure* from *Grammatical Structure*, and *Semantic Units* from *Grammatical Units*. This tutorial will focus on the "concept" as a semantic unit; we will expand into other kinds of semantic units in subsequent tutorials.

In previous tutorials, we have mentioned the importance of distinguishing between Form and Meaning. It is essential that we clearly recognize:

- The Grammatical Structure (Form)
- The Semantic Structure (Meaning)
- The Skewing Between Them[1]

One of the most common reasons for miscommunication in a cross-cultural context is a lack of understanding of the distinction between the *form* and the *meaning* of the message. Often this contrast becomes blurred, and we link the *meaning* too closely with the *form*.

Meaning apart from Form

We have seen the Standard Transfer Model, which illustrates the translation process.[2] We start with the *Source Language* Text and dig beneath the surface to discover the meaning. Then we re-express that meaning in appropriate *Receptor Language* forms. But sometimes we wrongly equate the meaning with the form—as if the form itself *is* the meaning.

---

1. "Skewing" will be explained and illustrated later in this tutorial. See: Mildred L. Larson, Meaning Based Translation: a guide to cross-language equivalence, revised edition, (Lanham, MD: University Press of America, 1998), pp. 97-105.
2. Larson, Meaning Based Translation, p. 4 display 1.1; see also: Katharine Barnwell, Introduction to Semantics and Translation (Horsleys Green, UK: Summer Institute of Linguistics, 1974, 1980), p.14.

THE SEMANTIC STRUCTURE OF LANGUAGE

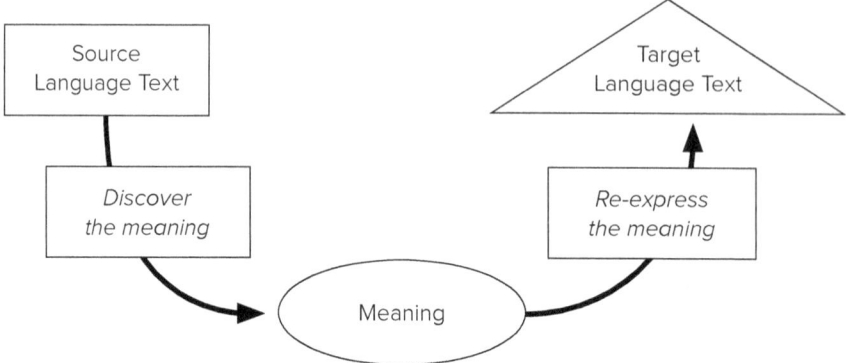

For example, in Mark 2:9, where it reads: "*Jesus said, '…pick up your bed and walk,'*" what is the meaning? Is the meaning "*Jesus said, '…pick up your bed and walk,'*"? No. If that were true, our translation of this verse into a receptor language would be:

- A *proper noun*
- Then a *verb* (3rd-person-singular-past-tense)
- Next a *verb phrase* (2nd-person-imperative)
- And a *pronoun* (2nd-person-possessive)
- Followed by another *noun*
- Then a *conjunction*
- Ending with a *verb* (2nd-person-imperative)

However, we need to remember that the words themselves are not the meaning! The real meaning is the *picture* we envision in our minds apart from any words that could be used to express it.

This *picture* is the *meaning* that needs to be translated from the Source Language to the Receptor Language. If we do our job correctly as translators, the picture should basically be the same no matter what language we translate into. Of course, some of the unspecified details could be seen differently by various target-language hearers—for example, a person's height or the color of their clothing—but the essential elements of the picture would be the same in every language. This picture is the Semantics.

Which Language?

Those of you who speak more than one language fluently can probably identify with me when I say there have been times that I heard someone say something, but later, when I thought about it, I wasn't sure what language they were speaking, because that person and I share more than one language. The meaning was very clear to me, but the actual form had escaped me—even to the point that I didn't remember what language the person was speaking.

Peering Inside the Magic Eye®

Clearly perceiving *Meaning* apart from *Form* could be likened to looking at a picture in one of those Magic Eye® picture books. Buried deep inside of the multicolored shapes and patterns is an intricate three-dimensional image. In order to see the three-dimensional image, you need to look past the forms on the surface. If you concentrate on the actual forms and shapes themselves, you will not be able to see the hidden picture.

Depth Perception

We all have various degrees of "depth perception"—the ability to see the *meaning* that is buried beneath the surface-level *forms*. Generally, this is something we have developed over time. Our natural tendency is to tie meaning closely to the forms of our own language—linking the surface-level forms with the underlying meaning. For most people, this link between *meaning* and *form* grows stronger as they move from childhood to adulthood.

Easier for Children

Children generally have an easier time than adults do when it comes to understanding meaning apart from form. A very small child will begin to grasp the meaning of things that directly affect him before he fully understands the spoken language all around him. Even after a child is old enough to talk, he still will *not* have the same deep-seated link in his mind between underlying meaning and the surface-level forms that most adults have.

Several years ago, I was on an Air Niugini flight in Papua New Guinea with my son, when he was about 4 years old. The flight attendant gave a full explanation of the seat belt, the life vest, the oxygen mask, etc. She said it one time through in English, and then a second time through in New Guinea Pidgin. When she finished, my son leaned over to me and asked, *"Why did she say all of that twice?"*

The *form* of the explanation in both languages was completely familiar to him, since he is fluent in both English and Pidgin. But his focus wasn't on the form—it was on the meaning. He knew that the meaning was the same both times; he just didn't happen to notice that the form was different—even to the point that it was in a different language.

Grammatical & Semantic Structure[3]

When we describe the grammatical structure of language, we have a full set of grammatical terms to designate each grammatical element, including words like *noun*, *verb*, *subject*, *object*, etc. So it is with the semantic structure of language. There is a completely separate set of terms used to describe semantic structure.

The smallest semantic unit is called a "meaning component." The meaning component on the semantic side often corresponds to the "morpheme" on the grammatical side.

The "word" level on the grammatical side often corresponds to a semantic unit called the "concept." Semantic "concepts" are classified into four groups: Things, Events, Attributes and Relations.

Concepts	Definition & Examples
Thing	All animate beings, natural and supernatural and all inanimate entities. Examples: boy, ghost, angel, stone, galaxy, blood
Event	All actions, changes of state (process), and experiences. Examples: eat, run, think, melt, stretch, smile
Attribute	All those attributes of quality and quantity ascribed to any Thing or Event. Examples: long, thick, soft, rough, slowly, suddenly, few, all
Relation	All those relations posited between any two of the above semantic units. Examples: with, by, because, since, and, therefore, after, or

Just as a "concept" on the semantic side often corresponds with a "word" on the grammatical side, so semantic *things*, *events*, *attributes* and *relations* on the semantic side correspond to certain kinds of *words* on the grammatical side. (See the following chart)

---

3. Larson, Meaning Based Translation, pp. 59-70.

Semantic Structure	Grammatical Structure
meaning component	morpheme
Concept	Word
Things	Nouns, pronouns
Events	Verbs
Attributes	Adjectives, adverbs
Relations	conjunctions, prepositions

Why do we need two lists?[4]

You may be wondering why there are two separate sets of terms: one for *grammatical* units and another for *semantic* units. Why can't we just use the grammatical terms—*noun*, *verb*, *adjective*, etc.—for both grammar and semantics? The reason is because of "skewing." *Skewing* is a mismatch between semantic units and grammatical units. Every language uses skewing.

We mentioned that a "noun" on the grammatical side often corresponds with a "thing" concept on the semantic side; but that is not always the case. Sometimes a grammatical *noun* may be a semantic *event*.

Consider this example:

"The work is difficult."

In this sentence, the word "work" is classified as a noun grammatically because it is the subject of the sentence. Semantically, however, "work" is an *event* which is an action. This is an example of skewing between the semantic and grammatical classes. "Work" in this context is not a "thing" that I put in my back pocket and carry around with me. Also, it is not something I would carry on a conversation with.

Remember, in the previous chart, we noted that semantic things are: Animate Beings (natural and supernatural) and Inanimate Entities.

---

4. Ibid., pp. 62-64.

More Examples (Note the Skewing)

Like a lamb that is led to slaughter (Is. 53:7)
— slaughter: E (NOUN)

They all condemned Him to be deserving of death (Mk. 14:64)
— death: E (NOUN)

The Lord was not in the earthquake.
— earthquake: E (NOUN)

Her singing is too loud.
— singing: E (NOUN)

Eating is very necessary.
— Eating: E (NOUN)

The man knifed him to death.
— death: E (NOUN)

Prayer comes first each day
— Prayer: E (NOUN)

Identify the Semantic Events (Mark 1:4)

"And so John the Baptist appeared in the wilderness, preaching a baptism of repentance for the forgiveness of sins." (Mark 1:4 NIV)

Of all these semantic EVENTS, only 2 of them are VERBS grammatically.

- appeared (verb)
- preaching (verb)
- baptism (noun)
- repentance (noun)
- forgiveness (noun)
- sins (noun)
- Baptist (noun)

One-to-one Correlation

We already noted that if there is no skewing, the one-to-one correlation of semantic concepts to grammatical words could be described as follows:

TUTORIAL 8.7

Semantic Terms (Concepts)	Grammatical Terms (Words)
Things	Nouns, pronouns
Events	Verbs
Attributes	Adjectives, adverbs
Relations	Conjunctions, prepositions, enclitics, etc.

The previous examples show that other grammatical forms can represent semantic events.

Here is the full chart of Semantic and Grammatical terms:

Semantic Terms	Grammatical Terms
Discourse	Text
Semantic part	Part
Episode cluster	Division
Episode	Section
Semantic paragraph	Paragraph
Propositional cluster	Sentence
Proposition	Clause
Concept Cluster	Phrase
Concept	Word
Meaning component	Morpheme (roots and affixes)

From the bottom upward

In this tutorial we will primarily focus on the Paragraph level and below. When you get above the paragraph level, the terminology varies from one author to another.

Meaning and Form

Sometimes it may seem like "Semantics" is mysterious and elusive—difficult to get a handle on. Actually, *semantics* (the "meaning") is the part of language that is universal and consistent. If we translate the meaning correctly, it should be the same in every language. It is the *Form* (grammar & lexicon) is inconsistent—different in every language.

THE SEMANTIC STRUCTURE OF LANGUAGE

Translation involves a double challenge: First we need to "un-skew" the source language text. Then we reconstruct the same meaning using appropriate receptor language skewing.

➡ ACTIVITIES

1. Identify the Semantic Events in Mark 1 and 2 – Use the *Tutorial 8.7 Activity Sheet - page 67*.

Remember: Due to skewing between grammar and semantics, some grammatical verbs may not be a semantic event; and some semantic events may not be a verb.

Tutorial 8.7 Activity Sheet

LOCATE and **MARK** all event concepts in Mark 1 and 2

- Place the letter **E** over each semantic event

....

Mark 1 (NASB)

¹The beginning of the gospel of Jesus Christ, the Son of God.

²As it is written in Isaiah the prophet: "BEHOLD, I SEND MY MESSENGER AHEAD OF YOU, WHO WILL PREPARE YOUR WAY;

³THE VOICE OF ONE CRYING IN THE WILDERNESS, 'MAKE READY THE WAY OF THE LORD, MAKE HIS PATHS STRAIGHT.' "

⁴John the Baptist appeared in the wilderness preaching a baptism of repentance for the forgiveness of sins.

⁵And all the country of Judea was going out to him, and all the people of Jerusalem; and they were being baptized by him in the Jordan River, confessing their sins.

⁶John was clothed with camel's hair and wore a leather belt around his waist, and his diet was locusts and wild honey.

⁷And he was preaching, and saying, "After me One is coming who is mightier than I, and I am not fit to stoop down and untie the thong of His sandals.

⁸I baptized you with water; but He will baptize you with the Holy Spirit."

⁹In those days Jesus came from Nazareth in Galilee and was baptized by John in the Jordan.

¹⁰Immediately coming up out of the water, He saw the heavens opening, and the Spirit like a dove descending upon Him;

¹¹and a voice came out of the heavens: "You are My beloved Son, in You I am well-pleased."

[12] Immediately the Spirit impelled Him to go out into the wilderness.

[13] And He was in the wilderness forty days being tempted by Satan; and He was with the wild beasts, and the angels were ministering to Him.

[14] Now after John had been taken into custody, Jesus came into Galilee, preaching the gospel of God,

[15] and saying, "The time is fulfilled, and the kingdom of God is at hand; repent and believe in the gospel."

[16] As He was going along by the Sea of Galilee, He saw Simon and Andrew, the brother of Simon, casting a net in the sea; for they were fishermen.

[17] And Jesus said to them, "Follow Me, and I will make you become fishers of men."

[18] Immediately they left their nets and followed Him.

[19] Going on a little farther, He saw James the son of Zebedee, and John his brother, who were also in the boat mending the nets.

[20] Immediately He called them; and they left their father Zebedee in the boat with the hired servants, and went away to follow Him.

[21] They went into Capernaum; and immediately on the Sabbath He entered the synagogue and began to teach.

[22] They were amazed at His teaching; for He was teaching them as one having authority, and not as the scribes.

[23] Just then there was a man in their synagogue with an unclean spirit; and he cried out,

[24] saying, "What business do we have with each other, Jesus of Nazareth? Have You come to destroy us? I know who You are—the Holy One of God!"

[25] And Jesus rebuked him, saying, "Be quiet, and come out of him!"

²⁶Throwing him into convulsions, the unclean spirit cried out with a loud voice and came out of him.

²⁷They were all amazed, so that they debated among themselves, saying, What is this? A new teaching with authority! He commands even the unclean spirits, and they obey Him.

²⁸Immediately the news about Him spread everywhere into all the surrounding district of Galilee.

²⁹And immediately after they came out of the synagogue, they came into the house of Simon and Andrew, with James and John.

³⁰Now Simon's mother-in-law was lying sick with a fever; and immediately they spoke to Jesus about her.

³¹And He came to her and raised her up, taking her by the hand, and the fever left her, and she waited on them.

³²When evening came, after the sun had set, they began bringing to Him all who were ill and those who were demon-possessed.

³³And the whole city had gathered at the door.

³⁴And He healed many who were ill with various diseases, and cast out many demons; and He was not permitting the demons to speak, because they knew who He was.

³⁵In the early morning, while it was still dark, Jesus got up, left the house, and went away to a secluded place, and was praying there.

³⁶Simon and his companions searched for Him;

³⁷they found Him, and said to Him, "Everyone is looking for You."

³⁸He said to them, "Let us go somewhere else to the towns nearby, so that I may preach there also; for that is what I came for."

³⁹And He went into their synagogues throughout all Galilee, preaching and casting out the demons.

⁴⁰And a leper came to Jesus, beseeching Him and falling on his knees before Him, and saying, "If You are willing, You can make me clean."

⁴¹Moved with compassion, Jesus stretched out His hand and touched him, and said to him, "I am willing; be cleansed."

⁴²Immediately the leprosy left him and he was cleansed.

⁴³And He sternly warned him and immediately sent him away,

⁴⁴and He said to him, "See that you say nothing to anyone; but go, show yourself to the priest and offer for your cleansing what Moses commanded, as a testimony to them."

⁴⁵But he went out and began to proclaim it freely and to spread the news around, to such an extent that Jesus could no longer publicly enter a city, but stayed out in unpopulated areas; and they were coming to Him from everywhere.

Mark 2 (NASB)

¹When He had come back to Capernaum several days afterward, it was heard that He was at home.

²And many were gathered together, so that there was no longer room, not even near the door; and He was speaking the word to them.

³And they came, bringing to Him a paralytic, carried by four men.

⁴Being unable to get to Him because of the crowd, they removed the roof above Him; and when they had dug an opening, they let down the pallet on which the paralytic was lying.

⁵And Jesus seeing their faith said to the paralytic, "Son, your sins are forgiven."

⁶But some of the scribes were sitting there and reasoning in their hearts,

⁷"Why does this man speak that way? He is blaspheming; who can forgive sins but God alone?"

[8]Immediately Jesus, aware in His spirit that they were reasoning that way within themselves, said to them, "Why are you reasoning about these things in your hearts?

[9]Which is easier, to say to the paralytic, 'Your sins are forgiven'; or to say, 'Get up, and pick up your pallet and walk'?

[10]But so that you may know that the Son of Man has authority on earth to forgive sins"—He said to the paralytic,

[11]"I say to you, get up, pick up your pallet and go home."

[12]And he got up and immediately picked up the pallet and went out in the sight of everyone, so that they were all amazed and were glorifying God, saying, "We have never seen anything like this."

[13]And He went out again by the seashore; and all the people were coming to Him, and He was teaching them.

[14]As He passed by, He saw Levi the son of Alphaeus sitting in the tax booth, and He said to him, "Follow Me!" And he got up and followed Him.

[15]And it happened that He was reclining at the table in his house, and many tax collectors and sinners were dining with Jesus and His disciples; for there were many of them, and they were following Him.

[16]When the scribes of the Pharisees saw that He was eating with the sinners and tax collectors, they said to His disciples, "Why is He eating and drinking with tax collectors and sinners?"

[17]And hearing this, Jesus said to them, "It is not those who are healthy who need a physician, but those who are sick; I did not come to call the righteous, but sinners."

[18]John's disciples and the Pharisees were fasting; and they came and said to Him, "Why do John's disciples and the disciples of the Pharisees fast, but Your disciples do not fast?"

[19]And Jesus said to them, "While the bridegroom is with them, the attendants of the bridegroom cannot fast, can they? So long as they have the bridegroom with them, they cannot fast.

²⁰But the days will come when the bridegroom is taken away from them, and then they will fast in that day.

²¹"No one sews a patch of unshrunk cloth on an old garment; otherwise the patch pulls away from it, the new from the old, and a worse tear results.

²²No one puts new wine into old wineskins; otherwise the wine will burst the skins, and the wine is lost and the skins as well; but one puts new wine into fresh wineskins."

²³And it happened that He was passing through the grainfields on the Sabbath, and His disciples began to make their way along while picking the heads of grain.

²⁴The Pharisees were saying to Him, "Look, why are they doing what is not lawful on the Sabbath?"

²⁵And He said to them, "Have you never read what David did when he was in need and he and his companions became hungry;

²⁶how he entered the house of God in the time of Abiathar the high priest, and ate the consecrated bread, which is not lawful for anyone to eat except the priests, and he also gave it to those who were with him?"

²⁷Jesus said to them, "The Sabbath was made for man, and not man for the Sabbath.

²⁸So the Son of Man is Lord even of the Sabbath."

8.8 Propositional structure 1

> **OBJECTIVES OF THIS TUTORIAL**
>
> In this tutorial, the learners will understand and describe the basic structure of semantic propositions, with special focus on EVENT propositions.

Structural Hierarchy (Grammatical & Semantic)[1]

We have talked about the fact that there is a structural hierarchy both in the *Grammar* (or "form") of language and also in the *Semantics* (or "meaning") of language. First, the Grammatical Hierarchy:

- Morphemes are grouped into words
- Words are grouped into phrases
- Phrases are grouped into clauses and sentences
- Sentences are grouped into paragraphs
- Paragraphs are grouped into higher discourse units

Just as there is a structured *grammatical* hierarchy, there is a parallel *semantic* hierarchy:

- Meaning components are grouped into concepts
- Concepts are grouped into propositions
- Propositions are grouped into propositional clusters
- Prepositional clusters are grouped into semantic paragraphs
- Semantic paragraphs are grouped into higher semantic units, such as episodes, episode clusters and discourse

---

1. Mildred L. Larson, Meaning Based Translation: a guide to cross-language equivalence, revised edition, (Lanham, MD: University Press of America, 1998), pp. 33-34.

Beyond the Concept Level

So far in our discussion of semantic structure, we have focused on Semantic *concepts*. As we noted, there are four kinds of semantic concepts: Things, Events, Attributes, & Relations. Now we are going to move above the Concept Level and talk about semantic *propositions*.

Semantic Propositions[2]

The *proposition* in semantics generally corresponds un-skewed with the grammatical clause or simple sentence. The proposition is a key pivotal element in the semantic hierarchy, because the proposition is the *smallest unit of communication*.[3] It is not the smallest unit of meaning. For Example, I can say, "*apple*." That has meaning. But no real communication has taken place. You would likely say to me, "What do you mean 'apple'? Apple what?"

Apple is a semantic concept—a *thing* concept. As a concept, it clearly has meaning, but when we say "apple" in isolation, totally outside of any kind of context, there is no real communication. However, if we say, "*He is eating an apple*," that is a proposition—which constitutes more than just meaning, it produces genuine communication. That is why the proposition is said to be the *smallest unit of communication*.

One Semantic Proposition—Many Grammatical Forms[4]

Often, a simple semantic proposition can be represented by several different forms, depending on the context. The following forms all express the same semantic proposition:

- John hit the ball.
- The ball was hit by John.
- The hitting of the ball by John…
- The ball, having been hit by John…

These utterances illustrate four possible ways that this single semantic proposition could be represented in English. The context would determine which one is applicable. The meaning is the picture we have in our mind of John hitting the ball.

---

2. Ibid., pp. 30-31, 207-17.
3. Ibid., p. 211.
4. Ibid., p. 209.

TUTORIAL 8.8

Analyzing the Proposition: "John hit the ball."
The central concept in this proposition is an **event**—the word "hit." And there are two **thing** concepts clustering around this single **event**: "John" and "ball." This particular proposition is made up of three semantic concepts.

Propositional Structure[5]

Here are a few key principles about semantic propositions:

- Every semantic proposition is composed of **at least two concepts**: Things, Events, and/or Attributes.
    - These concepts will be linked by some kind of definable semantic Relation.
- In every proposition, **one of the concepts is central**.
    - The other concept(s) cluster around the central concept and are linked to it by semantic relations. More concepts can cluster around those concepts.
- There are two kinds of propositions: **Event** propositions and **State** propositions.

Event Propositions
- An event proposition is one in which the central concept is an **event**.
- Every event proposition has one **event** plus at least one **thing**.
- There can be more thing and attribute concepts clustering around the central event.

State propositions
- State propositions are most often composed of a central **thing** concept with at least one **attribute** or one other **thing** concept attached to it.
- In some unique instances, an **event** or an **attribute** concept could be the central concept in a state proposition. Below are two examples:
    - "The work is difficult" is a **state** propostition; "work" (an event) is the central concept, and "difficult" (an attribute) is attached to it.
    - "The redness is intense" is another **state** proposition; "redness" (an attribute) is the central concept, and "intense" (another attribute) is attached to it.

---

5. Ibid., pp. 212-13.

Start with Event Propositions

When doing a semantic structural analysis of any given text, it is usually best to start by analyzing the event propositions. The first step in identifying event propositions is to identify and mark the event concepts in the text.

Almost every event concept is central to an event proposition. (Some may be embedded event propositions, or on rare occasions, an event may be part of a state proposition.) An event proposition is made up of an event concept along with at least one thing concept. Remember: events may be:

- Actions (run, hit, kill)
- Experiences (see, think, smell)
- Processes (die, rot, freeze)

Let's Look at Some Examples
What are the events in the following sentences?

- Like a lamb that is led to slaughter (Is. 53:7).
    - The semantic events are "led" and "slaughter".
    - That means this sentence is made up of TWO Event Propositions.
- They all condemned him to be deserving of death.
    - "condemned," "deserving," and "death"
- Her singing is too loud.
    - "singing"
- The man knifed him to death.
    - "knifed" (or stabbed with a knife), "death"
- Prayer comes first each day.
    - "prayer"

Next, Identify the Participants

Once you have identified the event concepts, the next step is to identify the participants (thing concepts) associated with each event. The participants are the persons or objects that do the action or to which the action is done. Every event proposition has one or more participant, but they may be implicit.

"Like a lamb that is led to slaughter."

- The first event is "led".
    - It has two associated thing concepts: "lamb" and "someone".
    - This first event proposition is *"Someone led the lamb"*.
- The next event is "slaughter."
    - It also has two associated things: "lamb" and "someone".
    - This second event proposition is *"Someone slaughtered the lamb"*.

The passive construction in this example points to the fact that *someone* did these two actions (leading and slaughtering), but it doesn't tell us who it was. In order to re-write these propositions in an un-skewed way, there needs to be an explicit reference to the participant who did the actions—even if we don't know who that was ("someone").

The Passive construction is a form of skewing. That is why we always eliminate passives when we rewrite the propositions of a text in their un-skewed form.

"They all condemned him to be deserving of death."

- The first event is "condemned".
    - It has two associated thing concepts: "they (all)" and "him".
    - The proposition is, "They all condemned Him".
- The next event is "deserving".
    - Its associated thing is "He".
    - The un-skewed proposition is "He deserves".
- The next event is "death".
    - The associated thing is "He".
    - The un-skewed proposition is "He dies".

PROPOSITIONAL STRUCTURE 1

The sentence in the example above has three event propositions. When we do a semantic structural analysis, we write each proposition on a separate line. This English sentence rewritten to express its basic, un-skewed semantic propositions, would be:

- They condemned him
- He deserves
- He dies

At this point, these three propositions sound disconnected from each other—as if they were totally unrelated. Of course, we know that these propositions are related to each other; but we will leave the relations undefined for now and come back to handle them later.

"Her singing is too loud."

- The event is "singing".
    - The associated thing concept is "her" (she).
    - The basic un-skewed event proposition is "She sings".
- But there's more here:
    - The phrase "too loud" is an attribute concept modifying "sings".
    - The word "too" is an attribute concept modifying "loudly".
    - So the complete proposition is "She sings too loudly".

Do you see how "*Her singing is too loud*" is skewed and "*She sings too loudly*" removes the skewing? The word "her" is a possessive pronoun, but in order to remove the skewing, we recast the word "her" as "she," a subject pronoun, since "she" is the one who did the event.

"The man knifed him to death."

- The first event is "knifed" (or stabbed with a knife).
    - The associated thing concept is "the man".
    - The un-skewed proposition is "The man knifed him".
- The second event is "death".
    - The associated thing concept is "him" (he).
    - The un-skewed proposition is "he died".

"Prayer comes first each day."

- The event is "prayer".
    - Grammatically, "Prayer" is a noun; but semantically, it is an event.
    - "Comes" is the only verb in the sentence, but in this case, it is not a semantic event.
- The associated thing concept is unspecified so we would use a general term:
    - Depending on the context, it could be:
        - "(Someone) prays"
        - OR: "(People) pray"
        - OR: "(We) pray"
        - OR: "(I) pray"
- The phrase "each day" is a semantic attribute attached to the event "pray".
    - "First" is another attribute attached to "pray".
- So the proposition here is "someone prays first each day" (or "we" or "I).

The reason we don't know the "who" of this proposition is that this example is taken out of context. That is a weakness of this kind of illustrative example. When you analyze an entire text, most of the participants will be clear from the context.

Let's look at Mark Chapter 1

We already identified the event concepts in verse 4. Now let's determine the thing concepts associated with each event.

- Appeared: "John the Baptist"
- Preaching: "John"
- Baptism: "John"
- Repentance: "people"
- Forgiveness: "God"
    - In Lamogai, "forgive" must be a **verb**.
    - And you must state **who** is forgiving **whom** of **what**.
- Sins: "people"

These Examples illustrate important principles:
- Every **event** proposition has an **event** concept.
  - It doesn't necessarily have any **verbs**.
- Every event proposition has one or more **participants** (semantic thing concepts).
  - It doesn't necessarily have any **nouns**.

Consider this Example:

"Did you eat an apple?"
"Yes."

In this context, the little word "yes" represents the event proposition "*Yes, I ate an apple.*" The semantic event is "ate," and the associated thing concepts are "I" and "an apple." These elements are not explicitly represented by any form on the surface, but semantically, they are part of the meaning.

Re-writing Event Propositions[6]
After identifying the Semantic events along with their associated thing and attribute concepts, we rewrite the Propositions in a basic, un-skewed form. Here are the guidelines for rewriting propositions:

- Use Active, Finite verbs
  - Passive voice is a form of skewing because often the participants (particularly the agent who does the action) are not explicitly mentioned.
  - Infinitives are also considered to be skewed for the same reason—because infinitives often do not explicitly mention the participants.
- Make all **participants** (semantic *thing* concepts) explicit
  - Even if it's not clear who or what the participants are.
  - In those cases use a non-specific term like "someone" or "something".
- Leave the **relations** for later

---
6. Ibid., p. 210.

"The destruction of the city was planned well"

- The semantic event concepts in this sentence are:
    - "destruction"
    - "planned"
- The event propositions are:
    - (Someone) destroyed the city
    - (Someone) planned well

However, there is one more element of skewing here. The propositions are not in their true sequential order. The real order of these events is:

- (Someone) planned well.
- (Someone) destroyed the city.

"John rejected Peter's offer"

- The semantic event concepts are:
    - "rejected"
    - "offer"
- The event propositions are:
    - John rejected (what Peter offered)
    - Peter offered (something)

Again, the propositions are out of chronological order. The order should be:

- Peter offered (something)
- John rejected (what Peter offered)

"His graduation depended on her help"

This one is a little bit trickier than some of the other examples.

- What are the EVENTS?
    - "graduation"
    - "help"
- Who are the PARTICIPANTS?
    - "He"
    - "Her"
- What are the propositions?
    - He graduated
    - She helped him

Again we need to adjust the chronological sequence, because she helped him first, then he graduated afterwards. In this example, both semantic events are grammatical nouns. The only verb in this sentence is the word "depended," which represents the semantic *cause-and-effect* relation between the events.

"Disobedience brings much suffering"

- What are the semantic events?
    - "disobedience"
    - "suffering"
- What are the semantic propositions?
    - (Someone) disobeys
    - (Someone) suffers much
        - "much" is an attribute describing the event "suffering"

This time the propositions are already in their correct sequential order. As with the previous example, the only verb in this sentence ("brings") does not represent a semantic event. It communicates the semantic relation between the two event propositions.

"The compliment was well received by Mary"

- What are the EVENTS?
    - "compliment"
    - "received"
- What are the propositions?
    - (Someone) complimented Mary
    - Mary received (the compliment)

The phrase "the compliment" is placed within parentheses because it represents skewing. Sometimes it is necessary to include come information that is skewed in our rewritten propositions. That "skewed" information should always be placed within parentheses as in this example.

ACTIVITIES

This tutorial (8.8 – *Propositional Structure I*) is directly related to the next tutorial (8.9 – *Propositional Structure II*).

The assignment at the end of that tutorial covers the material from tutorials 8.8 and 8.9 together.

8.9 Propositional structure 2

 OBJECTIVES OF THIS TUTORIAL

This tutorial builds upon the material contained in Tutorial 8.8 (*Propositional Structure I*), giving further instruction on the structure of semantic propositions.

We Learned in the Previous Tutorial that:[1]

- A proposition is the smallest unit of communication.[2]
- There are two kinds of Semantic PROPOSITIONS
    - EVENT propositions
    - STATE propositions
- Every proposition is made up of two or more concepts and one of the semantic concepts is the central concept of the proposition.
- **Event** propositions have an event as the central concept.
    - There must be at least one thing concept associated with the event.
    - There can be other thing concepts and/or attribute concepts.
- **State** propositions generally have a Semantic thing as the central concept.
    - There must be at least one other attribute or thing concept associated with the central concept.

---

1. Mildred L. Larson, Meaning Based Translation: a guide to cross-language equivalence, revised edition, (Lanham, MD: University Press of America, 1998), pp. 30-31, 207-17.
2. Ibid., p. 211.

PROPOSITIONAL STRUCTURE 2

State propositions[3]

State Propositions have two main parts:

- The **Topic** – the central concept that is being talked about.
- The **Comment** – what is said about the topic.

For Example:

- The man is a chief
- She is pregnant
- This is a bowl of rice
- Jesus was at home (Mk 2:1)

When we analyze **state** propositions, as with event propositions, the semantic structure (i.e., the *meaning*) remains the same no matter what language we are working in. It is the grammar (i.e., the *form*) that changes. The grammatical forms used to communicate the state propositions are language-specific.

Remember: Every **state** proposition is made up of a **topic** and a **comment**—with some sort of semantic **relation** between them. Here are some examples of state propositions:

Proposition	Topic ... relation ... Comment
	CAR ... ownership ... ME
English	This car is mine.
Otomi	This is my car.
Gahuku	My-car exists.
Lamogai	Car here mine it.
Tok Pisin	This car it [possession word] me.

---

3. Ibid., pp. 213-14.

TUTORIAL 8.9

	Topic ... relation ... Comment
Proposition	DOG ... naming ... FIDO
English	The dog's name is Fido.
Otomi	Dog he-is-named the Fido.
Gahuku	Dog name - (phrase-closure-marker) Fido-is.
Lamogai	Dog name-its Fido.
Tok Pisin	Dog name [possession word] it Fido.

	Topic ... relation ... Comment
Proposition	JOHN ... location ... HOUSE
English	John is in the house.
Otomi	John lives there in the house.
Gahuku	John - (phrase-closure-marker) house-in is-he.
Lamogai	John exists at house inside.
Tok Pisin	John he [predicate marker] exists in house.

	Topic ... relation ... Comment
Proposition	FRED ... description ... BIG
English	Fred is big.
Otomi	Is big the Fred.
Gahuku	Fred - (phrase-closure-marker) man big is-he.
Lamogai	Fred big he.
Tok Pisin	Fred he [predicate marker] big.

Situational Meanings of Propositions[4]

The situational meaning of a proposition reflects the purpose of the author by answering these questions:

- Is he making a statement?
  (To give information to the hearer)
- Is he asking a question?
  (To gain information from the hearer)
- Is he giving a command?
  (to prescribe a course of action)

In the baseball example we looked at earlier, the **situational meaning** could be one of these three possibilities:

JOHN ... HIT ... BALL	
Statement:	John hit the ball.
Question:	Did John hit the ball?
Command:	John, hit the ball!

All three examples in the above chart represent the same semantic proposition. The **situational** meaning is superimposed over the proposition by the context.

Event and **state** Propositions may occur with all three of these situational meanings. Every proposition expresses a command, a question, or a statement. This is called the **illocutionary force** of the proposition.

Form & Function of Situational Meaning[5]

The semantic term for situational meaning is **illocutionary force**. The corresponding grammatical term is **mood**. If there is no Skewing:

- A Semantic **statement** would be reflected grammatically in the **declarative** mood.
- A Semantic **question** would be reflected in the **interrogative** mood.
- A Semantic **command** would be reflected in the **imperative** mood.

---

4. Ibid., pp. 214-17.
5. Ibid., pp. 215-16.

Implications for translation:
Each language has its own grammatical forms for indicating illocutionary force. We cannot assume that the surface level features we are familiar with in our own language will carry across into other languages.

In English, two common surface level devices used to indicate illocutionary force are **word order** and **intonation**.

Word Order Marking Illocutionary Force
In the following English example, the two sentences have the *same three words* and the *same intonation*, but *different word order*. The change in word order indicates a change in illocutionary force. (The curved line over the last word of each sentence indicates a falling intonation at the end of the sentence.)

- John is going   (declarative)

- Is John going   (interrogative)

Notice that I did not include punctuation in these two sentences. Punctuation generally marks intonation. In this case, the two sentences can be said with identical intonation. The different word order is all that is necessary to make the distinction between a **statement** and a **question**.

Intonation Marking Illocutionary Force
In the following English example, the two sentences have the *same three words* and the *same word order*, but *different intonation*. We noted above that intonation in written speech is often marked by punctuation. In this example the change in intonation is all that is necessary to mark a change in illocutionary force. (The upward and downward curved lines over the last word of each sentence indicate a rising or falling intonation.)

- John is going.   (declarative)

- John is going?   (interrogative)

Language-specific Forms
Every language has its own way of differentiating between a statement, a question, and a command. We have seen that English often uses word order and intonation. English also uses **interrogative adverbs** (also called "question words") such as Who, What, Where, When, Why, How, How Much, etc.

Marking Illocutionary Force in Lamogai

The Lamogai language of PNG has question words that correspond to the interrogative adverbs in English. However, when dealing with questions in Lamogai that do *not* have an interrogative adverb, it can be tricky.

When we first started learning the Lamogai language, we quickly realized that it is often a challenge to tell the difference between statements and questions. In Lamogai questions, there is no change of word order. They use intonation only to differentiate between questions and statements in sentences that do not have an interrogative adverb.

The problem for us as we were trying to learn the Lamogai language is that the intonation pattern for questions sounds quite similar to the intonation for statements. As in English, we use punctuation to mark Lamogai Intonation. Here is an Example:

- Jon la konong?   (Did John go already?)

- Jon la konong.   (John went already.)

With the question above, the intonation only falls part of the way down; but with the statement, it falls all the way down. Listen to the difference on the recorded tutorial lesson.

Below are a couple more examples:

- Ti vasek ovul?   (Did they plant bananas?)

- Ti vasek ovul.   (They planted bananas.)

The words used and the word order are identical; the only change is a slightly different intonation pattern.

- Jisas ma me?   (Will Jesus come?)

- Jisas ma me.   (Jesus will come.)

Skewing and Illocutionary Force[6]

As we noted above, when there is no skewing of the Illocutionary Force:

- A semantic **statement** would be a **declarative** construction grammatically.
- A semantic **question** would be an **interrogative** construction grammatically.
- A semantic **command** would be an **imperative** construction grammatically.

With illocutionary force, as with most semantic features, there can often be skewing. A declarative clause could represent a semantic command as in this example:

"You didn't make your bed yet."

Or an interrogative clause could represent a semantic statement or command. That would be a rhetorical question.

Rhetorical Questions

When you encounter a **question** within a text the first thing you need to determine is whether or not it is a true question semantically—in other words, was the question asked in order to gain information? If not that means it is a rhetorical question.

When we determine that a particular question is a "rhetorical question," that means it uses the grammatical form of a question (interrogative), but it is not really a question semantically.

When we consider the Illocutionary Force of a proposition, there are only three possibilities: It must be a statement, question, or command. If it is not asking a question to elicit information, then it must be one of the other two.

Anytime you recognize that a particular question is actually a rhetorical question, the first thing you need to do is determine whether it is semantically a statement or a command. Here are some examples:

- In John 18:25 Pilate asked Jesus, *"Am I a Jew?"*
    - Clearly, Pilate was not trying to figure out whether or not he was a Jew.
    - He used this rhetorical question to make an emphatic statement:
        - *"I am NOT a Jew!"*

---

6. Ibid., pp. 257-69.

- In Mark 2:6-7 the scribes thought to themselves, *"Who can forgive sins but God alone?"*
  - Were they trying to figure out who besides God can forgive sins?
  - No. They, too, were making an emphatic statement:
    - *"No one can forgive sins but God alone!"*

- In Mark 4:40 Jesus said, *"Why are you so afraid? Do you still have no faith?"*
  - There are two rhetorical questions here, both apparently emphatic commands.
    - *"Don't be afraid!"*
    - *"You need to have faith!"*

Translation of Rhetorical Questions

Rhetorical questions cannot always be transferred literally from one language to another. In order to understand how to translate a rhetorical question, we need to determine its purpose in the source language. In the three examples of rhetorical questions mentioned above, the purpose seems to be emphasis. Putting those semantic statements and commands into the form of a grammatical question makes them more emphatic.

When we translate the rhetorical questions in these verses into any other language, we need to make sure we adequately relay the *emphasis* indicated by the rhetorical question, even if it is not possible to retain the form of the rhetorical question in a particular target language.

TUTORIAL 8.9

ACTIVITIES

1. Rewrite the semantic propositions (event and state) in Mark 2:1-12, removing the skewing. (See sample below)

- Put each proposition on a separate line.
- Use active, finite verbs for event propositions.
- In other words, do not use passive constructions or infinitive verbs.
- Include all participants explicitly even if you don't know who they are.
- Use nonspecific terms like "someone" or "people" if necessary.
- Leave the relations between the propositions for later.

> Jesus came back to Capernaum several days afterward
> People heard
> Jesus was at home
> Many people gathered together

8.10 Concept relations within propositions

OBJECTIVES OF THIS TUTORIAL

Learners will identify the meaningful relations between semantic concepts within propositions.

Relations within Propositions[1]

We have talked about semantic **things**, **events**, and **attributes**. Now we're going to talk about semantic **relations**. How are things, events, and attributes related to one another within a proposition?

We know that every proposition is made up of at least two semantic concepts. In the proposition represented in the baseball example, the event is "hit"; one of the semantic thing concepts in this proposition is "John," and the other semantic thing concept is "ball."

In every proposition there are semantically significant relations between the concepts. In event propositions, these relations are called case roles. In the baseball proposition, the case role relation between "John" and "Hit" is an agent Relation. John is the agent that actually does the action. He is the doer of the event.

Why not just say he is the "Subject"? Because the grammatical subject of a sentence is not always the semantic agent. We can't mix the grammatical and the semantic terms. Why? Because of skewing. Here's an example:

---

1. Mildred L. Larson, Meaning Based Translation: a guide to cross-language equivalence, revised edition, (Lanham, MD: University Press of America, 1998), pp. 219-234.

"Jesus was baptized by John."

- Jesus is the grammatical subject of this sentence.
    - But he is not the semantic agent.
- The semantic agent is John.
    - He is the one who did the action (baptizing) even though he is not the grammatical subject of the sentence.

The case role relation between "ball" and "Hit" in the baseball example is an **affected** Relation. The "ball" is directly affected by the action.[2]

Case Roles within Event Propositions[3]

The agent is the thing concept that does the action—the person or the object which is the doer of the event. Examples:

- **John** ran fast.
- **The deer** jumped over the fence.
- **The water** flowed swiftly.

The **affected** is the semantic thing concept that undergoes the event, or is directly affected by the event. Examples:

- The dog ate **the meat**.
- John hit **the ball**.

The **goal** is the thing concept toward which an event is directed.

- John prayed **to God**.
- John laughed **at Peter**.
- Peter threw the rock **at the fence post**.
- Jesus said **to the paralytic**:

---

2. Various authors use different labels to designate these relations. The terminology we will use in this module comes from Mildred L. Larson, Meaning Based Translation.
3. Mildred L. Larson, Meaning Based Translation, pp. 219-33.

The **beneficiary** is the thing concept that is advantaged or disadvantaged by the event. The beneficiary is not affected as directly as the affected.

- John sold the car **for a friend**.
- Mary bought a present **for Tom**.

The **accompaniment** is the thing concept which participates in close association with the agent, causer, or affected in an event.

- John went to the park **with his dog**.
- I went out to dinner **with my family**.

The **instrument** is the thing concept used to carry out an event.

- Mary wrote **with a pencil**.
- She covered the child **with a blanket**.
- The workmen widened the road **with a bulldozer**.

The **location** is a thing concept that identifies the spatial placement of an event

- Jane ran away **from home**.
- John flew in **from Chicago**.
- She went **to the store**.

The **time** identifies the temporal placement of the event.

- John went to college **three weeks ago**.
- Her mother stayed **for three weeks**.
- **Soon** someone will come for us.

The **manner** is the qualification of the event.

- The man ran **quickly**.
- John wrote the letter **perfectly**.
- The plant grew **rapidly**.

The **measure** is the quantification of the event.

- Jane prays **frequently**.
- They widened the road **by twenty feet**.
- The corn had grown **three inches**.

Case Roles and Skewing

In the examples above, there is no skewing between the form and the meaning. For example, the **agent** is the subject of the sentence in "John ran fast." And the **accompaniment** occurs as the object of the proposition "with" in the sentence, "I ate dinner with my family."

We have learned that there is a great deal of skewing between form and meaning in every language. Translators will often find that the skewing between form and meaning in the source language is not the same as the skewing between form and meaning in the target language.

The translator must consider it from both sides:

- Analyze the original text to discover the meaning without source-language skewing.
- Re-express the meaning in the target language, using appropriate target-language skewing.

Example of Skewing in the Encoding of Case Roles in English:[4]

One Case Role can be encoded in several different Forms. The clauses listed in the table below all represent the same semantic proposition. The context determines the various ways the proposition is worded:

Peter ate the apple	Object	⇐ NO Skewing
The apple was eaten by Peter	Subject	
The apple which Peter ate		
The eating of the apple by Peter…	Object of a proposition	⇐ SKEWED
Peter's eating of the apple.		

---

4. Ibid., pp. 245-55.

In the sentence, "*Peter ate the apple*" there is no skewing. The semantic **agent** (Peter) is encoded as the grammatical **subject** and the semantic concept filling the role of **affected** (apple) is encoded as the grammatical **object**.

If we say, "*The apple was eaten by Peter*" or "*The apple which Peter ate...*" that represents the same semantic proposition, but there is skewing. The semantic concept in the **affected** role (apple) is now encoded as the grammatical subject. Or if we say, "*The eating of the apple by Peter...*" or "*Peter's eating of the apple...*" that is also skewed. The semantic concept filling the role of **affected** (apple) is now encoded as the object of a preposition.

Sometimes a single Form is used to encode several different Case Roles. For example:

- I ate ice cream **with my spoon**. (Instrument)
- I ate ice cream **with my pie**. (Accompaniment-Affected)
- I ate ice cream **with my wife**. (Accompaniment-Agent)

This word "with" is used to communicate three different Case Role relations. Grammatically, these three sentences are constructed the same, but semantically they are very different.

State Relations within State Propositions[5]

Every State Proposition has a **topic** and a **comment** and a **relation** between the two. Below are a few examples.

	Topic ... relation ... Comment
Proposition	CAR ... ownership ... ME
English	The car is mine.
	The car belongs to me.

	Topic ... relation ... Comment
Proposition	DOG ... naming ... FIDO
English	The dog's name is Fido.
	The dog is called Fido.

---

5. Ibid., pp. 235-44.

CONCEPT RELATIONS WITHIN PROPOSITIONS

	Topic ... relation ... Comment
Proposition	CAR ... location ... GARAGE
English	The car is in the garage.

	Topic ... relation ... Comment
Proposition	THAT TABLE ... substance ... WOOD
English	That wooden table.
English	That table is made of wood.

	Topic ... relation ... Comment
Proposition	BOOK ... description ... SMALL
English	The book is small.

	Topic ... relation ... Comment
Proposition	BAG ... containership ... RICE
English	The bag has rice in it.
English	The bag contains rice.

	Topic ... relation ... Comment
Proposition	AIR ... ambience ... HOT
English	It is hot.

	Topic ... relation ... Comment
Proposition	TIME ... (time) ... NOON
English	It is noon.

Multiple encoding of State Propositions

A single state proposition could be encoded several different ways, depending on the context. For example, with "ownership" it could be:

- John's house…
- John has a house.
- John owns a house.
- The house John owns…

Or with "containership" it could be:

- The water jug…
- The jug of water…
- The jug has water in it.
- The jug contains water.
- The jug with water in it…
- The jug containing water…
- The jug which contains water…

These all represent the same Semantic Proposition, but it is encoded in several different ways.

Simple & Complex Concepts

An example of a simple concept would be the word "dog." But "complex" concepts often include embedded state propositions. Here is an example:

"The big dog inside the wooden fence is named Fido."

- The main state proposition in this example is "*The dog is named Fido.*"
- But there are additional embedded state propositions:
    - The dog is big.
    - The dog is inside the fence.
    - The fence is wooden.

CONCEPT RELATIONS WITHIN PROPOSITIONS

ACTIVITIES

1. Make a copy of the document that lists your rewritten propositions for Mark 2:1-12 (the assignment from Tutorial 8.9).

On this new copy, identify and mark the Case Roles in Event Propositions.

Identify and mark the State Relations in State Propositions.

Follow the pattern below. The first two lines are **event propositions** and the third line is a **state proposition**.

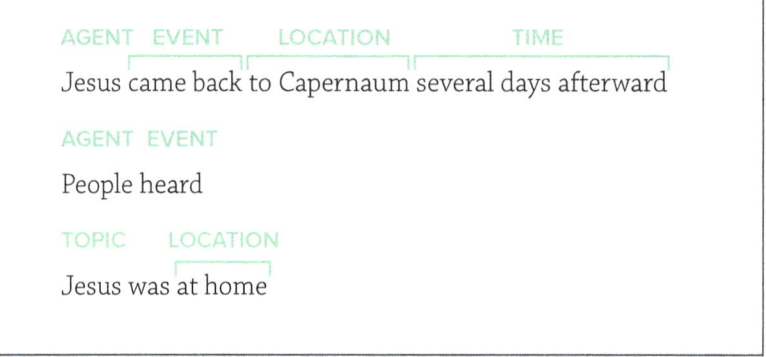

8.11 Communication relations

 OBJECTIVES OF THIS TUTORIAL

Learners will identify semantic relations between propositions and between larger semantic units.

Introduction

We have been looking at semantic **concepts** and the meaningful RELATIONS between them. With **event** propositions, the relations between the concepts are called **case roles**. With **state** propositions, the relations are called **state relations**.

Now we are going to focus on relations on higher levels. Our focus has been below the proposition level. Why is the Proposition such a key dividing line? Because the proposition is the smallest unit of Communication.[1] That's why relations between semantic units on the proposition level and higher are called "Communication Relations."

Propositions within their Context[2]

So far, as we have been looking at propositions, we have considered them outside of their context. When we consider propositions *within* their context, we will discover meaningful relationships between the propositions.

Propositions are joined together by "Inter-propositional Relations," sometimes abbreviated IPRs. Inter-propositional Relations (IPRs) are just one kind of Communication Relation. In this module we will use the broader term "Communication Relation" because it is more inclusive. The kinds of relations that we see between propositions on the proposition level can occur on other levels too.

Propositions often join together to form **propositional clusters**. Propositional clusters are related to one another by some of the same kids of communication relations that we find between propositions. As propositions and propositional clusters join together,

---

1. Ibid., p. 211.
2. Ibid., pp. 299-301.

they form semantic paragraphs. And paragraphs are joined together by communication relations to form larger discourse units.

It is these relations between propositions, propositional clusters, and paragraphs that we will be considering in this tutorial.

Examples of Communication Relations[3]

Here is a pair of semantic propositions:

> *Mary swept the floor*
>
> *The floor was dirty*

These two Propositions could be joined together with various kinds of communication relations:

A **reason**-RESULT relation would be:

> *Mary swept the floor because it was dirty.*

A **concession**-CONTRA-EXPECTATION relation (contrary to what is expected) would be:

> *Even though Mary swept the floor, the floor was dirty.*

A **condition**-CONSEQUENCE relation would be:

> *If the floor was dirty, Mary swept it.*

In each of these cases it is the same pair of semantic propositions. Only the relationship between the propositions is changed. Sometimes translators have succeeded in correctly translating the semantic propositions, but failed to correctly translate the relation between the propositions. The relation is part of the meaning that must be translated.

In a semantic structural analysis, a **reason**-RESULT relationship would be marked like this:

> [RESULT — *Mary swept the floor*
> [reason — *(because) it was dirty*

---

[3]. Ibid., pp. 300-301.

Head and Support Propositions[4]

Notice that one Proposition is marked with a term in UPPER CASE letters and the other is marked in lower case. The upper case letters represent the HEAD proposition when one is subordinate to the other. The lower case letters represent the support (also called the subordinate) proposition.

In some cases, a pair of propositions may be equal in prominence—not having a **HEAD-support** Relation. Neither proposition is subordinate to the other. In a case like that, both propositions would be described with either UPPER or lower case letters.

Here is an example:

Mary does the cleaning

And Jean does the cooking

Logical Relations[5]

Many of the Communication Relations we will be dealing with will be what we call **Logical Relations**. Logical Relations are **support-HEAD** relations where there is a **cause-and-EFFECT** relationship between the propositions. Here are some examples:

- reason-RESULT:
    - *John washed the car because it was dirty.*

Here is another way to communicate this same semantic relation:

- reason-RESULT:
    - *The car was dirty so John washed it.*

---

4. Ibid., pp. 299-317.
5. Ibid., pp. 235-51.

These two examples represent the same pair of propositions with the same relation. The only difference is the order.[6]

- means-RESULT:
    - By washing the car, John got it clean.
- purpose-MEANS:
    - John washed the car in order to get it clean.
- concession-CONTRA-EXPECTATION:
    - Although John washed the car, it isn't clean.
- grounds-CONCLUSION:
    - The car is clean, so John must have washed it.
- grounds-EXHORTATION:
    - The car is dirty, so you wash it, John.
- condition-CONSEQUENCE:
    - If the car is dirty, John will wash it.

Chronological Relations[7]

Sometimes the Relation between propositions is purely based on **time**, without a logically-oriented relation. These Time-based Propositions could be marked as:

- event^1
- event^2
- event^3
- event^4

For example:

> John went home
>
> he ate dinner
>
> and he went to bed

---

6. Ibid., pp. 344-45.
7. Ibid., pp. 309-10.

This example is **sequential**. Another kind of time-based relation is **simultaneous**. For example:

> *He played the piano*
>
> *While she sang*

Skewing of order[8]

A narrative discourse generally recounts a series of events which occurred in a certain order. However, these events may be reordered in the narrative in such a way that the order is not the same as the actual sequential order. This is a type of **skewing**. The form of the source language text may be non-sequential, but the actual meaning is sequential. No matter how those events happen to be ordered in written or spoken communication, they did occur in a certain sequence.

A translator may need to make adjustments in translation to make sure the correct meaning comes through clearly. In some languages (including many languages Papua New Guinea) it is often helpful to retain sequential order when translating a series of events.

When a translator approaches a complex series of events, written in a way that does not follow the actual sequential order, it may be helpful to think through the situation to figure out the order in which the events actually occurred. Even if the translator doesn't end up reordering the events in the translation, it can still be a valuable exercise to list the events in their true sequential order to paint a clear picture of what happened.

What is the real order of events in this text?[9]

Below is a sample text in which the events are not all told in their true sequential order:

> *John went into the house, leaving the people standing out in the cold. He returned to comfort them again, after discussing the whole situation with his wife and telling her the whole story.*

Here's written order of the semantic propositions included in this story (non-sequential):

> *John went into the house*

---

8. Ibid., pp. 310-12.
9. Ibid., p. 311.

John left the people

The people were standing out in the cold.

John returned (outside)

John comforted them again

John discussed the whole situation with his wife

John told her the whole story.

Now, here's the true sequential order of the events in this series of propositions:

John left the people

The people were standing out in the cold.

John went into the house

John told her the whole story.

John discussed the whole situation with his wife

John returned (outside)

John comforted them again

The written order is skewed, but the true sequential order is not skewed.

More Communication Relations

Earlier in this tutorial we noted that some communication relations are **support-HEAD** relations, also called **subordinate relations,** In because one of the propositions (or larger semantic units) is subordinate to the other. We already looked at one kind of **support-HEAD** relation called **logical relations**. With logical relations, there is always a **cause-EFFECT** relationship between the propositions. The Logical Relations we listed are:

- Reason-RESULT
- Means-RESULT
- Purpose-MEANS
- Concession-CONTRA-EXPECTATION
- Grounds-CONCLUSION
- Grounds-EXHORTATION
- Condition-CONSEQUENCE

Now we will consider two kinds of **support-HEAD** relations that are not classified as logical relations: Clarification Relations and Orientation Relations.

Clarification Relations[10]

When a pair of propositions is said to be linked by a **clarification relation**, the two propositions say basically the same thing from two different angles. The support proposition expand the information of the HEAD proposition. Below are three kinds of clarification relations:

HEAD-equivalence:
- The two units convey the same meaning
- Example: *Believe and do not doubt.*

HEAD-amplification:
- One of the units communicates some of the information that is in the other plus some further information
- Example: *He practices medicine; he practices at the clinic in town.*

GENERIC-specific:
- The specific part gives more precise detail
- Example: *He cut up the meat; he chopped the meat into small pieces.*

---

10. Ibid., pp. 324-30.

COMMUNICATION RELATIONS

These three Clarification Relations are closely related with a certain amount of overlap. In some cases, more than one of these three relations may adequately describe the connection between a pair of propositions.

Orientation Relations[11]

Another category of support-HEAD relations is called **orientation relations**. This includes circumstance-HEAD relations and orienter-CONTENT relations.

circumstance-HEAD Relations[12]

The circumstance provides some background information related to the HEAD proposition (or larger unit).

- Example: *Walking along the cliff top she saw Bill.*
    - (Could also be called **location-HEAD**)
- Example: *As the sun began to rise they left the village.*
    - (Could also be called **time-HEAD**)

orienter-CONTENT Relations[13]

Another very important and frequently used orientation relation is **orienter-CONTENT**. The proposition which is the **orienter** serves to introduce the CONTENT. There are several kinds of orienter-CONTENT Relations:

- Speech
- Perceptual
- Cognitive
- Volitional
- Evaluative

---

11. Ibid., pp. 319-23.
12. Ibid., pp. 321-23.
13. Ibid., pp. 321-23.

Speech orienter-CONTENT relations

Some sample event words used for to orient **speech** are "said," "commanded," "warned," "promised," etc.

Tell him not to go.

- **orienter**: You tell him
- CONTENT: Do not go

Jesus said, "Pick up your bed and walk!"

- **orienter**: Jesus said
- CONTENT: You pick up your bed
- CONTENT: You walk

The **orienter-CONTENT** "speech" relation is very common in dialogue.

Perceptual orienter-CONTENT relations (The Five Senses)

Some sample event words used to orient **perceptual** content are "saw," "heard," "felt," "smelled," and "tasted."

I saw him do it.

- **orienter**: I saw him
- CONTENT: He did it

I heard them talking.

- **orienter**: I heard them
- CONTENT: They were talking

Cognitive orienter-CONTENT relations

Some sample event words used to orient content that is **cognitive** in nature are "knew," "remembered," "thought," "agreed."

Did they agree to go.

- **orienter**: Did they agree?
- CONTENT: They will go?

I know where the prize is.

- **orienter**: I know
- CONTENT: where the prize is.

Volitional orienter-CONTENT relations

Some sample event words used to orient **volitional** content are "decided," "willed," "wanted," "purposed."

I want you to come.

- **orienter**: I want
- CONTENT: that you come.

I decided not to go.

- **orienter**: I decided
- CONTENT: I will not go.

Evaluative orienter-CONTENT relations

Some sample event words used to orient **evaluative** content are "is good," "is true," "is false."

It is good that it rained today.

- **orienter**: It is good
- CONTENT: that it rained today.

It is wrong to lie.

- **orienter**: It is wrong
- CONTENT: that someone lies.

When you mark **orienter-CONTENT** relations in the assignment for this tutorial, you do not need to classify the various kinds of orienter-CONTENT relations as **speech**, **perceptual**, **cognitive**, etc. Just mark them as **orienter-CONTENT** relations. The specific terms "speech, "perceptual," etc. are just meant to clarify the scope of orienter-CONTENT relations.

Multiple Functions of Grammatical Relation Markers[14]

A common mistake that translators make in dealing with communication relations is focusing too much on matching the Receptor Language forms. Focusing on the forms will cause problems because a single relation marker can often be used to represent various semantic relations. We need to make sure we match the semantic relationship—not the form of the relation marker.

For example, the relation marker "if" in English, has the primary meaning of "condition" in condition-CONSEQUENCE relations, as in the sentence, *"If the car is dirty, we will wash it."* However, "if" can also represent "grounds" in the grounds-CONCLUSION relation, as in the sentence, *"If the light is on, Mary must be home."* The area of meaning of the English word "if" does not match the area of meaning of any single word in many other languages.

Some languages may have separate markers for each of the following:

- If, and it IS true...
- If, and it is NOT true...
- If, and it may or may not be true...

When a translator learning another language discovers the target language word for "if" as it occurs in one of these semantic relationships, he or she may wrongly assume that that form can be used in all other contexts where the English word "if" is used.

We need to focus on the meaningful semantic relationships—not the specific relation markers. And in Scripture Translation, we need to be careful to faithfully translate all of those semantic relationships because they truly are part of the meaning. If we try to match the form of the target language relation markers, we may actually corrupt God's inspired meaning.

---

14. Ibid., pp. 330-31; 348-49.

COMMUNICATION RELATIONS

➡ ACTIVITIES

1. In this activity you will identify the communication relations for Mark 2:1-12.

- First, make a copy of your "Rewritten Propositions" in a landscape-orientation.
- Place each proposition on a separate line (See illustration below).
- Move all the propositions toward the right side of the page.
  - Keep a straight, consistent left margin.
  - Move the text as far to the right as the longest proposition will allow.
  - This will leave space on the left for the Communication Relations.

2. Pause at each illustration to make sure you understand it before moving on.

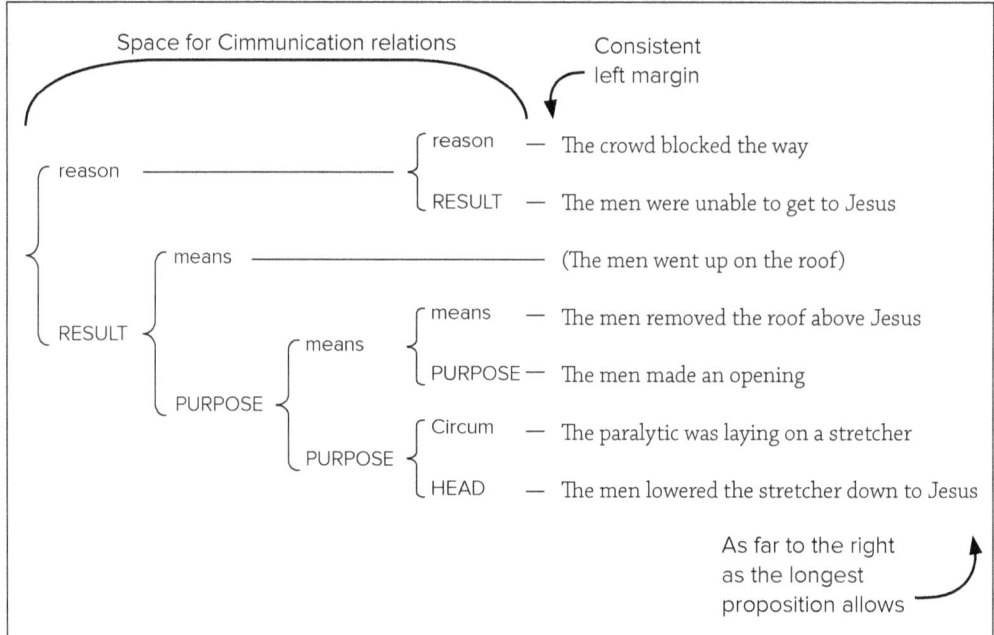

3. Identifying the Paragraphs.

- The first step is to identify and mark the semantic paragraph divisions. (Remember: *There is not just one correct way to divide the paragraphs; English versions do not all divide the paragraphs in the same places.*)
- For this exercise, let's call the first two verses (Mark 2:1-2) paragraph #1.
- And let's call the next three verses (Mark 2:3-5) paragraph #2.
- I will walk you through the process of analyzing some of the communication relations in paragraph #2; then you will work through the rest of the passage on your own.

4. Analyze one paragraph at a time.

It is important to identify the paragraph breaks before analyzing the communication relations, and each paragraph must be analyzed individually. Otherwise, you may inadvertently try to link a proposition at the end of one paragraph with a proposition at the beginning of the next paragraph, when they do not connect on that level.

5. Here are the steps for analyzing communication relations:

- First divide the passage into semantic units, from the largest (i.e., paragraphs) to the smallest (i.e., pairs of propositions that are directly connected to each other).
- Then define the communication relations starting on the lowest level (i.e., pairs of connected propositions) and working step-by-step through the levels of propositional clusters until you reach the highest level in the passage: the paragraph level.

6. Once you have identified the semantic paragraphs, next look for natural divisions within each paragraph indicating the major propositional clusters.

- I divided this paragraph into 15 propositions (You may have done it differently).
    - The first ten propositions form one major propositional cluster.
    - And the next five propositions form another major propositional cluster.

7. Pause to make sure you understand why I divided it the way I did.

	People came
	People brought the paralytic to Jesus
	Four men carried the paralytic
	The crowd blocked the way
Major Propositional Cluster	The men were unable to get to Jesus
	(The men went up on the roof)
	The men removed the roof above Jesus
	The men made an opening
	The paralytic was laying on a stretcher
	The men lowered the stretcher down to Jesus
	Jesus saw
	The men believed (Jesus could heal)
Major Propositional Cluster	Jesus said to the paralytic
	You have sinned
	I forgive you

8. Next we will look at each major propositional cluster individually to see where it divides into smaller propositional clusters.

The first major propositional cluster (see above) divides into two smaller clusters like this:

	People came
Propositional Cluster	People brought the paralytic to Jesus
	Four men carried the paralytic
	The crowd blocked the way
	The men were unable to get to Jesus
	(The men went up on the roof)
Propositional Cluster	The men removed the roof above Jesus
	The men made an opening
	The paralytic was laying on a stretcher
	The men lowered the stretcher down to Jesus

9. We are almost ready to start defining the communication relations. First we need to find pairs of closely connected propositions within these propositional clusters.

- This is where we will begin defining the communication relations between pairs of closely connected propositions.
- Then we will work our way up to the higher levels, defining the communication relations on each successive level.

10. There are four pairs of closely connected propositions within these propositional clusters:

- The first pair is connected by a **HEAD—amplification** communication relation
- The second is **reason—RESULT**
- The third is **means—PURPOSE**
- The fourth is **circumstance—HEAD**

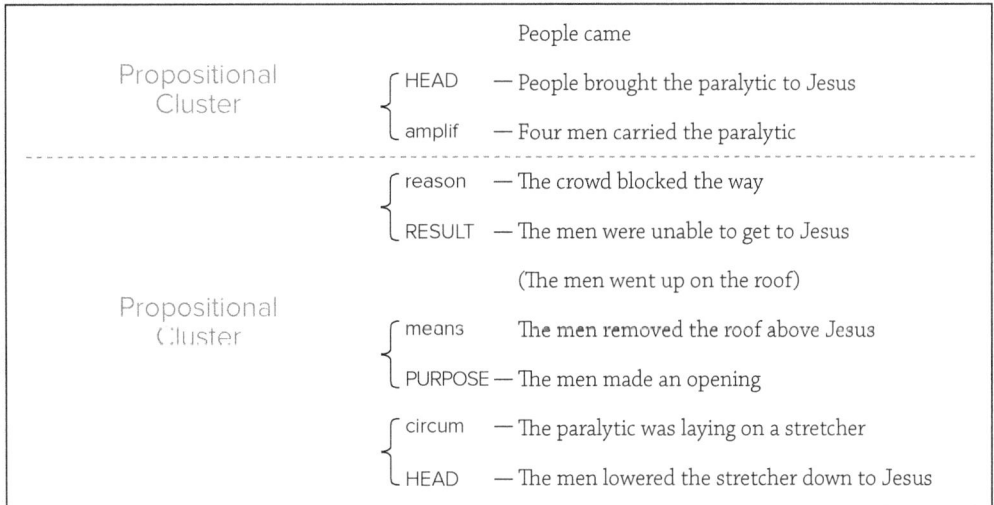

11. Pause to consider each of these four pairs of propositions above to make sure you understand why I chose these particular communication relations to describe the semantic connections.

COMMUNICATION RELATIONS

12. Now define the rest of the communication relations within these propositional clusters.

- Then, define the relations between the propositional clusters themselves.
- After that, continue defining the relationships, from the lower levels all the way up to the highest levels.

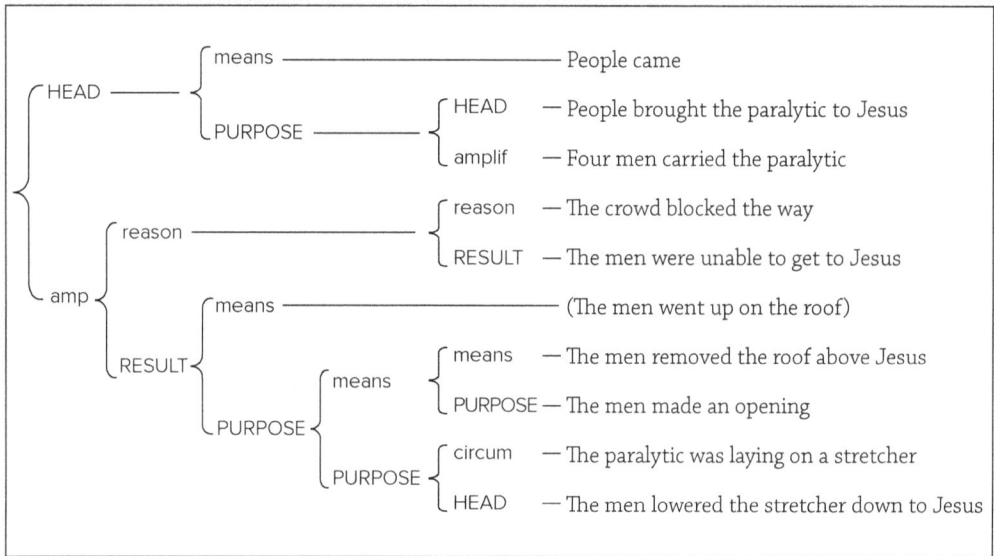

8.12 The translation process

 OBJECTIVES OF THIS TUTORIAL

Learners will take into account the importance of considering their target audience when translating key terms and other features of language. They will think through the process of translating Mark 2:1-12 for a specified target audience.

Feeling the Dilemma of the Translator

By now it should be clear that Bible translation is a very complex process. It's not an *impossible* process, but it is a *difficult* process requiring a serious commitment of time and effort. A major focus of this module up to this point has been to allow you to work through some of the steps a translator would work through and experiences some of the challenges a translator would face.

If some of the steps in these Bible translation tutorials have seemed a bit daunting—or even overwhelming—that is okay. I want you to feel a bit of the dilemma that translators face—not to discourage you, but to give you a more realistic understanding of what is really involved in Bible translation. I want you to realize that in Bible translation, there will often *not* be easy answers to the questions you will face. But even through the answers are not easy, there will indeed be an answer to every question.

The sobering weight of the task of Bible translation often drove me to my knees in prayer. I was constantly reminded of the huge responsibility I had taken on. But God was faithful every step of the way. When the Lamogai New Testament was finally published and put into the hands of the Lamogai believers, I can honestly say that I felt good about every translation decision we had made. I won't pretend that the Lamogai translation is perfect. There is no such thing as a perfect translation in any language. But I honestly believe that by God's grace, we were able to give the Lamogai church a translation of the Scriptures that is faithful and clear.

THE TRANSLATION PROCESS

Up to this point, our focus has been on exegesis—unpacking the meaning of the original. In this module, you will get a chance to try your hand at actually translating, but first there are a couple more steps that we need to take care of: **target audience** and **key terms**.

Source Text and Target Audience

The activity worksheets for this module all use the *New American Standard Bible* (NASB). The NASB translators leaned heavily toward the literal side of the translation spectrum. That means that even though the NASB is a good translation, it often does not follow conventional English literary style. No one actually speaks "NASB English," but hopefully we can all understand NASB English well enough to use it as our source language text for the simulated translation exercises in this module.

If the NASB is our source language text, then who is our target audience? I am going to leave that up to each of you to decide. I want you to choose a target audience, but it must be a target audience of English speakers. For example, you may choose a particular age group: a five year old child, a ten year old, a high school student. Or you may choose another category of English speakers like un-churched university students or inner-city adults with little or no education. As you work your way through this simulated translation process you will need to keep your specified target audience in mind with each translational decision you make.

Key Terms

Before you begin translating, you need to consider a few key terms included in our passage, Mark 2:1-12. You need to be sure you translate each term in a way that will be clear and natural to your specified target audience. Below are a few terms to consider:

Capernaum
When we translated for the Lamogai people we knew they would not automatically know that "Capernaum" was the name of a place. For that reason we translated it "the city called Capernaum" or "the place called Capernaum."

Paralytic
Will your target audience be familiar with this word? If not, you may need to translate it "a man who was paralyzed" or "a man who could not walk" or something similar.

Pallet
What does this word mean to you? When I hear the word "pallet" I think of a wooden skid used for transporting cargo, or a painter's pallet with primary colors of paint.

Depending on your target audience, some better options may be "mat," "stretcher," or "bedroll."

Scribes

Originally, "scribes" were copyists. They were the ones who painstakingly made handwritten copies of the Hebrew Scriptures because they had no printing presses. By Jesus's day, however, the scribes were much more than mere copyists. Since they spent more time with the Scriptures than anyone else did, they became the experts in the written word (which was often referred to as "the Law"). They ended up being the teachers and religious leaders of the Jews. Depending on your target audience, you may choose to translate this word as "Teachers of the Law" or "Jewish leaders," or something similar.

Blaspheme

Is this a word your target audience will understand? In Scripture "blaspheme" means to "speak badly to or about God" or to "try to take the place of God." One point to remember is that "blaspheme" is an extremely strong term. You need to make sure your translation of this term conveys the intensity of the original term.

Other Terms

There are several other terms you will need to consider specifically with your target audience in mind. Will they clearly understand words like "faith," "sin," "forgive," and "glorify"?

Son of Man

This is one of the more difficult terms translators often have to face when translating for a minority language like Lamogai. For the purpose of this simulated exercise, I will not ask you to try to unpack this term; just translate it "Son of Man." However, you may need to consider whether or not your audience will correctly understand the way Jesus used this term. He used it as a third-person reference, which could sound like he was talking about someone else—not himself. If necessary, it would certainly be appropriate to translate it "*I, the Son of Man*" to make sure it is clear who Jesus was talking about.

Dug [an opening in the roof]

Don't get hung up on the word "dug." If "dug" is the best word to paint the correct picture of this event for your specific target audience, that is fine. But you should know that "dug" is not the only correct way to translate the Greek word used here. This Greek word only occurs one other place in the New Testament, in Galatians 4:15, where it is translated "plucked out" in some versions: "*...I bear you witness that, if possible, you would have plucked out your eyes and given them to me.*" (In that context, "plucked out" sounds bad enough—I'm glad no one translated it "dug out," even though that would have been an acceptable rendering.)

Reasoning in their hearts

Again, don't get hung up on literally translating "reasoned in their hearts" if that will not sound natural to your audience. What does it mean to "reason in our hearts"? Even the highly-literal NASB often chose not to translate this phrase literally. Here are a couple examples:

- Genesis 27:41
    - HEBREW: "*Esau said in his heart*"
    - NASB: "*Esau said to himself.*"
- 1 Samuel 27:1
    - HEBREW: "*David said in his heart*"
    - NASB: "*David said to himself.*"

Ambiguity

There is an ambiguous statement in this passage. Some translations interpreted it one way and others interpreted it another way. The ambiguity is in verse 3, where it says, "*And they came, bringing Him a paralytic, carried by four men.*" How many people came with the paralytic? Was it only the four who carried him, or was there a larger group of people and just four of them were carrying him? The way this is worded in the original, it could mean either of these possibilities. As a translator, you may have to choose one.

Translating the Text

So far, our focus in this module has been on the "downward arrow" of the translation model illustration. We have been trying to discover and unpack all of the meaning. Some of the features we have considered are:

- Communication Situation
- Discourse Genre
- Groupings: Cohesion and Boundaries
- Skewing
- Semantic Paragraphs
- Semantic Propositions
- Case Roles and State Relations
- Key Terms

TUTORIAL 8.12

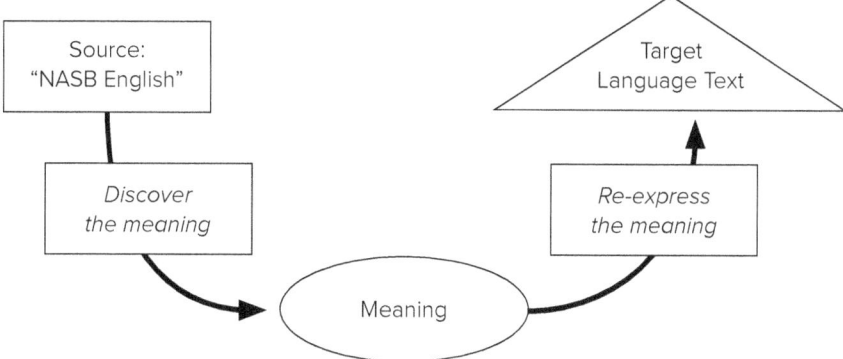

Now we will shift our focus to the "upward arrow"—re-expressing the meaning we have discovered, using forms that are appropriate for our selected target audience of English speakers. As we worked through the previous tutorials in this module, we produced some useful tools that can help us translate this passage. But along with these tools, we need to go back to the source (in this case, the NASB translation). In translating this passage you will work from the Scriptures and use the analytical tools we have created as a supplement.

Three Key Roles in Translation

When a team of translators undertakes an actual translation project, the team must include individuals with proficiency in the following three areas:

- The Target Language
- Biblical Exegesis
- Translation Principles

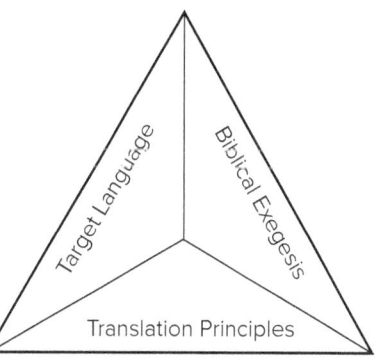

The Target Language

The mother-tongue speakers of the target language should always be recognized as the experts in their own language. This is true from the beginning of a translation project all the way through to the end. No matter how many years a non-native speaker has spent learning and speaking a particular target language, he or she will *not* be an expert in that language in the way a mother-tongue speaker will be.

Biblical Exegesis

In many cases, one or more of the non-native (expatriate) members of the translation team will be expected to be the "experts" in biblical exegesis. That does not mean they have to be true experts in all aspects of the Bible; but they should have direct access to the writings of qualified biblical scholars.

Translation Principles
Initially, when a new translation project is launched, the non-native (expatriate) team members will normally take the lead in properly applying translation principles. It is their job to know how to correctly transfer the meaning of the source language text into the target language. However, as the translation project progresses, the mother-tongue speakers on the team will grow in their understanding of translation principles. Ideally, the responsibility for properly applying translation principles will eventually be shared equally between the mother-tongue speakers and the non-native members of the team.

A Shared Effort
Even though the mother-tongue speakers are the *experts* in the target language, non-native members of the team who have learned the language can give input into the wording of the translation. Also, even though the non-native (expatriate) members of the team often have greater access to the writings of biblical scholars, the mother-tongue speakers can make a significant contribution toward making sure the translation reflects the pure biblical message. This will especially be true once the mother-tongue speakers have been well-taught in biblical truth and have begun teaching it to others.

Some expatriate translators have overestimated their proficiency in the target language, translating the Scriptures on their own and then reading the translation to a mother-tongue speaker to see if it sounds okay. Generally, that strategy produces a substandard translation. Also, there have been cases where mother-tongue speakers were given more responsibility for *biblical exegesis* and *translation principles* than they were equipped to handle. Each member of the translation team needs to recognize his or her particular areas of proficiency and use those proficiencies, joining with the other team members, to produce a high-quality translation of God's Word.

TUTORIAL 8.12

➡ ACTIVITIES

1. Choose a specific target audience of English speakers. Then translate Mark 2:1-12 into an appropriate form in English with your chosen target audience in mind. This will be your initial "rough" draft.

- Work from the Scriptures and also from the semantic analysis tools you have created.
- At the top of the page, specify your target audience.
- Include verse numbers within the text.
- Use appropriate paragraphing, based on the paragraph divisions you found. In other words, do not just put each verse on a separate line.

8.13 Assessing the translation

OBJECTIVES OF THIS TUTORIAL

Learners will be introduced to the process and purpose of conducting a *Content Check* and a *Comprehension Check* of translated Scripture.

Quality Control

The goal of every serious Bible translator is to translate the truths of Scripture accurately, clearly and naturally.[1] It is essential that all translated materials be carefully assessed in order to assure that this goal is fully reached. There are two main kinds of assessments: *Content Checks* and *Comprehension Checks*.

The Content Check

The purpose of a content check is to make sure the "content" of the translated materials lines up with the "content" of Scripture. A content check is done by comparing the translated materials side-by-side with the source text.

Some questions that may be raised in a content check are as follows:

- Has any of the content of this Scripture portion been inadvertently left out of the translation?
- Has extra content been added without reason?
- Has the meaning of the source text been changed?
- Does the translation convey the same force and intensity of the source text, or is it unduly weak or unduly strong?
- Does the translation contain unnecessary ambiguities that could cloud the meaning?
- Does the translation include distracting connotations that may be inappropriately humorous or offensive?

---

1. See: John Beekman and John Callow, Translating the Word of God (Grand Rapids: Zondervan, 1974), pp. 34, 39-43, 58-62. See also Dave Brunn, One Bible, Many Versions: Are All Translations Created Equal? (Downers Grove, IL: InterVarsity Press, 2013), chap. 5, pp. 85-98.

Each portion of translated Scripture will likely go through the content checking process several times before it is finished. When I was translating the New Testament into Lamogai, I would do a content check of every translated passage at several points during the translation process, carefully weighing the translation against the source text. Some content checks were focused on low-level details, and some were focused on higher-level discourse features, such as cohesion and boundaries in paragraphs and other large semantic units.

Once I was confident that the "content" of a portion of translated Scripture was basically what it needed to be, I would begin doing comprehension checks of the same portion.

The Comprehension Check

The purpose of a comprehension check is to make sure the mother-tongue speakers can clearly understand the intended meaning of a translated portion of Scripture. When we do a comprehension check, we generally read a section of the translation aloud to a mother-tongue speaker and ask them relevant questions to determine how well they understand the meaning. When it becomes apparent in a particular verse or passage, that the meaning is not coming through clearly, the translator will work with target language speakers to determine what is hindering clear communication of the meaning.

Ultimately, our goal is that the translation will communicate clearly to a reasonable cross-section of our target audience, including men and women, older and younger people, those living nearby as well as those living farther away. Here are some sample comprehension check questions for Mark 2:

- In this story, why were there so many the people gathered together?
- Why were the four men trying to bring their friend to Jesus?
- Why were the scribes upset with Jesus?

Finding the Right Balance

Obviously, there are details that the original readers understood that the average reader of a present-day translation will not know without teaching. It is not possible (nor is it advisable) to try to include every detail of meaning that the original audience may have known. However, we want to include enough details to make sure the translation paints a fair approximation of the picture perceived by the original readers and hearers.

A worthwhile exercise is to study a passage of Scripture to be translated, noting concepts that the original readers would have known. That does not mean every one of those details should be explicitly included in the translation. But working through that exercise can help the translator keep the perspective of the original readers in mind while translating that section.

See the sample "Culture Notes" chart for Mark 1 and 2 at the end of this tutorial.

The Consultant Check

When a translator has finished translating a book of the Bible and has completed the necessary content checks and comprehension checks, the next step is to schedule a check administered by a Bible translation consultant.

In most cases the consultant will not be familiar with the target language, so the translator will need to create a "back translation." A *back translation* is a fairly literal representation of the target language translation, turned back into English or another language that the consultant knows. The term "back-translation" is commonly abbreviated BT, or sometimes BTE ("back to English"), for a back-translation in English.

Below is a sample back-translation of the first part of Genesis chapter 1 from a real language. In creating a back-translation it is not necessary to strictly follow English grammar rules. Also, it does not need to be stylistically natural in English. The back-translation will likely reflect the style and grammar of the target language.

Senesise 1

This is the very origin of the various other things that God created

[1]In the very first origin God created the sky and the ground on which we live. [2]That ground which he created did not resemble the appearance of the ground which we now see. For that ground did not have various things, it was just there nothing. Above the ground there was deep water, then above that deep water there was darkness. And God Heart (the Holy Spirit) above the deep water was going gliding/soaring.

[3]Then God said that, It must be light, he said. And so in the way in which he said, it was light. [4]God, having seen that light, he said that, That light is good, he said. And so God separated into two the light and the darkness that were there. [5]Having separated them into two God, having seen the light, he said its name is light. Then having seen the darkness its name is darkness he said. That afternoon having finished, then the new morning having dawned that very first day began existing.

The consultant will use the *back translation* to do a content check of the translation, making sure nothing has been left out, or added unnecessarily, or changed. (See the list of content check considerations previously mentioned.) Based on this content check,

ASSESSING THE TRANSLATION

the consultant will write up a list of questions and comments identifying places where it appears that the "content" of the translation does not line up with the "content" of the source text. The consultant will send this write-up to the translator, who will work through the list of comments and suggestions, making adjustments where necessary. The consultant will also make affirming, positive comments about the translation where appropriate.

Content Check: Mark 1-8

Language: ------------
Translator: ------------
Consultant: Dave Brunn

Mk 1:3 – I see that your term for "wilderness" is "place where there are no people." In your back translation (BT) it sounds kind of peculiar where it says: "*That man will yell where there are no people, 'You people…'*" If the phrase "*where there are no people*" is a dead metaphor meaning "*wilderness*," that's fine, but if it will be interpreted literally that there really are no people there, it may seem odd that John the Baptist was yelling out to "people" where there are no people.

Mk 1:4-15 – I like the way you handled the discourse-level transitions in these verses. I can tell you were taking the big picture of the passage into consideration.

Mk 1:16 – Your BT says: "*Jesus walked TO the shore of the lake.*"

The SL says: "*Jesus walked ALONGSIDE the shore of the lake.*"

Mk 1:30 – OMITTED: "laying sick"

Mk 7:37 – DYNAMICS: Your word "startled" seems perhaps a bit weak for "astonished beyond measure." Can you intensify it?

Next, the consultant will schedule a face-to-face comprehension check with the translator. In this part of the check, the consultant will meet together with the translator and some mother-tongue speakers of the target language—usually two or three. The consultant will ask the translator to read a few verses aloud, and then the target language speakers will be asked to explain the meaning of what was read. The consultant will follow up with more questions, digging deeper if necessary, to make sure the correct meaning is coming through clearly to the target language speakers. If a certain part of the translation is unintelligible, or if the target language speakers misinterpret what it is supposed to mean, the consultant, along with the translator and the mother-tongue speakers, will try to determine what the problem is and propose a possible solution.

Consultant checks are not foolproof, but they can be valuable for improving the quality of translated materials.

ACTIVITIES

1. Exchange your "rough draft" translation of Mark 2:1-12 with a fellow student. If you don't know of any other students, you can contact the *AccessTruth* team.

2. Do a content check of the other student's rough draft translation.

- Refer to the list of content check considerations near the beginning of this tutorial.
- Be sure to make some positive comments along with your critique of the translation.

3. Devise comprehension check questions for *your own* translation of Mark 2:1-12, to determine how well your translation is communicating.

4. If possible, find someone within your designated target audience and conduct a comprehension check. Read a few lines of your translation of Mark 2:1-12 and ask comprehension check questions that pertain to that section, to find out how well the hearer understands.

8.14 What is literacy? Is it important?

 OBJECTIVES OF THIS TUTORIAL

This tutorial introduces literacy - an aspect of church development and growth that should be carefully considered. We will look at what literacy is, how it is viewed in the world today, and why it is an important part of the picture for a church.

What is literacy?

The English word literate, originally, and for most of its history, meant 'to be familiar with literature', 'well educated', or 'learned'. Only since the late nineteenth century has it also come to refer to the ability to read and write text. Today when most of us think of 'literacy', it is simply the ability a person has to read and write.

Here is a definition of literacy that is helpful because it gives a comprehensive view:

> *Literacy is the ability to read and write and use written information and to write appropriately in a range of contexts. It also involves the integration of speaking, listening, viewing and critical thinking with reading and writing, and includes the cultural knowledge which enables a speaker, writer or reader to recognize and use language appropriate to different social situations*[1].

So, although literacy is fundamentally about reading and writing skills, it also means much more for the individuals or communities concerned. Literacy brings with it an ability to have access to, and to use, information about the wider world. It gives people and communities the ability to evaluate influences or pressures on them, and to make wise decisions about them or even to resist them if they decide to. It also gives them a real voice and opportunities to influence and to benefit from the wider world.

---

1. A definition of literacy agreed to by Australian and New Zealand State and Federal ministers in 1997.

The literacy picture in the world today

Most of us come from highly literate societies, where there is a huge amount of 'environmental text'; such as street signs, food packaging, restaurant menus, instructions, notices - and where we are surrounded from childhood by an almost overwhelming amount of written materials, both print and digital. This can make it difficult for us to understand some of the issues surrounding literacy in societies that are not so rich in literate resources.

Literacy is not only the ability to read and write, but it also involves an individual's capacity to put their reading and writing skills to work: in shaping the course of their own life or the lives of their family and community. In the cultures most of us come from, putting literacy skills to work seems like a very natural consequence of everyday life - we have so much immediately available and easily accessible to read - and it is necessary to engage with written materials on a daily basis. In other, much less literate societies, there is little or no 'environmental text' and there are few written materials in the classrooms or at home. This makes the illiteracy cycle difficult to break, and it takes a determined and multi-faceted effort - motivating people to learn, providing post-literacy reading materials, making an effort to include adults and children - to see a community eventually come to embrace, enjoy and benefit from their literacy skills. Even though literacy programs require a lot of effort, they are often very much desired and supported by the community itself.

The chart below shows world literacy rates (orange areas have the lowest literacy levels):

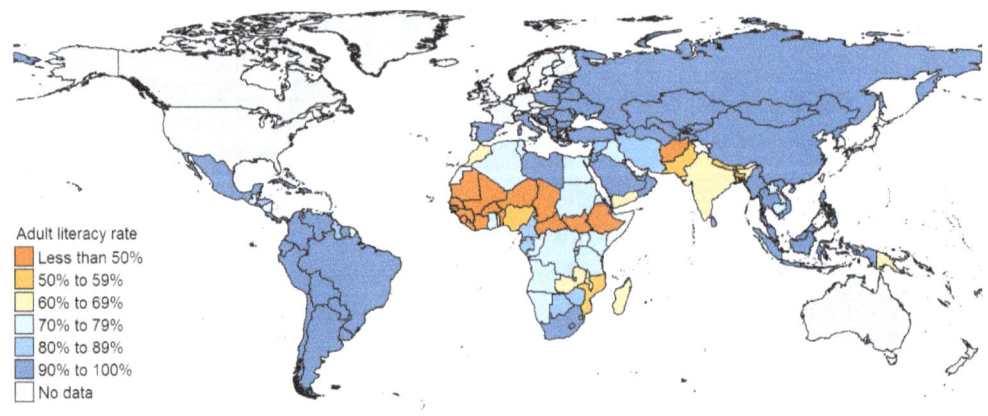

UNESCO Institute for Statistics, September 2013

The UNESCO Institute for Statistics, International Literacy Data 2014 says:

> The global adult literacy rate, for the population 15 years and older, is 80% for women and 89% for men.

> *Despite these gains, 781 million adults still could not read or write – two-thirds of them (496 million) were women. In more than a dozen countries, mostly in sub-Saharan Africa, fewer than half of all adults had basic literacy skills. Even though the size of the global illiterate population is shrinking, the female proportion has remained virtually steady at 63% to 64%.*

How are literacy programs viewed?

Later we will see how the literacy level in a community is a major factor affecting the healthy growth and development of a local church. Experience shows that effective and long-lived church planting efforts include literacy programs as a part of their initial strategy of community involvement and the ongoing life and outreach of the church. Almost universally, governments and local communities view literacy projects in a very positive way - literacy and other educational work is greatly appreciated. It can help to provide a platform for positive community relationships for a local church.

Why is literacy important for a church?

Anyone who has been involved in a literacy project will know that implementing, sustaining and passing it on to local teachers and administrators is a long-term undertaking. But even so, what an immense privilege and joy it is to see a newly literate person quietly sitting and reading their Creator's Word, and knowing that they are now able to benefit from the miracle of 'hearing' His voice - speaking directly to them - through that Word. A lot of people today do not have that privilege, either because they don't have a Bible translation in their language, or because they are unable to read, or both.

Thinking about individual believers learning to read God's Word in their own language is probably a compelling enough reason for us to want to be involved in making the Word accessible as part of a church planting effort, but we will probably be even more convinced when we look at the whole picture of what literacy brings to the life and function of a local church. Literacy is only one thread in the whole fabric of a church planting effort.

A group of team leaders in an area of the world where literacy levels are very low in the general population, wrote:

> *'We want to encourage our church planting teams to see the purpose of literacy to be much more than just teaching people how to read. It is the way that individuals can keep their souls fed with truth. If the church is to be strong, literacy must be strong. Literacy must be recognized in its importance as a tool God will use.'*

If we are involved in church planting work we should ask:

- Are the believers able to access the Bible in a form that clearly and faithfully communicates God's revelation to them?
- Are they increasingly able to make use of God's Word as He intends for His children and His Church?

Reading and writing prepares believers to participate in the life of the Church by allowing them to:

- Help with Bible lesson and curriculum development initially and into the future.
- Interact with believers from other local churches in a greater variety of ways.
- Teach Bible studies and write praise and worship songs.
- Teach literacy classes and be a part of developing and teaching material specifically for children.
- Have the opportunity to read God's Word for themselves and to grow spiritually through the ministry of the Holy Spirit.
- Have direct access to God's Word, not just rely on a few 'interpreters of truth'.
- Take part in outreach activities including education programs and teaching programs.

Having the tools of reading and writing, and written materials available, helps in these ways also:

- The authority of the Word of God is established through the idea of the unchanging written Word.
- It is God's Word, not man's teaching - the truth of the Bible and Bible teaching is given more authority and is verified by the written Word, rather than authority being based on human teachers or leaders.
- If everyone has access to God's Word, not just a few 'educated' leaders or teachers, it fosters unity, as everyone has more opportunity to be involved in the life of the Church, and it also fosters maturity because leaders and believers together are relying on guidance from the Lord and can support one another.
- Taught faithfully by local teachers who are able to refer to the written Scripture, God's Word is better contextualized for the Church – they know the deep issues in the community and have the relationships, understanding and empathy to

- help the believers to apply truth.
- The deep worldview changes that are made are based on the believers' own understanding of Scripture, and God's work directly in and through His Word in that culture, not on outside pressure to change. This protects against syncretism developing in the church, when it is God's Word itself that is changing people's minds and hearts.
- It helps in the discipleship process – when each believer is reading and growing spiritually, and each teacher or leader is equipped with the whole Word of God.

Literacy is vital to each of the key growth and development areas of a church.

Planting a seed...

"The gospel is to be planted as a seed that will sprout within and be nourished by the rain and nutrients in the cultural soil of the receiving peoples. What sprouts from true gospel seed may look quite different above ground from the way it looked in the sending society, but beneath the ground, at the worldview level, the roots are to be the same and the life comes from the same source." Charles H. Kraft

"Now the parable is this: The seed is the Word of God..." Luke 8:11 (NASB)

"For the word of God is living and active and sharper than any two-edged sword, and piercing as far as the division of soul and spirit, of both joints and marrow, and able to judge the thoughts and intentions of the heart." Hebrews 4:12 (NASB)

The fundamental reason to place a high value on literacy in church planting or development work is because it is the power of His Word that changes lives... *'that your faith should not be in the wisdom of men but in the power of God'* (1 Corinthians 2:5 NKJV).

God's Word has the power to change lives, so we should give 'free reign' to that power, by allowing a person or local body of believers to engage with it in its written form as well. God then has the opportunity to speak directly to people through His word as they read it for themselves. The 'seed' should be planted in such a way that it has the best possible chance to grow into a healthy, functioning, fruitful, mature church that will stand on its own and be able to fulfill the ongoing role that God has for it in a community. Literacy is an important part of that process of growth.

WHAT IS LITERACY? IS IT IMPORTANT?

? DISCUSSION POINTS

1. Have you thought much about literacy before? If not, do you think this might skew your view of the issues surrounding literacy in a less literate society? If you have thought about it before, how much do you empathize with those who are illiterate and can you imagine what it is like for them in today's world?

2. Do you think that every person should have the right to learn to read and write if they choose to do so, or do you feel that there are some 'non-literate' cultures that should be left that way? Explain.

➡ ACTIVITIES

1. During one normal day in your life, make a journal of every time you use your literacy skills, either to read or to write. Note also *how* you used your literacy skills, e.g., reading subtitles or news headlines on TV, reading a street sign, writing a note to a friend on Facebook, reading a book, sending a text message, etc. (Hopefully you'll be surprised by how much you have to note down.)

2. Look at the diagram below, and try to imagine, for each of the areas in an illiterate person's life, all the things such a person can do, but also all the things that are denied to them or that they might have difficulties with in each area. Take no more than twenty minutes to think about it and write down the things you think of.

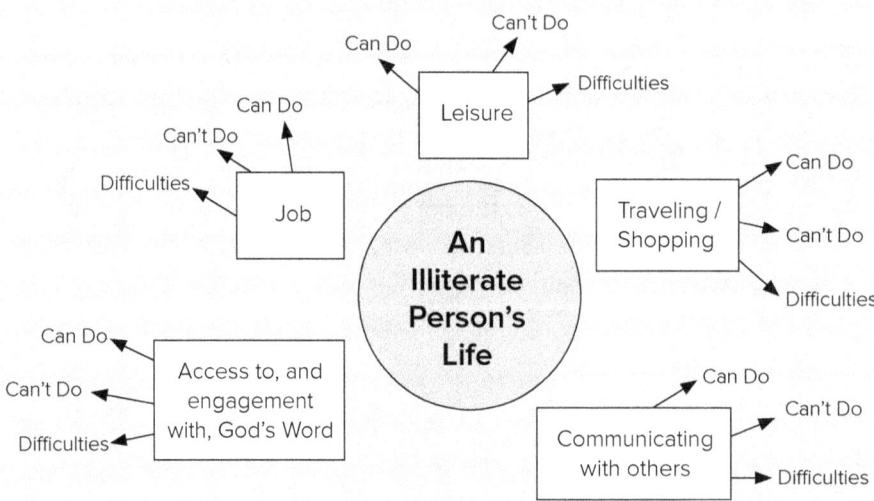

3. Do some online research about current literacy initiatives, the view of literacy by Governments, and the organizations that are involved in literacy work. (One example of a video to watch is; *Literacy as Freedom - UN Literacy Decade 2003-2012*).

8.15 Assessing literacy needs

✓ OBJECTIVES OF THIS TUTORIAL

It can be difficult to answer the question; "Is there a need for a literacy project here or not?" because there are so many factors to consider. In this tutorial we will look at some of the major things that should be taken into account when deciding to get involved in a literacy project in a community.

Introduction

The decision to be involved in some way in a community literacy project is a major one. For those who are the initial driving force behind the project, it will require careful planning and preparation of materials, as well as the motivating and training of local people to see them buy into the project and to eventually take it on as their own. As we saw in the last tutorial, a literacy project can be a very positive factor - some would say essential - in the growth and development of the community and the church.

So, how can a good decision be made? And if we do decide to initiate a literacy project, how can we decide what level or type of program is needed? There are a lot of factors to take into consideration, so we will separate them into these three major steps:

1. Understanding the role of literacy
2. Doing socio-linguistic research
3. Deciding on the type of program needed

1. Understanding the role of literacy

Firstly, are we convinced in the first place that an adequate level of literacy is even necessary? We discussed in the last tutorial that literacy is important for a community, and looked at all that literacy brings to a church. However, not everyone is convinced that all people should have the opportunity to become literate.

"Orality"

Over the last decade or so, there has been a growing trend away from literacy and toward visual or oral learning. Ravi Zacharias, a Christian apologist and defender of rational thinking with regard to spiritual truth, frequently expresses his concern about this trend. He talks about our being in a time where there is a "humiliation of the word" and an "exaltation of the image." He states, "More and more we are knowing less and less about the printed tradition. The ability for abstract reasoning is diminishing in our time, because [people] come to their conclusions on the basis of images. Their capacity for abstract reasoning is gone." (Ravi Zacharias, *Mind Games in a World of Images*)

John Piper asks the following question[1]: "Will we labor to reverse the Western cultural trend away from reading, in the conviction that, when one moves away from reading, one moves away from a precious, God-given, edifying, stabilizing connection with God's written word?"

In the area of church planting and development work, *literate* and *oral* approaches have often been pitted against one another, creating the idea that we have to decide on either one approach or the other. One of the results of this has been the growth of a strong "orality movement" and the implementation by some major missions organizations, among other things, of Biblical storytelling without any expository teaching, and to encourage the development of an "Oral Bible" rather than putting work into a written Bible translation.

Some people have gone so far as to say that it is actually wrong to teach people to read and write when they have traditionally been "oral peoples". We won't go into the details of the long and involved arguments here, but we can say that after some years of seeing the results of totally oral approaches in real communities, many of these more extreme methodologies have been reconsidered, and several major organizations have shifted their view back toward more careful and long-term approaches - again encouraging their workers to learn the heart language of the people and to develop written materials, including Bible translations, as part of their strategies.

Other organizations that have traditionally had a more 'literate' approach, have benefited from the research into oral communication that has come to light, and have reassessed their methodologies to include more of the storytelling features of the indigenous language and culture to increase the clarity of communication, and have put Scripture into use through songs, drama and other local cultural means that the local people enjoy and find beneficial.

---

1. John Piper, http://www.desiringgod.org/articles/missions-orality-and-the-bible

A comprehensive approach

The reality is that both oral and literate methods of communication are beneficial when planting a church and seeing it grow and develop in a community. Oral and literate methods are not mutually exclusive, but should be part of a comprehensive approach to passing on truth in the clearest and most compelling way possible.

God has created all peoples of the world to be oral communicators and He has also clearly used the tool of literacy as a complementary communication method throughout history in order to communicate Himself through His servants to the world. He has made a richness of communication available to human beings - we are able to use all of our senses in an almost endless variety and subtlety of communication techniques.

Communication with people whose life and interaction has been primarily or entirely oral should be in the style and naturalness of oral speaking - whether that is in daily communication, teaching, or in written materials including the translation of the Scriptures. Oral traditions of ethnic peoples are a rich resource for understanding how they communicate, and studying them will help us to introduce new information and truth into the society in the best way to deepen the understanding of the Message.

The key role of the narrative in many pre-literate societies provides a great opportunity for effective foundational, narrative Bible Teaching because it provides cohesion to the presentation of truth that the local people readily understand. In fact, it is something that seems to be universal across cultures - people enjoy and generally learn better from narrative style teaching. However, in our presentation of the true story of God's Word, we need to establish that the authority of our teaching is the written Word of God (if not, how does it differ from any other story that has been passed down through the ages?). The Word of God translated into the local language of the people is the visual evidence that God Himself is interested in communicating His Word to all peoples. We demonstrate our claim that God earnestly desires to communicate with man when we do the difficult work of Bible translation and if necessary, literacy program development.

But beyond the initial church planting effort, there are huge advantages for a local church whose members and leaders have the skill of literacy in their 'communication arsenal'. They will then be able to make use of the technological and communication developments impacting all parts of the world in order to reach out more effectively and grow in their ability to impact the wider community. They can also grow on to maturity and develop a healthy interdependence with other branches of the Church to partner effectively in ministry, not being limited only to ministry opportunities that do not require literacy skills.

2. Doing socio-linguistic research

Finding out the literacy level in a community is not as simple as just finding out how many people can read and write. There are many complex factors, including such things as:

- In an area where several languages are spoken, is one the primary language of education and trade, but not the language most people speak at home? In which language are people more literate?
- What are the domains of literacy for various people? Are some people only able to function in the arena of buying and selling, can they only sign their name, read newspaper headlines, etc.?
- What is the status of literacy? For people living in a resource-poor country, literacy equals both social and economic capital. Being literate allows them to participate more fully in society and to access better jobs. People who have higher reading and writing levels also typically have higher income levels.
- What access to education does the community already have? Are there other organizations with the primary goal of education or literacy, and what programs are they running?

Doing a socio-linguistic survey should help to answer these and many other questions, and provide essential information to make a decision about the need for literacy and the type of program needed. There are a variety of research outlines available, three good ones are included on the website for you to download and read.

3. Deciding on the type of program needed

Based on the information gathered in a socio-linguistic survey, and other research, an adequate response to the need may be starting a full-blown literacy project in the community. However, it could simply mean developing more interesting reading material in the language and encouraging people to improve their reading and writing skills, or supporting an existing education program. In most developing communities there will be a need for some form of education or literacy program, so that eventually the whole community will have full access to God's Word.

For the sake of giving the most helpful and comprehensive information on all of the steps involved in literacy program development, in the following three tutorials we will be looking at the process of developing a literacy project 'from the ground up', in a context where there is initially a very low level of literacy in the community, with no existing written language, and where all materials need to be developed so people can learn to read and write in their own language. We will discuss the process of developing an orthography (alphabet), developing literacy materials, doing pre-literacy activities, the issues surrounding teaching either adults or children, teaching the literacy program and training teachers, and the development of an adequate post-literacy reading and fluency program.

There are still many contexts in the world today where this kind of program would be an adequate response to their need. In fact millions of people live in this kind of situation: in rural areas where they are cut off from education and development (and often from the Truth as well). There are also many other contexts where there is some degree of education available to some or all of the community. Workers in those situations will have to carefully research and work with the community to decide on the type of literacy development that is needed.

Often too, the needs and motivation of a community change over time, and a literacy strategy should to be dynamic and flexible to keep up with the community and the particular people involved.

ASSESSING LITERACY NEEDS

? DISCUSSION POINTS

1. What are some of the ways you can think of where God has used the tool of literacy as a complementary communication method throughout history in order to communicate Himself through His servants to the world?

→ ACTIVITIES

1. Read '*A Short History of how God's Word came to Ata*' (on the following pages). The literacy needs in this community may seem obvious, with an illiteracy rate for the people group population in 1990 at 97%, and a high degree of 'felt need' for education among community members. As you read this account, note particularly the role that literacy had in the growth of the church, and in the ability of the local people to become involved in teaching and outreach.

You can also watch a video of the Ata people telling their story on the AccessTruth website.

2. Can you think of any creative ways that today's technology could have been used in the Ata situation, to equip the church and to help them to reach out more effectively?

Take a look at the following socio-linguistic surveys to see the kind of information that is gathered:

- Socio-Linguistic Research for Literacy Projects - Page 165
- Background Study Guide For Literacy Projects (developed specifically for the Philippines) - Page 171
- Literacy Survey (a questionnaire to ask individual community members) - Page 180

A Short History of how God's Word came to Ata

Paul was very familiar with cross-cultural village ministry because his parents were missionaries and he grew up in the Philippines in several village locations. After returning to Australia, Paul went to high school in Sydney. Paul and Linda met and married in 1983, and eventually decided to begin to get equipped for overseas cross-cultural work.

They moved in 1990 to the island of New Britain in Papua New Guinea where they studied the trade language of Pidgin before moving into the Ata people group. The Ata lived in about twelve villages in an isolated river valley in the center of the island. They lived in houses made of jungle materials and did slash and burn agriculture on the steep mountain sides around their villages. Paul, Linda and their daughter Dania, spent about eleven years living with the Ata in several of their villages. They began the work there by systematically studying the language and culture of the Ata people and they became very close to many of the people there. They hiked in and out of the village with the people, and lived their daily lives with the people. After two years, they were fluent in the language and understood the deeper aspects of Ata culture. They developed a written language for the Ata and taught them to read and write using literacy materials that they wrote.

They then prepared a curriculum of Bible teaching in the Ata language, beginning in Genesis and going through the Old Testament stories that prepared the people for hearing about Christ. After more than three months of teaching each day, many Ata people heard what Christ had done for them and they believed. Since that first time of teaching, many other groups of Ata and Mamusi (a neighboring language group) have been taught from the beginning and on through the Epistles and have formed healthy, growing local churches. Local Ata men teach the Bible material and both women and men teach the literacy classes. Paul and a local man, Kaikou, finished the translation of the Ata New Testament into the Ata language in 2000.

Today, there are many villages in the Ata and Mamusi area that have local village churches with leadership in place. They have had an important role in God's work on the island of New Britain and wider in PNG, traveling to help local and ex-patriate church planting teams with their work in the areas of literacy teaching and Bible teaching. They have also had a role in liaising with the government to develop preschool reading programs for local children. The Ata and Mamusi men now develop their own ongoing Bible teaching materials.

ASSESSING LITERACY NEEDS

The following are excerpts of newsletters and other publications – which include the date of writing or publication.

July 1989 - We will be finished our training about the middle of December this year. Our plans are to spend the four months between then and April next year preparing to go to the island of New Britain (In Papua New Guinea). We are hoping to spend some time in Sydney and Newcastle: not only in practical preparation for moving overseas but also with people who we see as being a vital part of what we are doing. It is not a task we feel capable of doing on our own. The enormity of moving to a different country and into a village location in a people group can be overwhelming at times - we really value your prayers for the future.

May 1990 - Yes, we did make it to the right island - New Britain. We are now in Hoskins ... six hours of every day are taken up with learning Pidgin English. On May 26th Paul and three other guys will be hiking into the 'Psokhok' people group in the mountains of West New Britain. They will be looking for a possible place for us to locate. Please pray as we look for the Lord's will for our location in a people group.

June 1990 - Psokhok survey report: ... We encountered only one man living with his family in an extremely remote and isolated place. It seems as though the main concentration of the people group is on the south coast in an area which is already being worked in by another group.

July 1990 - Our Pidgin study has been progressing well... we plan to finish the course on the 1st August. At the beginning of August we will be visiting the Ata people group in East New Britain. The work in this area was started in February this year. Two families moved in and built their houses. One of these families had to go home recently because of sickness, leaving the other family without partners in the people group. We will be staying in Ata for about three weeks and are praying about whether this will be our permanent location. We would appreciate your prayers as we make this important decision.

August 1990 - Ata tribal visit report:

The Ata people live in the Nakanai Mountains of East New Britain. They live on steep mountain ridges in villages of about thirty to fifty houses. Their houses are made of bush materials with dirt floors, and they have few possessions. They are subsistence farmers and also raise pigs and a few chickens. Sweet potato is their staple food but they also eat tapioca root, taro and many types of greens.

Standing at the top of the pass which separates the two narrow river valleys, it is possible to see nearly all of the traditional land of the Ata. Only one village is accessible by road. There is almost no flat ground anywhere... the trails are very steep, and criss-cross the rivers many times. There is nowhere to build an airstrip, so the family already living in Kaikou rely on the helicopter, as the only alternative is the (at least) ten-hour hike. As a result, this is one of the most isolated and expensive locations on the island.

With the helicopter costing over $1000.00, the decision for us to hike both ways was an easy one. The hike itself was not so easy. We had very willing Ata carriers for our provisions and for our daughter, but still it was a testing time especially for Linda who was still recovering from an attack of malaria when we went in. After sleeping at Wasilau, we reached YauYau by early afternoon where we stayed the night. The next morning we hiked into Kaikou, to a warm welcome from the villagers.

After spending a fortnight...we do indeed feel that Kaikou is where God is leading us as a family to live. The Ata are a gentle and friendly people, among whom we felt immediately at home. They invited us to come and live in the area and immediately cleared and leveled a house site for us.

November 1990 - We arrived in Kaikou on the 20th September, and are now well settled into our temporary house in the village. Paul has finished framing our house ... many people from Kaikou and the next village, Kukulu have been helping with materials and building.

We have been doing the first stage of language learning, "phonetic warm-up".

Linda was sitting with a group of ladies the other day and was telling them that we would first learn their language and then tell the whole of "God's Talk" so they would understand clearly. They said, 'You must learn our language quickly.'

February 1991 - Paul has almost completed the house now and we were able to move in early January. Our house perches on a ridge that juts into a narrow river valley. The river is about 500m below. We have begun full time language and culture study. A large part of our study will be to investigate many different areas of the Ata culture - particularly the spiritual aspects.

Linda began doing medical work each day with the help of some of the Ata ladies.

March 1991 - Our language study includes time spent with the people; in the village, in their gardens, hunting, fishing or hiking to other villages. We collect and study language and culture information in the form of taped dialogues, written stories and drawings of cultural objects.

Recently we hiked to a neighboring people group with four men and two ladies from Kukulu village. The trail was very slippery, steep and difficult, but worth every step as we spent time with our friends and came to know just a little bit more about their lives. The first three hours were spent climbing a mountain that was 1000m above our starting point, and the scenery was spectacular. We stayed in the Ata village of Kai on the way, sleeping in a tribal house and cooking our tuna and rice on the fire. The next day we hiked through beautiful rainforest with huge, vine-covered trees. We saw and enormous overhanging rock beside the trail, with a blackened cave underneath. Our companions were afraid and told us to keep quiet as they hurried past the rock. They explained that evil spirits lived in the cave and had killed people in the past, and the blackened ceiling was from the smoke of the spirit's fires. We are looking forward to the time when the Ata people will hear the Truth that brings freedom from such fear.

July 1991 - The Lord is answering our prayers and the people are becoming more excited about the future teaching of His Word. As we question them about their beliefs concerning the origin of the world, evil spirits and many other things, they are increasingly looking forward to hearing and understanding what God's Word says.

The people encourage us to use their language more and more and each day we are able to learn something new. Praise the Lord for his provision of our good language helpers, Kaikou and his wife, Palava.

Since our last letter in March, our foreign co-workers have left. The future, as always, is in God's hands and we are waiting to see what He holds in store for the future as we continue to work in Kaikou.

August 1991 - The men from Kaikou and Kukulu built a combined meeting house/medical room in Kaikou.

September 1991 - Our first language checks were very encouraging; we will take our second in November. More and more people are moving back to Kaikou village - six new houses have been built in the last two months. Pray that the Lord would preserve the lives of the older people until they can hear his Word in their own language.

December 1991 - As we continue to delve deeper with our language and culture study, it is becoming clearer how much superstition and fear control the lives and thinking of the Ata. A few nights ago, we were about to go to bed, when four men armed with axes and spears knocked at our door. When we asked them to come in, they came quickly inside, obviously afraid of something outside. They told us that a "tomo" - an evil spirit - had been sighted by three people in the village and they were afraid it had come to kill someone. They had come to stay for the night with us to protect us, and it was impossible for us to reassure them. There are many more examples of such fear in their lives - of sorcery, evil spirits and ancestor spirits, lightning spirits, broken taboos and men with spiritual power.

January 1992 - We began a village newspaper to increase interest in literacy (only ten people in the whole people group can read anything at all at this stage).

April 1992 - Over the last week we have been able to complete our Ata literacy primers which will now be printed. Praise God we are on target for our goal of teaching our first literacy class in August or September. Men from Kaikou and Kukulu built the literacy classroom in Kaikou.

We heard a few days ago that one of the old men from Kaikou died while we have been out (at a two-week conference). Please pray that no one else will die before they hear the truth, and that the work would continue quickly so they can hear as soon as possible.

September 1992 - Wosau is able to read and write simple sentences for the first time. He is a father of three, and one of the ten men and three women who are students in the first Ata literacy class in Kaikou. Class is held every weekday morning for two hours, and will run for four months altogether. By the end of that time, the students will be able to read and write stories in their own language, and begin to read longer books in Ata when the Bible teaching begins in January, Wosau and the others from his class will be able to read Bible lessons and Scripture portions after they hear them taught.

Linda will train four of the students from this first class to be teachers for following classes. Our desire is to see the literacy program being taught exclusively by Ata teachers as soon as possible. At the moment, only a few Ata people are literate in Pidgin English, and none in their own Ata language - the only materials in the Ata language are ones that we have translated and printed.

Vali an old man from Kaikou village, had been having heart problems for over a year. A little while ago he became very ill and was unable to leave his house. Paul taught him each morning for a week, beginning in Genesis and continuing through the Old Testament and finishing in the New Testament with the life of Christ. At the end of the week, Vali knew that he was a sinner; unable to please God, but that God had provided a Way for him through Jesus Christ. Vali died in early September.

November 1992 - Excitement is building as the date for the start of the teaching comes closer. We have been telling the people for several months now when we will begin the teaching and we have asked them to tell others also to make sure they are in the village at the time (The Ata people are semi-nomadic, spending time in several different villages during the year. Many of the Kaikou people also have houses in other villages, down near the road).

December 1992 - The first literacy class is finished. The students wrote a book of their own stories and began to read other books that we have translated into Ata. Some of these give them background to the Bible - "Animals of Israel" and "The customs of the Jews" are two of them.

January 1993 - Paul began Bible teaching in Kaikou.

We wish you could be here in Kaikou now to see the way the Lord has begun to work in the lives of the people here. Paul has been teaching for one or two hours each weekday morning for five weeks now. He has taught in Ata from God's Word from the very beginning of Genesis, and is now about to begin teaching about Moses and the Children of Israel. The people's response has been much better than we expected, and we are thankful for such a good attendance. They were amazed at God's power as they heard the true account of Creation for the first time. Then they heard of the Fall of man, and God's first promise of the coming Deliverer. God's promises of the coming One were traced for them through the stories of Noah, Abraham and Isaac. This theme will continue through the life of Moses and the history of the Children of Israel and many other accounts of the things God did and recorded in the Old Testament.

We have had several requests from different villages for the teaching later on. The Kaikou people have been telling them about it and a lot of interest has been generated in YauYau, Lavuxi, Sale and Sege.

There are two full classes of students signed up to begin in the literacy school in April. Please pray for the six trainee teachers who will be teaching the next classes... five men and one lady... all are enthusiastically attending the Bible teaching each day.

March 1993 - Teaching of the Life of Christ started at the end of February. About one month will be spent in teaching the Life of Christ. The people have heard small portions of this before. Seventy people have been coming every day... it is a steep 45 minute walk for the Kukulu people. One old lady has a swollen foot, but after one meeting she stood up and said she didn't care about the hard walk over, she just wanted to hear how the Saviour was going to return a sinner like her to God.

During the teaching of the life of Christ, the Saviour's life and significance really came alive for the people as it was placed upon the foundation of the Old Testament. On the 24th March Paul taught the death, burial and resurrection of Christ, and the next day they heard of His return to His Father in heaven. On these two days, about 70 people became God's children as they accepted the payment Christ made for them.

April 1993 - Some personal testimonies of those in the first Bible teaching in Kaikou:

> Ue (Oldest man in the village, he believes God kept him alive to be able to hear the teaching. Was always very self-righteous because he gave money to the church in the past.) - After the teaching he said, "Before, I thought that God was happy with me, but I made a big mistake. Nothing I could do was good enough. My only way is through the Deliverer that God sent."

> Poxolo (Old Kaikou lady) - She was in tears as she said, "I always thought I was OK, but really God's Enemy held me tightly in his hand so I couldn't escape. Then today I saw what God's Son did for me. He carried the suffering that should have been mine."

> Woli (Father of three from Kaikou village, before the teaching began he asked Paul many questions about spiritual matters. Paul told him to wait for the teaching of God's Word and then God Himself would open his eyes.) - The day after he heard about Jesus' death, Woli came to Paul and said, "Just like you used to say, God Himself has opened my eyes and now I understand the Truth. I used to worry about where I would go when I died." Paul asked him, "So where are you going to go when you die?" Woli answered immediately, "I'll go to be with God!" Then he added, "Not because of anything I have done, but because the Deliverer died in my place."

> Iamulu (A young married man) - " I don't want to praise you and Linda I want to praise God, but I want to say that I'm happy that he sent you to teach us God's Word. Before, we had only heard small portions, and we were confused. Now we have heard it from the beginning all the way to the 'head of the talk', and we are clear in our understanding. The Savior Himself has returned us to God."

> Voloko (Young unmarried woman from Kukulu) - "Before, I thought God's word was worthless, but I came and heard and I couldn't sleep at night. Every day I came and heard, and every night I lay awake in my house and thought about what I had heard. I thought about the sin that is with me, and that I couldn't do anything myself to return to God. Now I know that the Savior has returned me to God, and I am very happy."

April 1993 - Ten more Kaikou people who had come too late for the first teaching began to hear the Bible teaching. Bible teaching to the new believers continues.

ASSESSING LITERACY NEEDS

May 1993 - Second literacy class began, with four Ata teachers. Paul began to train/disciple three men as Bible teachers.

June 1993 - The ten Kaikou people heard the gospel, believed the message they heard and became part of the Body of Christ in that place.

July 1993 - We left for furlough. Believers meetings continued in Kaikou and Kukulu. The Ata teachers finished teaching the second literacy class.

April 1994 - When we returned to Hoskins from a short furlough in Australia, we spoke to the Ata guys on the radio to prepare for our trip back into the bush. They said, "We hope you don't mind, but while you were away, we taught another group of people right through the teaching in the same way you taught us, and now they are God's children too." Of course we were thrilled.

When we returned to the village, we heard many of these fifty people give clear testimony of their faith in Christ. These new believers have been coming to the meetings in Kaikou to hear more Bible teaching, and are building houses between Kaikou and Kukulu.

Two new literacy classes have begun. The four Ata literacy teachers are training two more men to teach. In May, these new teachers will move to Xoi Ete area to begin literacy there.

The people from YauYau and Lavuxi villages are building a meeting house / literacy classroom between their two villages at Xoi Ete. Paul and the Ata men have decided to begin Bible teaching there in August.

People from Kukulu are building their own meeting house there (in Kukulu village) so they can have believer's meetings there.

We plan to move with three Ata families to Xoi Ete to take the Bible teaching there. This will probably happen in June.

Paul is teaching the believers in Kaikou and Kukulu through the book of Acts. The meetings are overflowing, many people staying hours afterward to discuss the lessons. Paul is training six more men to be Bible teachers - these are men who are now literate and can therefore read and teach others.

June 1994 - Our move from Kaikou to Xoi Ete went very quickly with the help of a team from our church in Australia. We were only out of our work for three weeks, which is incredible to pull down one house, move five hours walk away and put up another one!

Paul and Kaikou (his co-translator) finished the translation of Acts and are most of the way through Romans. The schedule is tight and Paul has to get up at 4:30 am to fit in his work for the day - translation study and exegesis, actual translation with Kaikou Bible lesson preparation and teaching time. He is now only teaching the material to Bible teachers and their families (although the meetings are often packed with many other people), and then the teachers take the lessons to the other villages and teach the believers there.

The Bible teacher training program is going extremely well. There are 14 Bible teachers and 8 trainees (or 'disciples' as the Ata call them). The teachers are 'posted' in five different villages now, where teaching has been done and there are believers. One of these is the Mamusi (a neighboring people group with an entirely different language) village of Morelona, which was reached by bilingual teachers.

Every Friday afternoon until Saturday noon, there is a Bible teacher's meeting. All the teachers and their families come, about 40 people in all. They come to discuss the work in each location and to talk about any other things they wish to. Many of the wives are very keen and attend all meetings too. They always write important discussion and prayer points on the board, and go through each one thoroughly. Paul has been leaving the meetings early, so they become more independent of having to have him right there with them. They tell him the results of their discussions the next day. On Saturday morning, they have the Lord's Supper and a prayer time together which one of the men will lead. After this, Paul teaches the new Bible lesson for the week, which the teachers will then take back to their own villages to teach there. (All lessons are printed up in fully fleshed-out form in booklets for the teachers.)

They have written hundreds of songs, with the traditional Ata melodies and instruments, but telling the story of Salvation right through the Old Testament to the Life of Christ. More songs are being composed all the time. There are some people who are more prolific songwriters than others, but many men and women of all ages have written songs. As a group, they are very musical. Their songs often directly quote Scripture, and often very clearly state the important points of a lesson or a Biblical theme, so they are a good teaching tool also, and a good testimony to unbelievers.

In some of the villages, the people have been meeting at night in small groups, to discuss how the Bible teaching applies to their everyday lives. The teachers say it is a good opportunity for those who would not normally talk in the larger meetings, to discuss and ask questions.

Many people have been learning memory verses. They are incredible in the amount they can remember, and really enjoy it. They do tests for one another, and also have a Bible memory time in their small groups. This is another instance of something that has just become part of their lives with no input from us.

Please pray for us, we are very busy with everything going on here... there is a lot of pressure. We are completely committed to getting the job done here in Ata but it is difficult to contemplate it stretching on endlessly into the future at this level of activity and workload and pressure...

August 1994 - An outreach to the village of Sale is planned for early 1995, but a group of old people insisted that a Bible teacher come and teach them before then, because they did not want to die before having a chance to hear. So now two teachers are living in Sale and teaching this group of seven old people.

The Bible teaching here in Xoi Ete began on the 1st August, and many are coming from surrounding villages also to hear. The lesson is repeated in the evening for the community school children. Paul is team teaching with three Ata men from Kaikou village.

The literacy program is steaming along well, all in the control of Ata teachers, except for the materials Linda provides for them. There are schools in Kaikou and Xoi Ete and a new one will open in Sale soon. There are two young Ata guys who photocopy every morning, as the materials for Bible lessons and literacy are in such demand.

September 1994 - The tremendous growth we are seeing here is exciting and we continue to praise the Lord for it.

In our location here at Xoi Ete, this is what goes on in one week:

About 150 believers are taught a Bible lesson on Sunday and again on Thursday. They also have a prayer and worship time and break sweet potato on Sunday (the Lord's Supper).

One hundred as yet non-believers are taught for an hour each morning - all this evangelistic teaching is now done entirely by Ata men, but we still attend every meeting.

Each morning after the Bible teaching, a literacy class is held for twenty people, taught by Ata teachers.

Each Tuesday, the literacy teachers meet with one of the Bible teachers for prayer and encouragement.

On Friday afternoon the Bible teachers meeting begins and continues on Saturday morning.

Paul and Kaikou spend each weekday morning in Bible translation work.

Each weekday morning the Bible lesson is recorded on to tape and copies are made, which are taken to nearby villages to be played in the afternoon.

In the afternoons, the young men photocopy printed materials and on some days, the Bible teachers prepare dramas to illustrate the next day's Bible lesson, or practice teaching the lesson for the next day.

All the printing is becoming a bit of a burden, we now have four literacy primers, seven literacy reading books, four teacher's manuals, comprehension questions and homework sheets for literacy and 94 Bible lesson booklets. At this stage, we need at least 200 copies of all of these, but we can see the whole thing 'snowballing' and we will need to send the printing out to be done soon, as we just won't cope with it in here. This is the one area that the Ata believers will have to rely on outside help to continue - we will have to think about it (and pray about it) more. However, in many other areas, we have had to rely on them increasingly and to delegate and pass on responsibility. They are in every way as much responsible for the work here as we are, and interestingly, they are more and more looking for areas where they can take over from us and are bringing them to our attention. At this stage we have handed over the following areas to the people:

All of the photocopying, all literacy teaching, keeping track of and ordering literacy materials (from Linda) day to day running of the literacy schools and setting up new schools, Bible teaching rosters, all Bible teaching except new material (Paul only teaches the Bible teachers now), running of the library for Bible lessons and Scripture portions, dramas for the Bible lessons (they provide all their own props, costumes, etc.), all important decisions concerning the church (future outreaches, appointments and training of literacy and Bible teachers, etc.).

Paul still provides leadership, and feels that although the Bible teachers are fulfilling many of the roles of elders and deacons, they have not been recognized as such, and this will happen some time in the future. They will need more teaching about the Christian life and about the qualifications and ministry of elders and deacons. We pray that God will raise up the right men, in his time.

We and the Ata believers are facing some opposition from "religious groups" in the area. Their activities are centerd on controlling the local people and collecting money from their adherents, and so they are threatened by the fact that so many people have left their groups since hearing the teaching of God's Word. Despite their opposition we have a number of openings for future outreaches in villages, once strongly held by these groups.

October 1994 - All of the old people in the group from Sale gave a clear testimony of salvation, and now other Sale villagers have built a meeting house / literacy building and want to be taught too. There is very strong opposition from a few young men in this village.

Over 100 people in Xoi Ete heard the 'head of the talk' (the last part of the Creation to Christ teaching about the death and resurrection of the Lord Jesus Christ) at the end of October. This was a very emotional and exciting time and the new believers are enthusiastic about hearing more teaching from God's Word. The Ata men who taught this outreach are thrilled by what God has done. Other believers from Kaikou played a major part in dramas and helping to review the lessons at night using cassettes.

People in the village of Sege are asking for teaching, the Ata men plan to go there as soon as possible.

A group of believers who heard the teaching in Kaikou and have moved back to their village in Wasilau are facing strong opposition and violence. However, some other Wasilau people have asked to be taught. We and the Ata are waiting for the Lord's timing.

The Bible teaching will begin soon in the Mamusi (neighboring people group) village of Morelona where the people have built a meeting house. The Ata men have not rushed over there as they wanted to think about and pray about the whole thing and make sure it is done properly.

About 150 believers from Kaikou, Kai and Kukulu meet twice a week to fellowship and hear more teaching from God's Word. The villagers from YauYau who were previously resistant to the gospel have now asked to be taught also.

December 1994 - Some of the new believers from Xoi Ete are training as Bible and Literacy teachers.

Some Bible teachers and their families from Kaikou have moved to Wasilau and Sege to teach the new believers there.

High School students who have returned to their villages for Christmas break will be taught through the lessons from Genesis to the Gospel. Some adults from other villages want to hear at that time too.

Bible teaching has begun in Morelona, where many people are coming every day to hear.

We feel our move from Kaikou to Xoi Ete has been profitable for God's work here, as the focus has been taken off one particular area of the people group. The emphasis of our work has shifted too, as we are more in contact with the Bible teachers only, and not with all of the believers (that would be impossible now). So it has become the Ata leaders who are dealing with problems and with different situations that come up among the believers and not us. They are learning so much by relying on God only and what they know from his Word, to deal with things.

The teachers are really being stretched with so many outreaches going on and so many believers to be taught. It has brought the whole aspect of teacher training and discipleship into focus. They are getting together a lot of good thoughts on the whole area and working on a teacher training manual based on Scripture so they can be consistent in the future with how they go about the whole process.

1995 - The literacy program continues on, with more literacy schools opening and more teachers being trained.

Bible teaching continues in all the Ata churches with Ata men teaching. Paul teaches the new material to the Bible teachers in a monthly meeting rather than weekly. Meetings for all the Bible teachers are now held for a few days each month, as some of the outreaches and churches are up to two days' hike away. This has proved to be much more efficient for Paul and the teachers too. He is able to teach enough material in a few days for them to continue teaching lessons twice a week (one review lesson a week) for the month back in their villages.

Translation continues on well; Paul is very thankful to have such a great co-translator in Kaikou.

Believers who show they are interested and faithful are continually being brought into the teacher training program.

> The Peaceful Revolution (written by Paul in 1995)
>
> "The morning mists swirl amongst the tops of the trees in the narrow river valley. Roosters greet the sun while village dogs scavenge for anything even vaguely edible. A young child sees me coming and calls out to let the other know. A few men come out of their houses that are smoking with the first cooking fires of the day. They stretch and yawn and say good morning. I notice most of them have Bible Lessons in hand - some of them are Bible teachers studying for tomorrow's meeting, others are just going over familiar material. I wander on past the meeting house. It only has half-walls and I duck my head under the roof to locate the murmuring that comes from inside. I see two teenagers sitting together studying the week's memory verses. In another house there are three literacy teachers going over the lesson for the day that they will give to the 18 eager students who also want to be able to read God's Word in their own language.

The thought comes to me that a revolution is taking place here. Not a revolution of guns and violence as is happening in other similar jungle settings, but a revolution of paper and peace. It is about the overthrowing of a regime - the regime of ignorance, fear and darkness. It is a revolution in the hearts and minds of people who suddenly have a purpose for living. It is not principally about education nor about printed materials in their own language - although it is one of the means by which the changes are happening. It is about people hearing the Truth in their own "heart language". It is about them reading for themselves about the Creator, His Son, the story of salvation, and the riches that they now own as His children. It is a peaceful revolution that will bring eternal victories."

1996 - During this year, we have been able to have the use of a small apartment out at Hoskins, and have been spending some time out there to really get in some good time on the translation of the New Testament. The people do benefit a lot from having us out for a time too, as they are then more likely to rely on the Lord when problems come up. When we are out at Hoskins, we are in regular radio contact with them.

We have built a book storage room in a central location in the people group (Lavuxi village) for the Ata books and materials. We are now getting some printing done in Australia and some in Goroka here in PNG. It has really freed us up to have someone else doing the main bulk of the printing as it has become a huge amount of material. There are about 150 Bible lessons alone, and we need at least 300 copies of each lesson when we print it.

February 1997 - Paul taught all the Bible teachers through the books of 1 Timothy and Titus at a big meeting at Xoi Ete this month. We are praying that this teaching will pave the way for the Lord to guide the Ata teachers in forming a more structured church leadership over the next year or so.

March 1997 - Kaikou and his family will be coming to stay out at Hoskins for a month or so to begin work on the final quarter of the New Testament translation - the goal is to have it finished by the end of this year.

We have had a lot of boxes of lessons and Scripture, literacy materials and teacher training manuals delivered here ready to be transported into the bush and stored ready for use in the Book storage room. Believers and teachers from all nine Ata churches use the room, which is supervised by three ladies and one of the Bible teachers. A small amount is charged for each lesson, which is collected and every now and then deposited in the Ata Printing Account at Hoskins. This can then be used to purchase pens, pencils, paper, and other needs for the Ata. The men order or buy these from Hoskins when they are there.

There are more new outreaches, to the villages of Malasi and Vala, with many people coming to hear. There is very strong opposition in these areas closer to the road, but it doesn't stop people coming to hear the teaching.

More Mamusi (neighboring people group) villages are asking for teaching, and some villages that were once strongly opposed to the teaching are asking to hear. Pray for the Ata and Mamusi men as they work together to bring the Bible teaching to these villages as soon as possible. The Ata teachers are working toward training Mamusi men to teach their own people and provide leadership, so the Ata can 'phase out' of the work there.

April 1997 - In the last month, two new literacy schools have been set up by the Ata teachers. Over 900 people are now literate.

The Ata teachers received a letter from the village of Peiling in Mamusi requesting Bible teachers come to their village to teach them. The Ata guys are discussing the best way to meet the need - maybe wait till some Mamusi men are trained to teach and then send them.

April 1998 - There are over 50 Bible teachers and trainees who are teaching the Word in ten different Ata churches. The believers meet three times a week for teaching, sharing, praying and singing. They also share the Lord's Supper together at least once a week. The Bible teachers in each village meet every week, and then once a month they all meet together to discuss problems or to plan outreaches to new villages. We are so grateful for the way the Lord is leading and guiding the teachers and believers in his churches here.

We plan on having the New Testament translation completed by the end of this year. As the believers have taken on most of the responsibility for the work in the bush, we have been able to spend more and more time just on the translation project. When we began, we didn't really realize what a huge task it is. Paul and Kaikou translate each morning, and Linda does a content and spelling check. Kaikou and his wife Palava do another read-through check each afternoon. Then Paul writes the back-to-English translation, which Linda reads through and checks for content and spelling also. Then the real checking process with a translation consultant can begin.

August 1998 - Kaikou and several other Ata leaders made a visit to the Mamusi area last month to see how things are progressing there. They reported that the Bible teaching is going very well, and the 300 or so Mamusi believers are hungry for God's Word. There are Mamusi literacy classes and some enthusiastic Mamusi men are training as Bible teachers. People from other villages continue to ask to be taught also.

ASSESSING LITERACY NEEDS

Wasilau village has been a center of opposition in the Ata area for years, but there has been a real breakthrough there recently, and many children and adults are coming to be taught God's Word.

The only books left to be translated are the Gospel of John, 1&2 Peter, 1,2&3 John and Jude. The New Testament should be all checked and ready for printing in July next year.

October 1998 - Things have improved in Wasilau to the point where the Ata guys have decided to hold their next big teachers meeting there this week. Many unbelievers are planning to come and check it out. Paul will be teaching through the 1 Thessalonians lessons and we will stay in Wasilau for several days. The Ata men said that they are no longer worried about opposition any more, because they are used to it (up till now, there have been four meeting houses burnt down, and many people yelled at and physically assaulted - mainly in the villages near the road.)

Mamusi people in another big village have built a meeting house and asked for Bible teachers to come. The Ata and Mamusi guys are trying to organize to fill the need there.

We have sort of lost count, but there are now approximately 1200 Ata believers and almost 1000 who are literate. All the Bible lessons are written up to the book of Revelation and are printed and in the hands of the teachers who continue to teach in all the churches. Our planned 'phase out' from our direct involvement in the work is going very well, and we see that the completed New Testament will be one of the final stages. However, we do plan to continue to make regular visits to the Ata churches.

A small printshop has now been set up in Hoskins, and a couple from Australia are coming soon to permanently be available to print materials for village churches. This will be a fulfilment of a great need for the Ata who will now just be able to order the books they want and come to Hoskins to pick them up.

December 1998 - Paul and Kaikou finished the New Testament translation last week. Kaikou and his family moved back to the bush from Hoskins a few days ago, where they will have an itinerate ministry encouraging the Bible teachers and believers in the Ata and Mamusi churches.

One more translation check with a consultant is planned for January and then Linda will work on the final formatting before sending the New Testament to the USA where it will be prepared for printing. We are so thankful to the Lord for all He has done to make it possible for the New Testament to be completed, for all his provision and protection over the years of translation work.

We have been praying about our future direction and there are several possibilities that we are considering before the Lord. We will possibly be based in Australia for a time, and traveling to other countries to help people working in other areas.

July 1999 - The Ata New Testaments are being printed right now in the USA and should be on their way to PNG by September. Paul will visit the Ata later this year to do more teaching, and then we will all go in early 2000 when the New Testaments arrive by ship.

April 2000 - For one week in April the Ata and Mamusi believers gathered in the Xoi Ete valley to thank the Lord for the New Testament. The books arrived safely and there was great joy and thankfulness and also a strong commitment to read and apply God's Word and to continue to reach out to those who have not yet heard the gospel. One of the teachers who spoke during the meetings said, " We praise the Lord for His plan for us, the Ata people. Through His Word, we have come to know Him, and his character - we know that it has always been his desire for all people to have His Word in their own language, so that they can also know Him, His way and his will. We praise Him, because of the way His Word came first to many other languages, and then to us, the Ata people. We have the joy and responsibility to take God's Word to other languages and other people also."

December 2000 - We speak to one of the Ata elders (there are now six appointed elders) on the radio every few months to catch up on the latest news from there. The last time we spoke to them, they were extremely encouraged with how things were going, and said the believers were still hungry for God's word and still reaching out to others. There is now another language group - the Nakanai - where several people have been saved through Ata outreach, and others who want to hear.

The couple from Australia are doing a great job in the small printshop in Hoskins, and the Ata are able to order Bible lessons or any printed materials over the radio very easily.

We have been able to get back to visit them every six months or so, and continue to write Bible study materials for them to use.

We look forward to another visit into Ata next year.

August 2001 – We visited the Ata and stayed at the village of Sege. Paul taught through the book of Hebrews, and the Bible teachers read from the Hebrews lessons that had been prepared earlier and printed up into books at the Hoskins printshop. The Ata teachers will now teach this book in all the village churches.

The elders are encouraged with the growth in the churches, and are discipling six more men to be brought into eldership in the future. The literacy program is expanding again, with many of the old people now learning to read and write, and the program beginning to be taught in the government-run elementary schools in the area also.

August 2013 – The Ata continue to meet as groups of believers in individual village churches and influence the community around them. They have had influence in many other efforts to reach other areas in PNG, giving input and help to new churches in people groups in New Britain and also on the mainland in various areas, helping in the areas of literacy, Bible teaching programs, leadership and outreach strategy, and translation projects. Recent major changes in the Ata area, are the introduction of cell phones and the rapid growth of the oil palm industry, both of which have brought cultural changes. We enjoy being able to talk to them regularly by phone and catch up with how the churches and individuals are going. The elders in the church have been guided by the Lord as they face new challenges and help the church there to move ahead by faith and be used by Him to continue to reach out with the Truth.

TUTORIAL 8.15

Socio-Linguistic Research for Literacy Projects

The notes below give suggestions for finding out pertinent information about different aspects of the particular people group or community:

1. Geography
2. Linguistics
3. Education
4. Sociology
5. Economy
6. Politics

1. Geography:

Make a map of the area and describe:
- The area size
- Physical and political borders
- The villages, the population and the languages spoken in the area
- The linguistic areas
- The dialect areas (if already established)
- Distance between villages and transportation available
- Important buildings in area (missions, churches, schools, government offices etc.)

Note any other facts that should be taken into consideration for the literacy program.

2. Linguistics:

Language and speakers:
- Which languages/dialects could best be utilized for teaching literacy?
- If several languages/dialects are spoken in the area how widely are they understood?
- Is there a bilingual relationship between the languages spoken in the area? (E.g.,

Mother language, trade and official languages?)
- What is the attitude towards the mother language by the different age groups? Is there a specific situation that one language is preferred instead of the other? Do the people want to learn to read in the mother language?
- List the dialect differences. Can you use the same material? What is the attitude towards the "standard" spoken language?

Linguistic Analysis:
- Who did the language analysis? List the linguists involved. How many of them speak the language?
- Are there any publications or reports of their work? List them.
- Give the linguistic aspects (or facts) that are particularly important for literacy purposes.

Alphabet and Orthography:
- Which alphabet is going to be used? Is there a chance it will be changed?
- Who proposed the orthography used for the literacy material? Was it accepted by the community, by the university or by the authorities responsible for literacy? Who has developed it?
- Is there some other competing orthography? If so, which is the best at the present time? Which one is the most read? And the easiest to read? What is the people's attitude towards this situation? Who could be used as an agent of unification of the orthography?
- Which area of the proposed orthography presents problems?
    - According to the linguists?
    - According to the native speakers?
    - According to others?

3. Education:
Traditional Education

- What system (if any) of education is already in place? What is taught? Who teaches whom, with what purpose and using which method? Is the teacher paid? How are the learners motivated? How is achievement recognized (e.g. awards, certificates etc.)? Is individual progress encouraged? Alternatively, is group

progress more encouraged? Does competitiveness motivate or not?
- What is the approximate percentage of speakers who are already literate or semi-literate?

Formal Education

- What is the teaching proposed (mono or bi-lingual)?
- Who is in charge of the schools? The government, Christian missions or who else?
- Do the teachers speak the language?
- Would they be open and like to be helped to learn and teach that particular language?
- What percentage of children start school and what percentage drop out of school?

Non-formal education

- What other literacy programmes are going on in the area? In what language? What materials are being used? What is the result? What part of the population has been touched by it?
- What literacy programmes have been started in the past?
    - Among the literates, by whom?
    - Among the semi-literates, by whom?
- Talk about successes and failures, giving reasons. Talk about the methods and the curriculum used.
- List all the organizations or persons in the area who are in charge of education (main leadership; local authority; leaders in agriculture or health; churches; missions etc.).

Essential components for literacy teaching

- What are the materials available for teaching?
- Who are the competent people available to do the teaching?
- Could we use equipment or buildings that are already in place?

Literature in the local language

- What are the materials available in the local language? (Give title, date, author,

editor and distributor.) How many titles are available? Was the publication a success?
- Did people express a desire to see some publication? Which one? What was their main interest?
- How do they get published books?

Bible Translation

- Is there an existing Bible translation? If so:
    - Who did it (and what was their process for translating)?
    - What language is it in?
    - Is it in the language that Bible teaching will take place in - the heart language of the people?
    - Do people or groups use it already and how much is it understood?
- Is there a planned Bible translation project? If so:
    - What language will it be in?
    - What orthography will be used?

Local authors

- Give a list of persons or groups who had materials published in the language? Who are the creative authors?
- Make a list of the people that could possibly be trained as authors. Mention their abilities in detail.

Production, promotion and distribution

- Are there local means of production available for the people to use? (e.g. typewriters, computers, photocopiers etc.) What is the quality level required in order to distribute the final product?
- How and where could we promote and sell the new books and booklets? (Stores, market, churches, door-to-door, libraries, other?)

4. Sociology:

Problems and needs of the people

- What are the expressed and pressing needs of the people? Who talks about these needs and how do they talk about it?
- Are the people looking for external help to satisfy some of their needs?
- By what means could we trigger interest for literacy among the people?
- In which area of their lives do they feel the disadvantage of being illiterate?

Interest

- What are the main subjects of discussion at home, in community groups, at different seasons of the year?
- What impassions people and what motivates them to act?
- List the goods or objects people would like to bargain for or save money to buy.
- In humorous stories, what subjects are talked about?
- Are the people interested in certain aspects of their history? Among certain groups in the community (e.g. Christians, members of organizations etc.) are there some interests that could motivate them to become literate and follow a literacy program?

Motivation

- Is there spiritual motivation to read religious literature or Bible translation?
- Do people have the desire to write or receive letters?
- List all the committees of individuals who have expressed a real interest in learning how to read (this information must be obtained by an internal investigation or from other contacts).
- For what reason do they wish to learn how to read? Is it a general attitude or just a few people?
- Who could benefit from being taught to read the mother tongue in order to learn the official language?

Attitude toward teaching

- What is the attitude of the traditional chiefs, in general, toward the education of adults and children (and females)?

- What is the attitude of other leaders (pastors and other)?
- What would the political leaders like to see as a result of a teaching program? According to them, how should this be achieved?

Responsibilities

- Where do the leaders stand concerning literacy? (Chief, government, church leaders etc.) What is their attitude towards the use of the language?
- Who makes the decisions and how? (Individuals, group, vote?)
- Who are the innovators? How do people perceive them?
- Who could trigger motivation? (Chief, priest, pastor etc.)

Reaction to changes

- How do the people react to changes?
- Who are the first to accept changes?
- What dangers do people see in changes?

5. Economy

- What is the main activity of the people? What is the average income of working people?
- Are there some other forms of wealth? Who is wealthy and how did they become wealthy?
- How do the people work? Do they work in groups? Do they divide chores according to gender, age, or how?

6. Politics

- Who is in charge to give authorizations, permits etc. Are they friendly?
- How could the teachers contribute to the national aspirations or to development socially, economically, spiritually, morally?
- Does a committee of study of the language exist? A cultural group? Where? What is their influence on the community?

Background Study Guide for Literacy Projects
Adapted from SIL, Philippines

A. MAP
- Show municipalities and villages and their centers.
- Show rivers and mountain ranges.
- Show locations of schools, churches, clinics/hospitals, roads.

B. DEMOGRAPHY
- Name each municipality.
- Name each village.
- How many communities are there in each village?
- What is the population by municipality and village?
- What is the ethnic group population of each municipality and village?
- What is the adult population (15 years +) of the ethnic group?

C. LITERACY RATE
- How many adults (15 +) are literate? What percentage of total adults does this represent?
- How many adults are semi-literate and what percentage does this represent?
- How many adults are illiterate and what percentage does this represent?
- What percentage of illiterates are men?
- What percentage of illiterates are women?
- Is there a significant difference between the number of men and women illiterates?
- What percentage of the illiterates are between 15-30 years?
- What percentage of the illiterates are 30+ years?
- Are there significant differences between the 15-30 and the 30+ groups or illiterates?

NOTE: When using the Census Information to gather literacy rates, assume that all adults with no grade completed are illiterate; adults who completed grades 1-3 are semi-literate; and the rest are literate. This will result in a conservative estimate of illiteracy.

ASSESSING LITERACY NEEDS

D. LANGUAGE
- What language do people speak?
- In what language do the people prefer to read?
- Are there specific situations in which one language is preferred over another?
- How many people own books? In what language? How much did they pay for them?
- How many people own radios or tape recorders?

E. EDUCATIONAL FACTORS
- Name each school.
- What is the highest grade level of each school?
- What percentage of the students are members of the ethnic target group?
- What percentage of the target ethnic group complete grade 3?
- What percentage of the ethnic target group complete grade 6?
- What percentage of the ethnic target group complete high school?
- What is the actual medium of instruction in the schools?

F. HEALTH PROBLEMS
- What health personnel are available in the area? (This refers to the "scientific," private or government licensed workers.) Give their location and means of transport to them. What are the practical barriers to the actual delivery of health care by these people?
- List type and number of traditional healers available and distance involved in obtaining their services; i.e. traditional birth attendants, herbalists, spirit mediums, etc. What do the local believers feel about using each type?
- What is the number of patients seen per week by personnel involved in medical work? Approximately how many hours does this involve?
- Give a one-month account of the top five most common diseases) by diagnosis or major symptom); give the actual number of people seen in each category.
- How many deaths have there been in your village or area in the last year? Estimate the population that this statistic is taken from. List the assumed causes of death and the approximate age at death.

G. RELIGIOUS FACTORS

- What is the traditional religion? What percentage of the population adheres to the traditional religious practices exclusively? What percent of the population keeps traditional religious practices alongside of other newer religious practices?
- What is the dominant religion(s)? When was it introduced?
- What percentage of the population adheres to this religion?
- What churches and missions are in the area?
- How many members does each church have?
- Are there believers who are not affiliated with a particular church? How many?
- What is the attitude of church leaders to the use of the vernacular Scripture; to literacy education for church members; to community development as a Christian responsibility? What is the attitude of the church members to these things?

H. ECONOMIC FACTORS

- How is subsistence maintained?
- How much money/many goods would probably be exchanged in an average household in a month?
- What do people buy and sell?
- How are saleable goods distributed and vendors/sellers compensated?
- What services are exchanged?
- How is compensation for services made?
- How do people divide their time between work and leisure activities?
- What is the daily and yearly schedule of work and leisure activities for men, women, and children?

I. INFRASTRUCTURES

- What kinds of authority/social structures are there?
    - What traditional/cultural structures exist?
    - What religious/church structures exist?
    - What educational structures exist?
    - What political/governmental structures exist?
- What are the geographical and social-cultural boundaries of each infrastructure?

ASSESSING LITERACY NEEDS

What is the influence of each?
- How do these authority structures overlap?
- How do these authority structures interact?

For each authority structure, answer:
- Who makes decisions?
- How are decisions made?
- Whom do the decisions affect?
- How are the decisions enforced?

J. SOCIOLOGICAL FACTORS

Problems and Felt Needs

- What are the problems and felt needs as expressed by the people themselves? Comment on how these are expressed, by whom, to whom.
- Are there any felt needs concerning which the people are seeking outside help?
- Are there ways in which the team can foresee arousing a felt need for literacy?
- Are there any areas of their lives where people see themselves as disadvantage if the are not able to read and write?

Motivation

- Is there any spiritual motivation for reading religious writings?
- What desire is there to receive and send letters?
- Name any groups or individuals that have shown a real interest in learning to read. On the basis of your literacy survey, does it appear that one area is more ready/interested in learning to read than another area?
- What reasons has anyone given for wanting to learn to read?
- Is there any motivation for reading or learning to read the mother tongue in particular?
- What reasons so people give for not wanting to learn to read and write?
- Who could effectively stir motivation?

Attitudes toward Education

- What is the attitude of the traditional leaders toward education in general, and

for the adults and the children?
- What is the attitude of other leaders (c.f. infra-structures)?
- What would the leaders like to see accomplished as the result of an educational program?
- How would the leaders think that education should be acquired?

Reaction to Change

- Who are the innovators? How do they introduce new ideas?
- How do people react to innovations?
- Who accepts change first (particular groups, types of individuals)?
- What dangers do people see in accepting change?

SOURCES OF INFORMATION

A. SURVEY (Useful for gathering data in almost all areas of the background study.)

Types of Survey

1. Interview and test a random sampling of individuals
2. Interview a random sampling of individuals. Accept their answers at face value.
3. Interview selected individuals in the community.

Areas of Caution

1. The selection of respondents: the respondents are not representative of the community at large.
2. The bias of the interviewer: the interviewer's expectations color the results.
3. The expectations of the respondents: the respondent answers according to how he thinks he should rather than the way he actually thinks.

How much survey is "enough?"

In small groups, it may be possible to interview every person. In large groups, this, of course, is impossible. As a minimum, however, I suggest that you try to interview 50 people in at least 2 places. A better picture would be gained by interviewing 100 people in 5-10 places.

B. INTEGRATED CENSUS BOOKS (Useful for finding demographic information and literacy rates.)

A census report called Integrated Census of the Population and its Economic Activities, available through the National Census and Statistics Office, gives comprehensive data for broad categories of ethnic populations. If the ethnic group is small, the data is not available here. The latest census is 1980. The books are available by province.

C. PHILIPPINE GOVERNMENT OFFICES (Useful for gathering demographic information, information on social services, health, education, economy, etc.)

- Provincial and Municipal offices
- MEC Regional Data Bank
- MEC Division offices (Provincial level)

Note: Whenever you wish to use these sources of information, it is wise to have a letter of introduction from your Personnel Director.

D. PHILIPPINE COAST AND GEODETIC SURVEY (Map source)

Topographical maps can be obtained from the Philippine Coast and Geodetic Survey. The topography is excellent; place names are sometimes inaccurate. Maps are available by province and municipality (sometimes).

E. ETHNOLOGY NOTEBOOK (Useful for gathering most "value"/non-statistical information included in the background study, particularly on infrastructures, economic, religious, and sociological factors.)

By writing down your observations in an ethnology notebook, you should, over a period of time, begin to notice patterns of behavior. Every now and then, pull out the background study guide to reread the questions and jot down any thoughts you have on the subjects.

SO WHAT?

A. STEPS IN DATA PROCESSING

Data alone will not give us the clues we need to design an appropriate literacy-promotion program. These steps give us a way to process the data.

1. Compare the data across continuums:

Community A		Community B	
Men		Women	
Literates		Illiterates	
Illiterates (age 15-30)		Illiterates (30+)	
Example: 30% of illiterates are 15-30; 70% of illiterates are over 30.			
Grade 6 completion, ethnic group		Grade 6 completion, national average	
Example: 60% of ethnic students who enter school complete grade 6; 70% of all students nationally who enter school complete grade 6			
Conclusions drawn from literacy rate data		Conclusions drawn from education data	
Example: Illiteracy is dropping; grade 6 completion is close to national average.			

2. Make a judgment based on the comparison: Example, Literacy needs are being met through present educational services.

3. Draw a conclusion about the literacy promotion program: Example, The Literacy promotion program will not need to teach illiterates; if illiterates request services, the literacy program will be short-term.

B. WHERE THE DATA POINTS

Each category of information is related to every other category. Making comparisons, making judgments and drawing conclusions needs to be done for each category of information, and the conclusions themselves must be compared with each other to substantiate or reject a conclusion. It may be helpful, however, to see how such types of information contribute to our understanding of the literacy-promotion program design.

ASSESSING LITERACY NEEDS

A MAP AND DEMOGRAPHIC information show logistical factors which influence where the program might begin, how the program might expand, how much time will be needed to operate the program, and how large a program is needed. All this helps to define a "critical mass" of vernacular readers sufficient to create the momentum for an on-going distribution network. For example, the "critical mass" of vernacular readers will be significantly fewer for a group that lives in a few concentrated homogeneous villages than for a group of the same size that lives scattered across a wide area intermingled with lowlanders.

LITERACY RATE is useful in determining the focus of a program. For example, high illiteracy means that something must be done to teach reading skills, while a high semi-literacy rate says that, while educational services are adequate, reading opportunities are minimal, so the program will need to generate the necessary reading opportunities. By comparing age differences and the literacy rate, we can tell whether illiteracy is on the decline, which in turn indicates the possible length of a non-formal educational program.

LANGUAGE information on bilingualism and reading preference tells us how people view themselves and their language in relationship to other groups. Seeing people as they see themselves is essential in planning program goals and motivational activities.

EDUCATION, HEALTH, AND RELIGION profiles help us determine whether existing schools, health facilities, missions, and churches are meeting the basic educational, health care, and spiritual needs of the people. From this information we evaluate who should be included in the program's target group, what the program should try to accomplish, how long the program will need to function, how the program might assist existing services, and how the existing service agencies might assist the literacy-promotion program. For example, in a situation where there are no educational or health care facilities, we can predict that a comprehensive community-wide program to provide these services will be needed. In contrast to a situation where educational and health care facilities are available but are not used by the group, we can predict that the program will need to focus on building bridges between the community and the existing services.

Any program's success or failure is determined, in a large part, by how successfully the program design (goals and activities) has meshed with the ECONOMIC system and the local INFRASTRUCTURES/authority systems. Internal sponsorship and internal funding for a program can only be realized if we can understand how the "insides" work. For example, a program of salaried workers, whether they be teachers, paramedics, colporteurs, or writers, in a community where services are normally exchanged is likely to have, at best, short-lived success. Another example; if the field worker does not tag the "correct" community leaders to initiate a program, nothing will happen.

SOCIOLOGICAL FACTORS point out program direction. At the highest level, program goals are determined from a knowledge of the group's problems and felt needs, and their motivation for reading and writing. On another level, these same insights can suggest appropriate program activities which will allow the participants immediate and tangible reward for their expectations. If we use an understanding of the group's attitude toward change to identify the initial target group, we can expect to be more successful in generating snowballing momentum for the program as it expands to reach other clients.

ASSESSING LITERACY NEEDS

Literacy Survey

Date: Place:
Name: Sex: Age:
Birthplace: Residence:

Mother: Birthplace: Alive?

Father: Birthplace: Alive?

Spouse: Birthplace:
Schooling?   To Grade:

Children:
1. Schooling: To Grade: Reading:
   Residence: Spouse: # of children:

2. Schooling: To Grade: Reading:
   Residence: Spouse: # of children:

3. Schooling: To Grade: Reading:
   Residence: Spouse: # of children:

Personal Literacy Details

Schooling:	To Grade:		
Can Read?	Can write?		What language?
Tested?		Results:	
Owns radio?		Listens to?	
Owns books?	Number:	Languages:	

For Literates (or those who consider themselves literate):
Why did you strive to learn to read?

In your opinion, is there value in being able to read? What is it?

For those not literate:
Would you like to learn to read? Why?

In what language?

8.16 Developing an orthography

> **OBJECTIVES OF THIS TUTORIAL**
>
> This tutorial will give an introduction and some principles and tools for the development of an orthography (a writing system) in a previously unwritten language.

Introduction

In this and the following two tutorials we will be looking at the process of developing a literacy project 'from the ground up', in a context where there is initially a very low level of literacy in the community, with no existing written language, and where all materials need to be developed so people can learn to read and write in their own language. This tutorial focuses on the development of an alphabet, and other aspects of developing a writing system in a previously unwritten language.

What is an orthography?

Of the world's almost 7000 languages, less than half have an established writing system. Even though these languages have clear and complex rules of speech and established patterns of grammar, writing systems to record literature, or for people to communicate other than orally, have never been developed.

Writing is simply a method of representing language in a visual or tactile way, and consists of some kind of graphic marks on a durable or electronic surface. These marks must systematically relate to significant vocal sounds in the language so that readers can reconstruct a linguistic message and communication is achieved. The graphic marks used in writing are called 'graphemes', and they can be signs, characters, letters, diacritics, punctuation marks, etc.

DEVELOPING AN ORTHOGRAPHY

Left: A stone tablet from around 1100 AD, written using the Glagolitic Alphabet, an early Croatian alphabet. It records a donation of land made to a Benedictine abbey.

An orthography is the combination of a set of graphemes (also called an alphabet) with the set of rules that governs their use in writing a particular language. This set of rules or conventions can include rules for spelling, word boundaries, punctuation, capitalization, hyphenation or emphasis. English is written using the Latin or Roman alphabet, which has 52 letters (including upper and lower case), plus punctuation marks. There is a set of rules for how the Latin alphabet should be used when writing English, for example, names must always begin with a capital letter, and questions must end with a question mark. Many other languages also use the Latin alphabet, and add various notations, diacritics or ligatures (two letters joined together) to represent necessary features of the particular language being written.

The major writing systems used in the world today are shown on the following map[1] - the main ones are Latin, Cyrillic, Arabic and the Asian logographic scripts (like Chinese, where *units of meaning* are depicted rather than *sounds*). Each of these writing systems is used to represent many different languages. For example, the Cyrillic script that is used to write Russian is also used for around 100 other languages, the Chinese script is also used to write Japanese and other languages and dialects, and the Arabic script is used to write more than 40 separate languages.

Developing a writing system for an unwritten language is not simply a matter of analyzing the language and finding a linguistic solution. A writing system is always a significant social reality for a community of speakers, so sociolinguistic and political issues and the history and context of the community need to be taken into account as well. There are also other practical issues such as font availability and how easy it will be for people to learn to read and write.

---

1. *Writing systems worldwide*, English language Wikipedia, JWB

TUTORIAL 8.16

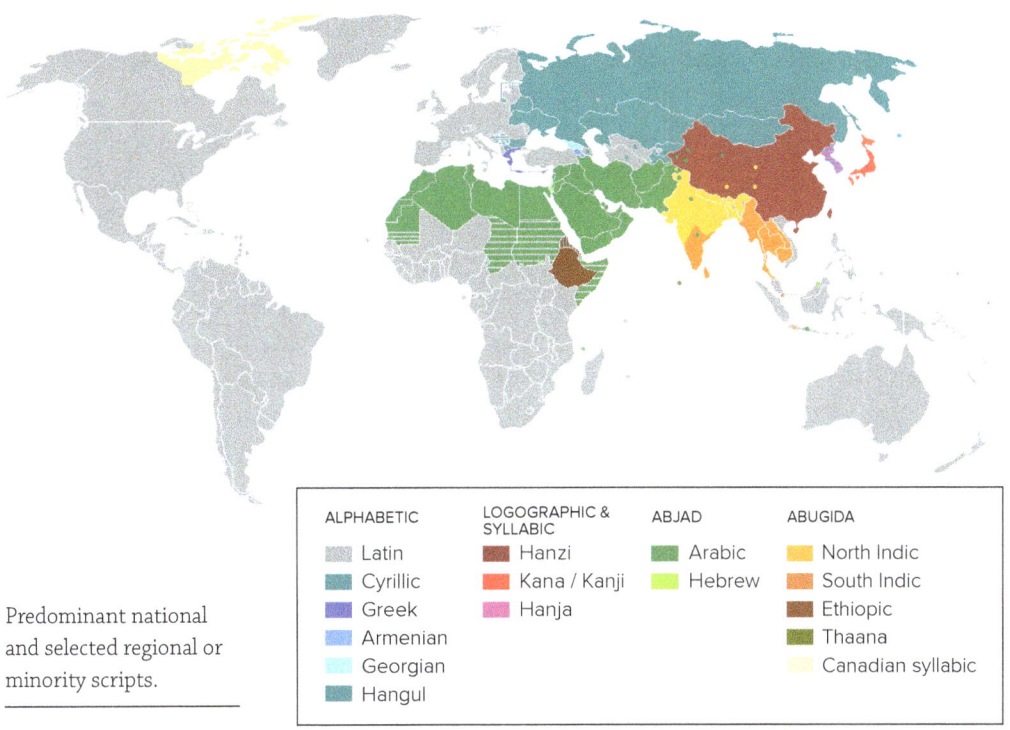

Predominant national and selected regional or minority scripts.

ALPHABETIC
- Latin
- Cyrillic
- Greek
- Armenian
- Georgian
- Hangul

LOGOGRAPHIC & SYLLABIC
- Hanzi
- Kana / Kanji
- Hanja

ABJAD
- Arabic
- Hebrew

ABUGIDA
- North Indic
- South Indic
- Ethiopic
- Thaana
- Canadian syllabic

Linguistic issues

A good writing system should seek to represent the language in an elegant and simple way. The first step is to do an analysis of the sounds of the language (this is called phonemic or phonological analysis - see Module 5, Tutorials 5.8 and 5.9 for an introduction). There are many good resources available to help you if you are involved in Phonological Analysis.

A phonological analysis will help you to decide:

- What are the distinctions of sound that must absolutely be represented in the language to avoid confusion? For example, [pit] and [bit] mean different things in English, and so it follows that /p/ and /b/ are different phonemes, and should be represented by different graphemes in the written language, otherwise meaning could not be communicated.

- How should the essential sounds be spelled? Should one sign represent one sound? Should each distinctive sound unit be represented by only one sign? For example, in English, /p/ in the initial position before a vowel is aspirated (i.e. is followed by a little puff of air, as in 'pin'), but it is unaspirated after /s/ (as in

183

'spin'). These two 'p' sounds are different, but they never make a difference in meaning in English and only change because of the contexts in which they occur. We say they are allophones of the same phoneme, so they can be represented by the same symbol or grapheme <p> in the written language.

- What is the grammatical structure of the language and how does this influence how the language is written? For example, decisions need to be made about where word breaks should be: in English, the word *walking* could possibly have been written as two separate words - *walk ing*.
- Does tone have to be represented, and are there any other units of meaning that must be written to convey a clear meaning? In many tonal languages there are a lot of words that would mean exactly the same thing if tone wasn't represented in the written language. Chinese is a tonal language, but it uses characters that represent meaning in a logographic way rather than phonemically (based on sound). In English, intonation is represented by punctuation, for example:

She's bought a car.   a statement of fact.

She's bought a car?   a question: is it true?

She's bought a car!   an exclamation: I don't believe it!

She's bought a car, …   an innuendo: …and that's not the end of it.

She's bought a "car".   an implication: it may not be a "normal" car.

Types of alphabets

Another major decision that has to be made is what *type* of alphabet will it be? For example an alphabet can be: a phonetic alphabet (where sounds are represented), a non-phonetic alphabet (like English), a syllable-based alphabet (meaning there is one character per syllable - Tibetan is of this type), or an abjad, (which is a consonant-only-alphabet, where all vowels are represented by diacritic marks - Hebrew and Arabic are examples of this type).

The decision about what type of writing system you will use will probably be influenced by socio-linguistic and practical issues, which we will look at now.

Sociolinguistic issues

Sociolinguistic and other political factors have to work together with linguistic considerations when developing an orthography. The orthography really belongs to the community: to the speakers and the eventual readers and writers of the language. It is crucial that local people are enthusiastic and accept the orthography so they feel ownership of it and will be motivated to learn to use it. Development, testing and making adjustments to an orthography should all involve consultation and discussion with local people - we will look in a later tutorial at how this kind of collaboration can be a natural part of a community literacy project.

During the development stages of an orthography, local people will be your main resource in understanding socio-linguistic and political factors that need to be considered, such as:

- *Attitudes toward other languages or dialects in relation to their language.* Do they feel their language is inferior or superior to other languages or dialects and, if so, why? Is there pressure on their language from another major language? Is there another language that has a high status or is of commercial or educational benefit?
- *The influence of other orthographies.* What are the other orthographies that people have come into contact with in their region (those used for the national language or other major languages)? How many people are literate in other orthographies? How do people feel about using an existing familiar orthography or would they prefer a new and unique orthography for their own language?
- *Government policies.* What are the government policies relating to literacy, education and alphabets or scripts? Are there any existing government policies or projects supporting particular orthographies?

Practical issues

Finally, there are a number of more practical issues to think about when developing an orthography, such as:

- *The utility, or practical simplicity of the orthography.* The orthography should naturally reflect the particular structure of the language in a way that makes sense to speakers of that language when they read it. A phonetic orthography, for example - where the written form represents the sound - will be easier for people to learn to read and write and will also allow younger members of the community to add new words - to spell them and write them phonetically, which helps the written language keep pace with natural language change.
- *Technical production issues.* What local fonts are most available for printing, word processing or other digital communication in the country? The representation of any characters other than those used in the major writing systems is going to be a problem because access to special fonts may not be available to the community. The safest option - to ensure usability of the orthography as well as

DEVELOPING AN ORTHOGRAPHY

safe long-term storage of digital files containing text written in that orthography - is to use only characters that can be found on a standard local keyboard or combinations of these characters (e.g. digraphs or combinations of letters with diacritics).

➤ ACTIVITIES

1. For detailed practical information and resources for developing an orthography, you can go to the *Resources for Developing Orthographies* link at the SIL (Summer Institute of Linguistics) website. Explore the website and the resources that are available there.

You will find a helpful step-by-step guide in *Writing unwritten languages*, drafted by Clinton Robinson with Karl Gadelii, December 2003.

For a wealth of information for further research, you can go to *Omniglot*, an online encyclopedia of writing systems and languages, or to the *Museum of the Alphabet*.

2. After you read the following information on *Colorbet*, answer these questions:

- What type of alphabet is *Colorbet*?
- If *Colorbet* was chosen as the writing system for a previously unwritten language, are there any potential issues can you think of that might come up in linguistic, socio-linguistic, political or practical areas? List any you can think of.

Colorbet

By Vitaly Vetash

Colorbet[1] is a color alphabet based on the International Phonetic Alphabet, and was developed by Vitaly Vetash, a Russian painter and linguist. The first variant of the color alphabet was done in 1983, on the basis of psycholinguistic investigations. Theoretically, any language can be written using Colorbet.

The model is based on the kinship of psychological meaning of sounds and colors. According to the system of Goete (which now is used in T.V. transmission), the whole variety of colors is based on a fusion of three main rays (red, yellow and blue), light and shadow. A similar law can be found in phonetics, where the variety of vowel comes from the combination of the triangle of the main sounds (A, I, U). Therefore, the colors of vowels are: A - red, I - blue, U - green (not yellow, but green, as used on TV).

According to psycholinguistic investigations, one can give to non-sonorous consonants darker colors than to sonorous ones, voiced ones have brighter colors than voiceless ones, and fricatives are more colored than plosives. That is, brightness depends on sonority: from rich colors (of sonants) to dry tints (of voiceless plosive sounds). Sonorous consonants, having more clear colors, are more close to vowels (R is ruby-colored, and burr R is orange; velar L is yellow-white and palatal L is white-rosy. Nasal vowels: mat-green M, mat-beige N, light-violet Y, dark-yellow W).

On the next page the color scheme according to the IPA (International Phonetic Alphabet) is represented. It shows that tints of kindred sounds are close. However, plain (flat) reproduction of sounds doesn't reflect the character of sounds exactly, because in the strict way one has to reproduce the texture also. Thus, colors of vowels must have additional luminescence, and consonants produce material sensations. For example, sibilants (S, Z, TS) could be reflected by metallic surface, and gutturals coincide with shaggy (wooden or board) surface. A dim, lacquered surface fits for resonant sounds (L,M,N etc.). Vowel sounds are written as longer colored sections, to distinguish them more easily from consonants, which are shorter.

---

1. Colorbet, by Vitaly Vetash, http://www.omniglot.com/conscripts/colorbet.php

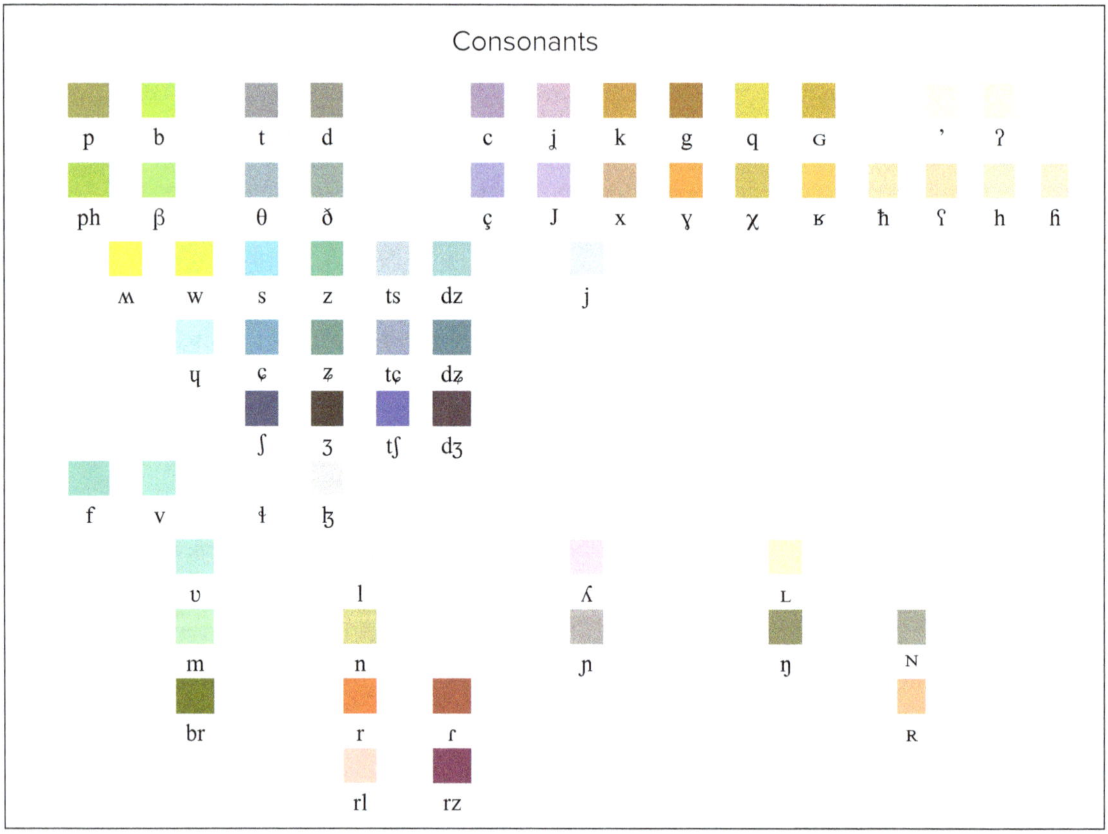

DEVELOPING AN ORTHOGRAPHY

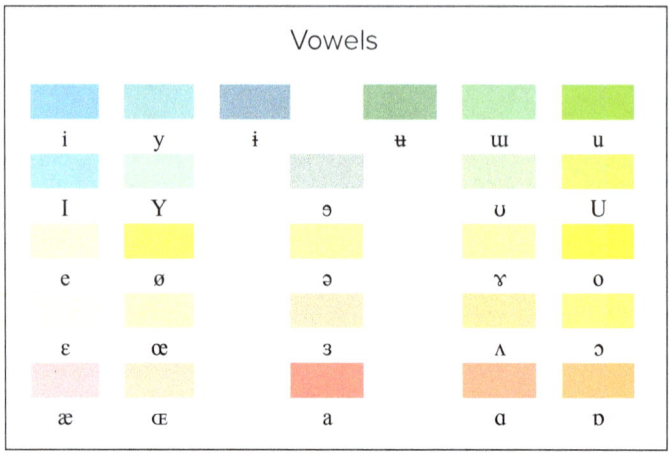

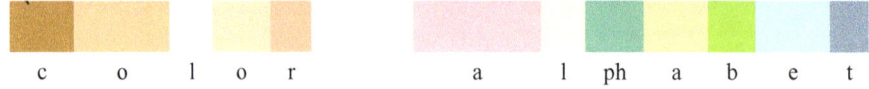

The example below of *Colorbet* writing says, "color alphabet":

8.17 Developing literacy materials

✓ OBJECTIVES OF THIS TUTORIAL

This tutorial will discuss principles to apply when developing materials for a literacy project and will give some examples of effective literacy materials.

Introduction

It probably goes without saying that your literacy materials - the teaching books, reading books, flashcards and classroom materials - are an important part of your program. If they are of good quality, they will be able to stand up to the scrutiny of government officials or others who may see them, and the students and local teachers need to be proud of their program so they will take it seriously and be motivated to take on the responsibility for it. Materials should also be reproducible so that the program is sustainable and locals can continue running the literacy program themselves in the years to come.

In this tutorial, as well as outlining some of the principles of literacy materials development, we will also look at examples of some actual materials used in a successful program (a primer-based syllable approach to literacy).

List your materials

The materials you will need for a literacy project will obviously depend on the kind of program you have planned. After you have done your research into the literacy needs of your community and have decided on the type of program needed - then you can make a plan to develop your materials.

You should develop a list of all the materials needed to run your program and have a plan in place to get them made, printed or produced before the beginning of your first literacy class. Below is an example of a set of materials needed for a syllable approach program[1]. You will also find detailed directions for developing each of these materials and examples of each of them later in the module.

---

1. Based off the NTM Literacy Manual (2001), pg. 9 - *Overview Of Major Literacy Materials to be developed*

DEVELOPING LITERACY MATERIALS

Your goal as a literacy worker is to write a complete set of literacy materials - from the start of pre-literacy, through the entire literacy course, and on into post-literacy.

Main literacy materials needed for a complete literacy program:

Pre-Reader
A pre-reader is used during the pre-literacy program. A pre-reader contains culturally appropriate pictures, shapes, numbers, etc. It does not contain words that will be read. Pre-readers are used to teach reading fundamentals, such as reading left to right and differentiating between similar pictures and shapes.

Primers
You will need to write approximately four primers. The number of primers will vary from three to six or more, depending on the needs of the language. These primers will be used to teach the students to read all the sounds in their language.

Local people in Africa with their set of six primers.

Teaching Aids
Teaching people to read involves much more than just primers. You will also be using the blackboard, flash cards, etc., to reinforce or emphasize what you will be teaching. Developing these teaching aids and equipment is a vital part of preparing to teach literacy.

Lesson Plans
Daily lesson plans explain in detail what is in each lesson and how the lesson material is to be taught. It is preferable for these lesson plans to be prepared in the vernacular.

Supplementary Materials
It is advisable to write a graded reader to follow each primer. Each graded reader provides the student with practice reading material that uses only what has been taught up

to that point. In addition, you may also wish to develop supplementary materials that you consider essential for the literacy program, such as homework, handouts, tests, etc.

Post-Literacy Reading Materials
Post-literacy reading materials help the students to gain fluency. They can include such things as indigenous stories, health and hygiene booklets, information about the world around them, and eventually Bible stories, Bible lessons and translated Scripture. These materials will carry the rewards of reading into the future.

Get the local people involved

Because it is your eventual goal to hand the program over to local people, you should try to get them involved as soon as possible. As you are developing your teaching and classroom materials try to think about ways to get others involved in designing, illustrating, writing stories, taking pictures, printing, photocopying, laminating, setting up a classroom - in any way you can. Even before the first actual literacy class begins, you can stimulate community involvement by setting up a community notice board or newspaper with the help of local people, and get their involvement in deciding where to teach and who to have in the first classes.

Do the best job you can

Literacy program development can be a daunting prospect for anyone to undertake, and many church planting teams or cross-cultural workers put it aside and don't take on the challenge of equipping the local community to read and write. Developing a literacy program from the ground up takes faith - faith that literacy is an important part of God's work to see his Word truly in the hands local people so that they have the ability to engage fully with it and are fully equipped to pass it on clearly to others. But it can be very easy to settle for something less. Making a commitment to giving time and effort to meeting the literacy needs of a community is an investment that is priceless for that community and something that the Lord also highly values as people gain a much greater ability to engage with his Word and pass it on to others.

Your materials need to express the high value you have for the project. Putting effort and time into developing good illustrations, having clear, consistent formatting and good-quality printing and laminating - making them look good - is actually very important. If you value the project and communicate that it is important for you and the community, then local people are more likely to value it as well. Your materials need to say, "this is a program we can be proud of and support as a community".

DEVELOPING LITERACY MATERIALS

Examples of real materials

To give you a more concrete idea of literacy materials development, the following is a description of the materials used in the Ata literacy program, from the Ata people group, Papua New Guinea.

The Ata literacy program began in 1992, and is still going strong today (2015). What began as an adult literacy, Ata language program, has now developed to also teach Pidgin and English literacy classes to both adults and children and to teach people from other language groups as well. Local Ata people have been administrating and teaching the program in a number of village schools and pre-schools since 1994. The same materials that were originally developed for the first program are the materials that are still reproduced and used today. Local people were involved in making, printing, designing and developing the reading materials, and they began to teach classes from the second class onward. Local people have done all teacher training since 1994, following the same classroom procedures and teacher lesson books that were first developed for the program. They now are involved in developing new materials for English and children's literacy programs and are involved in helping other language groups with their local literacy programs.

Pre-Reader

The Ata pre-reader takes one week to teach through for an adult class. It includes activities and exercises for those who have never been introduced to the concept of reading or writing before. The teacher's lesson book for the pre-reader clearly outlines the procedure for each day of teaching through the pre-reader. During the teaching of the pre-reader there are other activities to stimulate new pathways of thinking; color matching games, jigsaw puzzles using local themes, games using symbol matching, and practice writing symbols and numbers (without naming what those symbols stand for at this stage). The following picture shows a couple of pages from the Ata Pre-reader - these pages give students practice in beginning to distinguish between symbols that are slightly different from one another, and practice in moving their eyes from left to right on a page.

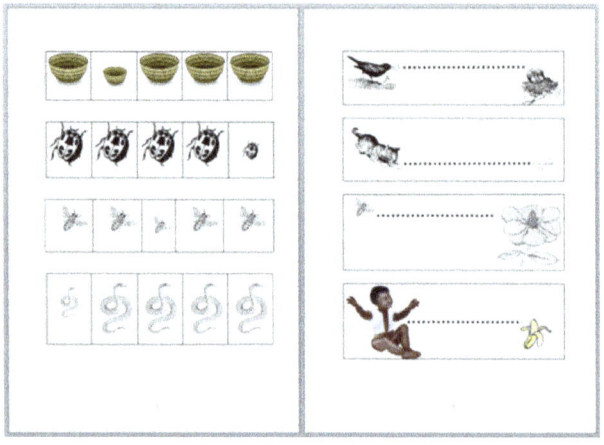

Ata Pre-reader

Primers

The Ata program has three primers which gradually teach all the sounds of the Ata language, and give systematic introduction and reading practice of all the syllables in Ata that use those sounds. The following illustration shows two pages from the second Ata primer - the teaching page for the new syllable "ua", using the key word "uaxa" (canoe), and a reading page giving some sentences for reading practice using the new syllable "ua" in a variety of words.

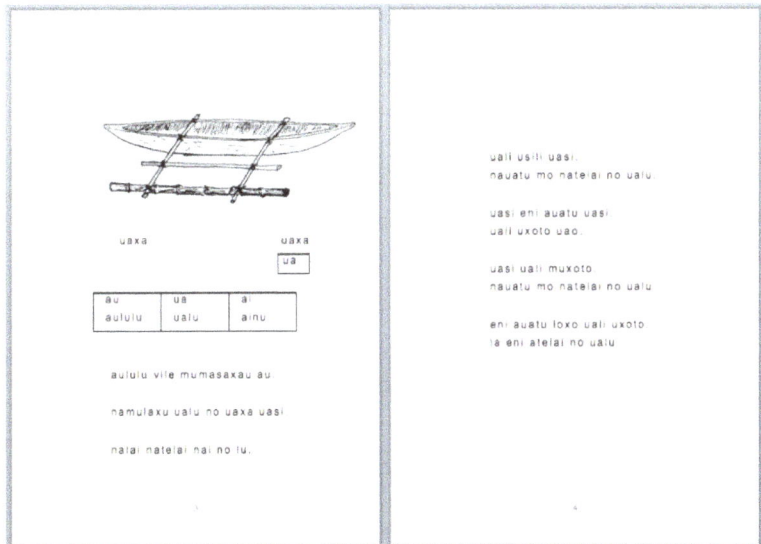

The second Ata Primer teaching the new syllable "ua"

Teaching Aids

Flashcards for both words and syllables are used as a regular part of classroom procedure to review and drill syllables and sounds. These are produced on colored card and laminated. The color of the flashcards matches the color of the primer cover in which the particular syllable was introduced. Flashcard kits for Ata village schools can be seen in the following picture. The picture on the right shows the first three Ata key word flashcards ('man', 'edible plant', 'string bag') ready to be printed on card and laminated for use.

Flashcard kit

Key word flashcard for 'man', 'edible plant', 'string bag'

mulu

lava

tiva

DEVELOPING LITERACY MATERIALS

Lesson Plans

Clear, easy to follow, step-by-step lesson plans that a newly literate teacher can use effectively to teach others have been a key element to the success of the program. Each primer has a matching teacher's lesson book that has a step-by-step guide for the teacher to follow each day, including reading and writing activities and the particular new sound to be taught.

The lesson plan below (written in the Ata language) gives the lesson number, the page of the primer to teach from, what syllables should be written on the blackboard, instructions for reading practice, writing exercises relating to that day's material and the homework sheet to use for that day.

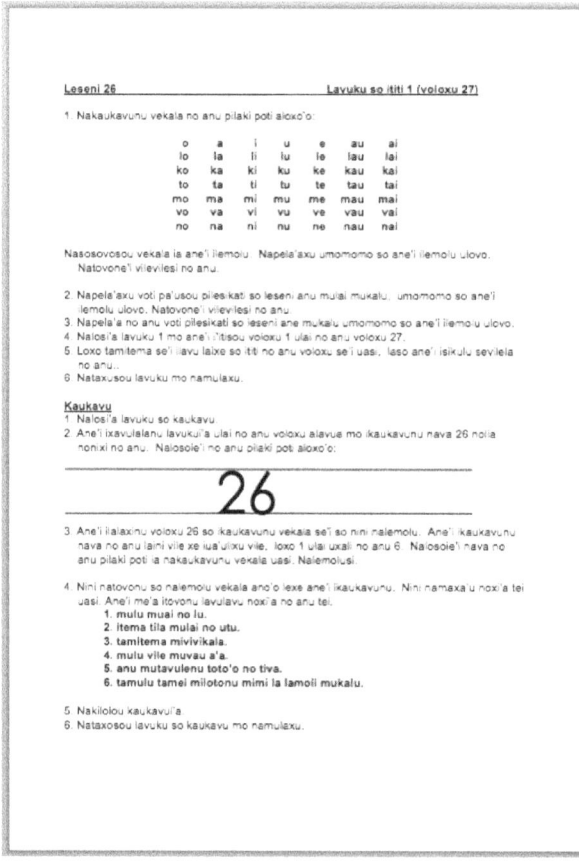

Ata Lesson Plan

Supplementary Materials

Using supplementary materials (extra reading materials and homework exercises) during the program motivates students and makes learning as effective as possible. The Ata program includes homework and activity sheets - some examples are shown below. The program includes extra activities such as practice with other community members, group fun days with literacy related games and the encouragement of newly literate believers to read the Bible publicly to show how they are progressing.

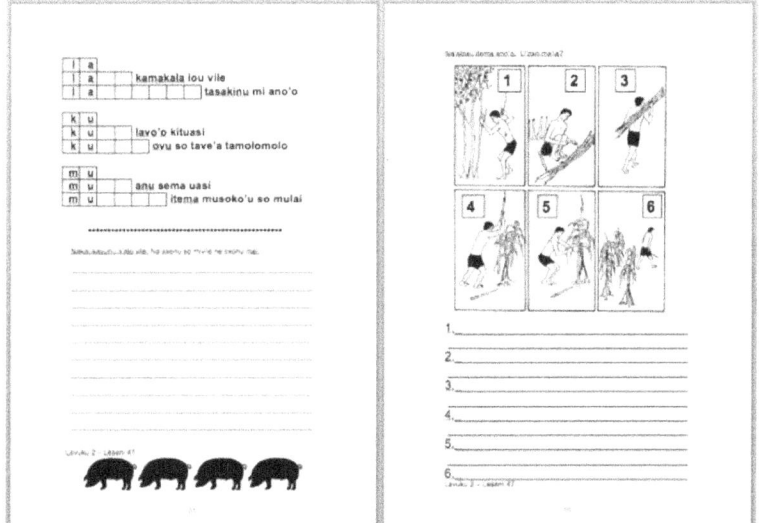

Homework and activity sheets

Post-Literacy Reading Materials

Having plenty of graded and varied reading materials available for the new literates to practice and improve their skills is essential. The Ata program includes translated booklets as well as stories written by local people about the history of their people, stories from the old people, and helpful materials as a background to Bible teaching. Students also write their own stories as soon as they are able to add to the store of future reading materials. The post literacy program is structured so that the teachers keep track of each student's progress and continue to give them encouragement as they read each book and answer comprehension questions about it. Bible Lessons and translated Scripture are available as the final reading material in the post literacy program. Extra fluency exercises or training are available for those who want or need them for their work in the local church. One of the important goals of the post-literacy program is to help students to understand the relationship of their new reading and writing skills to practical, everyday, useful activities in their lives and in God's work - to apply them and use them often.

Sustainability

For all the materials you eventually develop, you will need to establish a way for local literacy teachers to be able to finance printing, make corrections to materials, reprint and store materials. This will depend on the local infrastructure, economy, and other factors and the program may need your support for several years until it becomes self-sustaining. You should remember, particularly if your school is in a remote area, that they will need to replace or reproduce materials such as blackboards and chalk, exercise books for students, pens and pencils, erasers, pencil sharpeners, and of course the printed materials for the program itself. A good community project might be to establish a reading and storage room, so books and materials are kept well and local people can come to get reading materials, writing materials or re-stock their local literacy schools.

The following list is a translation (back to English from Ata) of a materials checklist that the Ata literacy administrators use to stock a new village literacy school. Each item on this list is something that the Ata are either able to source and buy themselves, or are able to order copies to be printed at a small print shop in a coastal town. They then travel out to town to pick up their copies and buy other supplies.

Things for the School
(for 20 students and 3 teachers)

For the Students
- ☐ 1 blackboard
- ☐ 2 blackboard erasers
- ☐ 1 box of chalk
- ☐ 1 clock
- ☐ 1 string with clothes pins (for hanging the flashcards up)
- ☐ 1 box flashcards
- ☐ 40 pencils
- ☐ 1 box of small pencil erasers (48)
- ☐ Small bits of plastic for covering up the pictures (pre-reader)
- ☐ 20 manila folders (for homework sheets)
- ☐ 20 exercise books (96 pages)
- ☐ 20 English pre-readers
- ☐ 20 Ata pre-readers
- ☐ 20 Primer 1
- ☐ 20 Primer 2
- ☐ 20 Primer 3
- ☐ Enough blank paper for homework
- ☐ 20 graduation certificates

For the Teachers
- ☐ 1 Roll Book (exercise book with ruled pages and names written)
- ☐ 3 Teacher's manuals for Pre-reader and each primer
- ☐ 3 red pens
- ☐ 3 clip-board folders

For the Post-literacy Course
- ☐ 5 "Stories about the ways of the Ata"
- ☐ 5 "Stories about the ways of the bigmen"
- ☐ 5 "Some true stories"
- ☐ 5 "Some stories by students"
- ☐ 5 "The story of transportation"
- ☐ 5 "Animals of Israel"
- ☐ 5 "How the Jews lived"
- ☐ 20 sets of comprehension questions for each reading book
- ☐ 1 checklist chart for marking off each student when he finishes a book and the questions.
- ☐ Blank paper for writing the question answers.

ACTIVITIES

1. Read the Tutorial 8.17 Reading Activity - *Introduction and Planning for Literacy*[1].

---

[1]. A modifed section from the NTM Literacy Manual (2001).

Tutorial 8.17 Reading Activity

Introduction and Planning for Literacy

The Importance of Literacy

Can you imagine life without being able to read and write? In all contexts, literacy opens the world of the printed word. Our desire is that literacy will open the written Word of God to all people groups.

The primary purpose of literacy programs is to enable the people to read translated Scripture and related materials in their own language. Literacy is crucial to the over-all church planting strategy of any given work. With this in mind, every effort needs to be made by the entire team to do what is necessary to assure a successful literacy program.

Planning

A good literacy program should be planned in its entirety. Before starting to teach literacy, we need to think through the whole strategy for literacy, including the following:

- Team involvement
- Motivating the people
- Developing literacy materials, including pre-primers, primers, and post-primer reading material
- Developing teaching aids
- Teaching the literacy program
- Indigenization of the literacy program

Preparation

Preparation is critically important in any literacy program.

- We need to prepare the people by instilling in them a desire to learn to read.
- We need to prepare the literacy materials that will teach the student to read and write in their own language. It is advisable to prepare all necessary literacy materials before actually starting to teach literacy.

Implementation

The literacy program is designed to teach the people in progressive steps toward reading Scripture.

- We will start by teaching pre-literacy. Pre-reading and pre-writing are integral parts of the whole literacy process.

- Then, we will move into teaching them to read and write, using primers along with a variety of teaching aids.

- The next step will be to take the student through the reading of post-literacy materials. These materials should move from the simple to the more complex and should provide the student with plenty of reading practice so that they will gain fluency and be able to read with understanding.

- Finally, the student will progress to being able to read translated Old Testament Scripture portions, Bible lessons, and the New Testament.

Indigenization

The people should be involved as much as possible in each stage of developing and implementing the literacy program. We want to turn the literacy program over to the people, and their involvement at each stage will prepare them to assume that responsibility. As the literacy program is indigenized, it will become an ongoing part of each work.

Preparing for Literacy during Language and Culture Study

Stimulate motivation for a future literacy program

From the day that initial contact is made with the people group, the missionary team should actively create an interest in literacy. These conscious efforts by the missionaries will, in most cases, motivate people to want to learn to read and to write.

Here are some suggestions to stimulate interest:

- Provide suitable magazines or scrapbooks of pictures for the people to browse through at leisure. Nature magazines, pictures of people of various lands, pictures of other people groups from their own country, and photos of them and of their environment will all create interest in the printed page. For people who have never seen pictures, you may need to teach them how to read pictures, how to hold pictures right side up, etc.

- Let the people see you, your family, and your teammates reading and writing at every opportunity.

- Send notes or letters to each other to prove to the people that the paper talks to you. For example, you could give a message-bearer a note containing a request for an item. Tell them that this note is asking for an item which they should bring to you. The receiver of the note should read it while the message-bearer watches. Then they should give the item to the message-bearer to take to the writer of the note.

- Consult books in their presence. For example, you could look in a medical book to find an answer to their medical problems. Let them see that you look to books for answers.

- Let them see your personal enjoyment of reading. Let them also see that the children on your team enjoy reading.

- Produce a newspaper with them about events that are important to them. Initially, you will have to read it to them. Use this as an opportunity to encourage them to learn to read. With the availability of scanners, digital cameras, smart phones etc., articles in a newspaper can include pictures of them and their lives, and therefore be a tremendous source of interest.

- Use a community bulletin board. Initially you may have to read to them what is posted on the bulletin board. Once some can read, their ability to read the bulletin board will show the value of the written word to those who cannot read. It will motivate students for later classes.

If the people among whom you work live in extreme isolation and have never had their concepts of life challenged by other ways of doing things, you may need to come up with additional motivational ideas. In rare cases, you may actually find that the people have no desire to become literate until after they become believers. Nevertheless, do everything you can to stimulate interest in reading and writing. Be creative, considering the people's culture, interests, and felt needs.

One of the biggest keys in motivating the people will be your own enthusiasm. Be excited about them becoming literate. Be excited about the opportunity you will have to teach them. Communicate your enthusiasm, and it will help to motivate them to want to learn to read and to write.

Keep literacy in mind as you choose computer software

Computers will be invaluable in your literacy program. The computer software that you use to record language and culture data should be chosen with literacy in mind.

DEVELOPING LITERACY MATERIALS

For ease in producing literacy mate- rials, the software you choose needs to be able to:

- Produce a complete dictionary of the vernacular.

- Enable manipulation of language data so that you can formulate word lists.

- Contain the ability to mark picturable words (that is, nouns which can be easily illustrated) so that they can be easily retrieved when writing the literacy primers.

Consider also software that will be best for the actual production of literacy primers and other literacy material. In general, any word processor or desktop publishing program can handle this job.

Start a picture file

Start a file of clear, easy-to-understand pictures. Gather the type of pictures that you would find in magazines, as well as the outline-type of drawings that you usually see in primers. Such pictures will be used in a myriad of ways. For example, you can use the pictures to make scrapbooks, puzzles, and games for use during pre-literacy. You can also use these pictures as reference material to draw illustrations for your primers.

All pictures that you will use during pre-literacy should be of complete objects, such as an entire tree, a whole person, a table with all its corners and legs visible. However, your picture file should also contain pictures of parts of things (for example, body parts, parts of a tree, etc.) for use later in the literacy program.

Pictures of objects will be the best for use in your literacy materials. However, if possible, include in your file pictures of easily recognizable actions (such as chopping down a tree, swimming, running, building, etc.) Also include pictures which show emotion (such as anger) or which would be descriptive (such as tall, or crooked).

Be sure to gather pictures of things that are important in their culture. For example, if you know that pigs are a big part of the people's culture, gather pictures of pigs.

Start a file of story ideas

As you are learning the language and culture, be alert to common, everyday activities, events, and topics which interest the local people. The people will enjoy reading about these things when you develop literacy readers.

You will be able to use your culture file and texts extensively as resources for story ideas. Texts which are gathered during language and culture study can later be edited and used as reading material.

Set goals

Although you won't be ready for extensive work on literacy during early language and culture study, your team should take the time to write out goals and hopes for the literacy program. Ideally, a literacy consultant will be able to sit down with your team and lead you through the process of setting up goals in the light of the whole church planting strategy.

Do not begin to write literacy materials until you have reached the appropriate level in your language and culture study. The more fluent you are in the language, the better. Yet, you cannot wait to begin literacy until you are fluent like a native speaker, because you probably never will be. Working closely with native speakers will help to compensate for any lack you may have in the language.

Your literacy consultant or field leadership can advise you as to when to begin preparation of literacy materials. In general, this is usually when you are between levels three and four (in a four-level program) in language and culture study. Ideally, by the time there are believers, there will also be people within the group who are literate.

Let the people know that you plan to teach them to read and write. Be general, rather than specific. Do not make promises that you cannot keep. For example, you may say something like, "We will teach you to write so you will be able to write letters to people who are in different areas." Or if there are believers, "We will teach you to read so you will be able to read the Word of God for yourselves. The Word of God is like food for us."

Determine 'customized' orthography

The people must like the look of their language. Once the linguistic work has been done, the orthography will need to be determined. Generally the linguist will determine this with tribal leadership and community input.

You as the literacy worker may have input because of student feedback that you hear and observe in the literacy classes.

Usually the people want their alphabet to look like the trade language. Jean Johnson[1] explains that while "one symbol for each sound" should be our rule of thumb, we can't ignore the preferences of the government and the people we are trying to help. If there are sounds in the vernacular which require an odd looking symbol, make inquiries as to how this should be represented as part of an alphabet that looks right both to the people and to government officials.

---

1. Jean Johnson was one of NTM's first literacy workers and for many years was NTM's only literacy consultant. She taught the literacy course at NTM's Language Institute for many years.

For example, in most South American countries, typically 'c' is used rather than 'k,' and 'que' and 'qui' are used to represent the phonemic 'ke' and 'ki.' Therefore, some literacy workers will prefer to follow that same pattern of 'ca, que, qui, co, cu' right from the start. Otherwise, they would end up teaching the people 'k' with all vowels and then doing transition teaching later. Usually, the closer you stick to the familiar, the better the government and the tribal people will like their alphabet.

Once the alphabet for a native language has been fairly well established, literacy preparations can begin. However, it is common for changes to be made in orthography after there are literate people, so start out with a small trial printing of the first literacy materials.

Understand literacy's "Big Picture"

Once the time comes to begin final preparations for literacy, it is vitally important that you understand the literacy program as a whole.

- The literacy program was already begun when your missionary team began to stimulate interest in reading and writing.

- The literacy program is now to be implemented through the efforts of the literacy worker, the team, and the literacy consultant.

- In the future, the literacy program will be carried on by native teachers of literacy, thus remaining with the people long after the missionary is gone.

Avoid mixing methods

Although other methods to literacy exist, the syllable method presented in this manual has been proven to meet the need of most works. Should you run into a unique problem, you may be able to glean ideas from other resources. Check first with your literacy consultant for guidance as to what resources to use. It is important not to mix methods. That would be confusing for the student, and probably for you as well.

Establish communicaiton with your literacy consultant

The process of establishing communication with the literacy consultant will vary according to your field's procedures. On some fields, the language learning consultant will let the literacy consultant know when you are ready to begin.

If your field does not have a literacy consultant, field leadership may be able to get consultant help for you. If you are going to follow the method presented in this manual, it is important that the person who helps you is someone who has developed their primers following the procedures of this method and has taught those primers.

You as the literacy worker need to keep the literacy consultant informed of plans, progress, consultant needs, etc., as the literacy effort develops.

The literacy consultant will, in turn, be able to offer ideas, resources, and experience, along with hands-on help at crucial stages of the literacy program development, particularly when you are writing primers and when you are learning how to teach the materials.

8.18 Teaching literacy & getting community involvement

 OBJECTIVES OF THIS TUTORIAL

This tutorial will give an overview of the principles involved in teaching and managing a literacy project in a community, with some practical ideas for encouraging community involvement in the ongoing program.

Introduction

How you teach literacy for the first time is going to be the model for the future. It will set the stage for local people to embrace the program as their own. Seeing a well-run and successful class, with good materials, a clear schedule, a confident teacher and motivated students will give them the confidence to take on the role of teaching the program for themselves and later expanding and administrating it for the long term… but how can all of that come together? In this tutorial we will look at some ways you can prepare and implement your literacy program to encourage that kind involvement from your local friends and coworkers.

Get local people involved at every stage

We mentioned in the last tutorial, that because it is your eventual goal to hand over the program to local people, you should try to get them excited and involved as soon, and as much as possible. Be creative and involve them at every stage, being positive about their contribution and about their ability to have a real part in the future of the program. If they see it as "your program" and not "their program" then you still have more work to do in motivating them to be involved!

Pre-literacy: motivating and preparing people for literacy

We talked in the last tutorial about stimulating community involvement by setting up a community notice board or newspaper with the help of local people. There are a lot of other creative ideas that have been successful in motivating people for literacy, here are just a few:

- Using dramas to depict the importance and benefits that literacy will have for them personally and for their community, and to bring a focus on literacy before the upcoming program.
- Using your own skills personally to demonstrate the benefits of reading and writing:
  - Reading a letter from a family member a long way away.
  - Reading labels on canned goods, medicine, instructions for vehicle maintenance, recipes or health information.
  - Reading maps of the local area or broader region.
  - Reading fluently in the local language, to the pre-literates for their enjoyment. (Choose text material or appropriate, interesting stories you have recorded from them and transcribed).
  - Reading Bible portions or passages in the local language - telling them that one day they will be able to read God's Word for themselves in their own language.
- Making reading materials with pictures available, so people become familiar with holding a book, turning pages, reading from top to bottom and left to right.
- Using jigsaw puzzles, dominoes, color matching games.
- Involving local leadership (Government, church or local political leaders) in making decisions for their community program - they can help to discuss with you:
  - Who to choose as possible people to train as teachers, or involve as helpers.
  - How to find space to set up a classroom and do any necessary work.
  - How to decide who the first students will be and how to choose or recruit students for following classes.
  - The best way to connect with the community to get them involved and excited about the literacy program.
  - When the classes should begin, what hours and what days should they be held, when to have breaks.

Teaching Literacy: encouraging local involvement

One of the most important elements in getting others involved in teaching literacy is having clear, easy to follow lesson plans in the local language, with a clear lesson process that new teachers can understand and use. The lesson process itself should be repetitive and become familiar to both teachers and students - they will not get bored because the new sounds and symbols they are learning within a familiar lesson framework will keep them interested and motivated. Teacher lesson plans that are easy to follow for newly literate people make it possible for them to imagine teaching it themselves - they can feel empowered by being able to read and follow the instructions in the lesson plans, while remembering the experience they have had in going through the literacy class as students themselves.

Try to avoid setting up a literacy program that requires a higher level of training or education for teachers than they will gain in the literacy class itself - that is a potential road-block to your grass-roots program spreading and growing on its own. Students who graduate from your program should be able to help in teaching the program straight away.

Lesson plans that follow the same basic pattern each day of exercises and activities - blackboard drills, introduction of new sounds using flashcards, reading practice, writing dictation, flashcard review time, homework time - allow people who are faster students to begin to help during the class to actually teach parts of the program. They can quickly be involved in helping other students by:

- reviewing the flashcards,
- writing the exercises on the blackboard,
- listening to others read,
- helping during dictation exercises,
- preparing the classroom before the class begins,
- storing materials and keeping class records.

This is a natural way for local teachers to develop at their own pace and in the context of the literacy class itself rather than in separate training classes, which makes teacher training accessible to many more potential teachers. Remember that you are not only teaching reading and writing skills, but encouraging and equipping future teachers, and ensuring the longevity of the program.

Post-literacy: linking literacy to life

It can be difficult for some students to make the "jump" at the end of formal literacy teaching to actually using reading and writing every day. Continued practice and use of literacy skills is very important for new literates, especially during their first literate year, or until it becomes a comfortable and integral part of their lives. They can be greatly helped in this process if they are actively guided into practical uses for reading and writing during the actual literacy program. The more they are given the opportunity to actually use what they are learning, the more it will help them to see a link between the theoretical classroom work and real life and see the practical purpose reading and writing now has for them in their life and within their community, society and culture. Some of these ideas will help:

- Having a graded post-literacy reading program that begins with simple material culture and stories and moves into more unfamiliar and complex material and finally ends with Bible lessons and Scripture.
- Making sure that translated Scripture, printed Bible lessons and other reading materials are available and accessible.
- Including comprehension questions for post-literacy books to which the students write answers that are checked and corrected personally by the teacher.
- Providing culturally interesting and relevant material that people want to read (e.g., local culture and history, an introduction to Jewish culture).
- Giving personal attention, encouragement and ideas to new literates to continue to use and practice their skills.

Here are some ideas to encourage new literates to use their skills and keep in practice.

- Using real-world text material to practice skills - reading newspapers to learn about the news, reading recipes in order to actually cook something. Other real-world text material would include work manuals, job applications, contracts, coupons, and of course Bible lesson and Scripture materials.
- Writing and sending real letters; to the children's school, to a government representative, to a friend or relative.
- Training to be a literacy teacher, meeting with other teachers and studying the teacher's manual and materials.
- Writing out Scripture verses. Doing regular Scripture memorization and daily Scripture reading.

- Using the Bible lessons and questions as reading and writing exercises.
- Writing books to be used as literacy reading material. Possible subjects include an important cultural event such as a wedding, school opening, community building project, natural disaster, etc. (Providing a series of photographs can help.) Students could also publish a collection of stories written by their class.

Administration of the program: handing it over

A literacy program that supports the work of the local church will have a solid foundation to continue on. Local church leaders will be motivated to see that the program continues if they can see the value it has in the life of the church. From the beginning you should be providing opportunities for members of the local church to assist and be a part of the literacy program in any way they are able and for leaders to gradually take on the decision-making responsibility for it in such areas as:

- providing administration for the entire program,
- organising the ordering and supply of printed materials,
- planning for the future of the program; new schools, continuing needs, longevity, etc.,
- training and assigning teachers,
- providing communication between schools and church leadership.
- developing a church outreach strategy that includes literacy teaching.

TEACHING LITERACY & GETTING COMMUNITY INVOLVEMENT

DISCUSSION POINTS

1. Think of all the different ways that a literacy project in a community might supplement or enhance a church planting work in that same community.

ACTIVITIES

1. Read the Tutorial 8.18 Reading Activity - *Teaching the Literacy Program*[1].

---

[1]. A modifed section from the NTM Literacy Manual (2001).

Tutorial 8.18 Reading Activity

Teaching the Literacy Program

What needs to be completed before starting to teach literacy

Preparing the materials for the whole program before starting to teach literacy may seem overwhelming. It does take time and effort to prepare everything. But once these things are done, you will not have to do them again, unless you make improvements. For example, laminated flash cards and primers with laminated covers can be used over and over again.

Take the time to organize and set the program up well. It will be worth the time and effort. Remember the purpose of your literacy program is to enable the people to read translated Scripture in their own language. The growth of the believers and the strength of the church is dependent on the believers being able to read the Word of God. And being able to read the Word of God is dependent on the effort you put into literacy. So take the time — make the effort — and do it with your whole heart, honoring the Lord.

If the following list of things to do seems overwhelming, concentrate on doing one step at a time. Check off as you complete each step.

- Prepare the pre-literacy materials.

- Write the primers. Check them with a consultant.

- Make all the flash cards which will be needed for each lesson. If possible, laminate them for durability.

- Determine and gather needed classroom vocabulary.

- Write and print the lesson plans for the entire literacy course. It is preferable for these lesson plans to be written in the vernacular. If possible, it would be helpful to have a literacy consultant check these lesson plans.

- Write and print the graded readers.

- Prepare any supplementary reading or writing activities that you plan to use.

- Write and print at least some post-literacy materials.

TEACHING LITERACY & GETTING COMMUNITY INVOLVEMENT

- Gather all classroom materials. If multiple literacy programs will be taught in more than one location, you will need the following items for each location:
    - A large blackboard (3' x 6' minimum). If you have a large class and space, two black-boards would be better.
    - Tables and seats for the students. Tables work the best for a writing surface, but lap boards or clipboards could also work.
    - A wide podium with a slight slant OR a table for the teacher. It is best if you have something that is large enough to lay out a day's teaching materials.
    - Chalk and blackboard erasers
    - Clock (optional, but helpful if you plan to teach them to tell time)
    - A cupboard or foot locker for book storage
    - A box with dividers, which will hold:
        - syllable flash cards
        - key word flash cards
        - built-word flash cards
        - lesson plans
    - Pencils (including red pencil for teacher), pencil sharpeners and erasers
    - Pre-reading and writing materials:
        - pre-readers
        - games and game pieces (optional)
        - puzzles (optional)
    - Primers for each student
    - Graded readers (You will need to decide if you want one for each student or a set number of library copies.)
    - Writing exercise books for each student, with at least 80 pages
    - Post-literacy reading materials
    - The lesson plans
    - Attendance sheets (Checking off attendance provides incentive for them to be there on time. Attendance sheets are used to fill out records.)
    - Certificates of achievement (Although these don't need to be completed until the end of the literacy program, you may wish to investigate what is available.)

Implementing the native literacy program

Be prepared
Have all the materials ready for the entire literacy program before you start teaching pre-literacy. Have plenty of materials prepared for the people to read before you start to teach them to read.

Set a date to begin
Do not set an actual date for the literacy program unless you know that you will be ready to start then. Setting a date prematurely and then having to postpone the program because you are not ready to teach could cause disappointment and disillusionment for people who are excited about learning to read and write. People who have been disillusioned will not easily be excited again. When you set a date to start teaching literacy, to them, you are making a promise. Set that date only when you know that you can keep your promise.

Determine how often the literacy classes will meet and for how long. Consider the following possibilities:

- Meet 5 days a week, for 2 hours per day.

- Meet 4 days a week, for 3 hours per day.

- Meet 3 days a week, for 4 hours per day.

- It is not recommended that you meet less than 3 days per week. When there are several days between classes, the students tend to forget. You need to meet frequently in order to make progress.

How frequently you have classes and for how long depends as much on the students' schedule as it does on yours. What will work best for them? Accommodate their needs. Consult with them about what they think would work for a class schedule.

Determine how long the entire literacy course should take. Many factors are involved in the length of time it takes to teach an entire literacy course. Obviously, how often the literacy class meets is one factor. How many primers you have and how densely they are packed with new material is another. And how quickly the students catch on is yet another. The people's yearly schedule is another major factor.

Because of these factors, it is impossible to give an estimate in this manual that would fit every situation. The following broad estimations may help you to plan, but be aware that it could take less time or more time:

- 3 primers — 3 to 5 months
- 4 primers — 5 to 7 months
- 5 or 6 primers — 6 to 10 months

Your estimate of how long the literacy program will take can be adjusted as the course is taught. As you determine when to begin the literacy class, keep in mind that your personal schedule should not include extended breaks away from the village while you are teaching Primer 1. An unnecessary absence during Primer 1 would indicate to the people that literacy is not important. In addition, the first primer should be taught straight through so that material learned will not be lost during an extended gap between sessions.

Breaks do need to be scheduled at intervals during the literacy program. This is for their sake as much as for yours. At the end of the first primer (between four to eight weeks), you may want to take a week's break. Then take breaks at appropriate places throughout the rest of the program. Try to plan the breaks around their schedule. For example, if they will be harvesting during a specific time, take your break then. This will allow them to do the work they need to do, and give them a rest from studying.

Decide who will be the first students

Your first class should include between six and ten students. This will allow you to give each of the students the time they need for individual help. Having a smaller class gives you more time to listen to each one read.

Take their culture into consideration as you decide who will be in the first literacy class.

- Consider kinship relationships.

- Consider the family group. Ideally, the first students should not all come from just one clan or family. You may also have to work around cliques.

- Consider if men and women in their culture can attend the same class at the same time. In some situations, men and women may need to be taught separately.

- Consider if it would cause problems if a wife were taught before her husband had been taught. Sometimes if a wife knows how to read before her husband does, it creates marriage problems. If women learn to read before men, they may take on a role in the family or in the church that is not acceptable in the culture.

- Consider if women who become literate would be allowed to become teachers of men.

- Consider if it is appropriate to teach adults and children in the same class. Often, it is not culturally acceptable. You should also be aware that children tend to learn faster than adults and thereby can cause adults to become discouraged with their slower progress. It is generally best to choose adults or teen males to be students in the first class.

If possible, some leaders should be in the first literacy class. However, often leaders feel they are too busy to attend classes. Encourage them to come, but you cannot make them attend.

You want a cross-section of ability in the class. Although you can't know at this point who will learn to read, you may have an idea of who in the village is above average and who is slow to learn. For this first literacy class, don't choose just the most intelligent. Try to choose some who will be average learners.

Try to include in your first class those who may be prime candidates to become teachers themselves. For example, you may be aware that a translation helper or a language and culture helper has potential to become a literacy teacher. Include them if possible, but do not tell them what you have in mind. You do not want to promise a person a certain position until you know they are capable, faithful, and have been trained.

Begin the literacy program

Ideally, the team member who developed the pre-reader and the primers should teach the first literacy program. If it is necessary to hand the teaching over to someone else, the one who wrote the literacy materials should be close enough to help as needed.

Remember to follow your daily lesson plans. These lesson plans will keep you on track.

Teach the whole program

Remember that the whole literacy program includes teaching (1) pre-literacy, (2) literacy, and (3) post- literacy.

Teach pre-literacy: Follow your pre-primer lesson plans closely as you teach the foundational reading skills through the pre-primer. You will teach Primer 1 immediately after finishing the pre-literacy program. Therefore, do not start to teach pre-literacy until you have primers ready.

Teach literacy: After you have taught pre-literacy, you will teach the people to read, using the primers and other teaching aids. Specific helps on teaching the people to read can be found in the chapter, "Teaching Procedures."

Teach post-literacy: The post-literacy program begins after the final primer has been finished. If possible, the post-literacy program should be a supervised reading program.

TEACHING LITERACY & GETTING COMMUNITY INVOLVEMENT

Ideally, the students will continue to come to the classroom and practice their reading. At each stage, you should check their reading ability, that is, listen to them read cultural materials, then non-cultural materials, then Scripture-related materials. If they are reading well, they can move on to the next stage. By the end of post-literacy, the new literate should be able to easily read translated Scripture and vernacular Bible lessons. (Please note that some new literates are so eager to read the Word of God for themselves that they begin reading it as soon as they finish the primers, without ever reading other post-literacy material. If they are motivated to read Scripture and it is available to them, do not stop them. However, because it is better for them to gain fluency *before* reading Scripture, be sure to have adequate post-literacy materials written *before* they finish their primers and graded readers.)

Revise as needed

Teaching the first literacy class will reveal mistakes that are certain to be found in the first edition of the literacy materials, especially in the primers. As you teach the first class, make notes about anything that needs to be changed. Use a red pen, so your notes are easily seen when you begin to revise. Be alert for the following:

- Typing errors

- Spelling inconsistencies

- Grammatical errors

- Unnatural language — this will be apparent when they try to read what is written, but add a word which is needed to make the sentence natural, or when they omit a word that is written, because it is not needed.

- Where they consistently have problems

- Whether they can read the story pages by themselves

- Which stories appeal to them

- Whether the day's lesson is too long or too short

Revision does not necessarily mean reprinting. You can do some "patchwork." For example, you can paste a replacement page over a page that has errors. Using white out is another option. Most of the revisions will probably be in Primer 1. You may find that you could have said more. You may find that they did not accept something so you need to take it out. You may find that you need more sight words, or fewer sight words. Hopefully, the revisions will be minimal. The checking process that you used as you wrote the primers should have caught most of the problems before they ever made it into the classroom.

Classroom procedures

Classroom procedure

Take attendance when the class is due to start, whether or not all students have arrived.

> You will need to determine before you start the literacy program how you will handle absentees. Determine how many sessions they can miss and still be a part of the class. Some literacy programs have set up the rule that students can only miss three classes. You will also need to determine how you will teach those who have missed a class. Probably the best thing is to work with them individually, but at the same time, you cannot neglect the rest of the class. If you have teacher helpers, perhaps they could work with the one who was absent.

Focus your teaching toward the average student[1].

> So that faster students do not get bored, give them extra work or use them as student teachers or teacher's helpers. Be sure to supervise and watch them closely as they help others. As you observe, correct on-the-spot anything that they are doing wrong.

> To encourage slower students[2], give them extra help outside of class time. Special tutoring should not be done at the expense of the other students' progress.

> Part way through Primer 1, you can divide the slower students from the faster students.

> If the slower students are holding the rest of the class back from making progress, you will need to put them into their own class.

> If you are an inexperienced teacher, it is not recommended that you try to handle two classes at the same time. An extra teacher or a student helper could work with one of the classes. Or, you may find it necessary to teach two separate classes each day.

> If the class is divided, the slower students should not be allowed to hang around to listen and observe the faster class. That would only confuse them and make learning to read harder.

---

1. To help handle different ability levels, some literacy teachers plan for a variety of activities that the students can do. For example, some students could play games with the syllable cards, or work on their writing, or do a worksheet, while the teacher listens to the individual students read.

2. Some students may never learn to read or write well. This has been true of some older people. Yet some older people have eventually learned to read well enough to read a few Bible verses on their own, and they have found great joy in that. Do not discourage such students from attending the literacy class, but you may want to drop their writing assignment in order to let them focus totally on reading.

Encourage your students to think. Do not allow them to "parrot" after the teacher or other students, except when the teacher feels it is necessary. They need to think and build the words and sentences them- selves. Encourage them to (1) look, (2) think, and (3) try to read it.

Classroom culture

You should do everything possible to fit your school procedures into their culture. However, sometimes instances come up when you need to have a classroom culture which is somewhat different from the broader culture. For example, in their culture, perhaps younger men would never teach older men. But younger men may become your helpers and eventually become the indigenous teachers. So they would be teaching older men in the classroom.

You can explain that, in order to have a good school, it is necessary to have a school culture within their culture.

- First express your appreciation for their culture.

- Then ask them if a school was part of their culture before the missionaries came. Most will recognize that the school was not previously part of their culture.

- Then explain that you will have a schoolroom culture. In other words, you will have a culture in the classroom that will not apply to the rest of their lives.

- On this basis, most groups will accept a separate classroom culture.

Classroom Etiquette

You may need to set down some simple rules for the classroom. You can explain that a school without rules and order will not be a good school.

Respect one another: The students will all have different abilities. Some will learn quickly, while others will take longer to learn. You may need to tell the students that they should not laugh at others when they are struggling and make mistakes. Laughing at a struggling student just makes it more difficult for him or her to try again, and that student could end up being shamed.

Listen to the teacher: You may need to establish a rule that there should be no talking among the students during class time. They need to be listening to the teacher. If there is something they need to know, they should ask the teacher, not one another.

Avoid distracting[3] other students: You should tell the students not to walk around in class or be running in and out. That can distract the other students. Of course, if they have an urgent need to go outside, they should be allowed to do so.

---

3. If you have students who are mothers, they may need to bring their children to class with them. Be aware that the

Record keeping

Keeping records of literacy statistics is very important. These records should be readily available for interested government officials.

Records are especially necessary if you are going to apply for government funding for your literacy school. In some countries, the government will provide funds for the literacy program if 60 percent of the students are women. Be aware, however, that if the government helps fund the literacy program, the government can claim control. Ideally, your literacy school should be connected to the church rather than the government so that the literacy program remains under the authority of church-appointed teachers.

Another reason to keep record of literacy statistics is in case you need to prove the validity of your work among a particular people. Remember that literacy in the vernacular preserves the culture of the people group.

When indigenous teachers are holding a class, each teacher should turn in properly written records with the information for each class. Their records are then added to the cumulative record.

Records can be easily set up on a computer database.

1. Records for each individual class should include the following information:

- The number of students

- The breakdown of male and female students

- The teacher's name

- The village name

- The class's graduation date

- The number of literate people per class. Remember, only the people who can read are literate. Not all of the students who take the course will become readers. When you record the number of literate people for a given class, you are only recording those who can actually read.

- Scores from exams

- The number of male literate people and number of female literate people

---

children can be quite disruptive to a literacy class. The best thing is for another villager, such as a grandmother or sister, to take care of the children outside the classroom. But if they will be inside the classroom, plan some activities to keep them occupied. Have some magazines or puzzles available for them to play with.

TEACHING LITERACY & GETTING COMMUNITY INVOLVEMENT

2. **Cumulative records** should include:

- The total number of literate people to date

- Number of literacy classes that have been conducted

Teaching Procedures

Before the class arrives[4]

- Get out all picture, word, and syllable flashcards that you will need for the day's lesson.

- Get out enough copies of the primer that you will be using for the day's lesson, along with the students' writing books.

- Get out pencils and erasers for the students[5]. Get your chalk and chalkboard eraser ready.

During class time
A. Using key word picture flash cards

- Hold up the picture flash card and point to the picture. Ask them what it is and wait for their answer. Of course, if they don't recognize it right away, you should say what it is. Then point to the word and tell them that it says the same as the picture.

- Use your hand or a blank card to cover up part of the word so that only the syllable being taught shows. For example, if you are teaching the syllable 'ka' from the word 'kame,' you would cover the 'me.' As you show only the syllable being taught, tell them what the syllable says. Use the phrase "This says...," or "This is the part that says...." Choose whichever phrase will be most meaningful to the people you are teaching. So, for the example above, 'kame,' you would cover the 'me' so that only the syllable 'ka' shows. And you would say, "This is the part that says 'ka'." As you continue, you would be able to cover the 'k' so that only the 'a' shows, and say, "This is the part that says 'a'."

- Lead the class through the entire procedure in unison. Then have each one go through the entire procedure individually as you point to the card and as you

---

4. As soon as possible, train the people to handle these jobs.
5. It may be best if the students bring their own pencils and erasers. Help them establish a supply chain that does not involve the missionaries.

divide it. This takes time until they learn how to do it, and then it moves very quickly.

- Make sure all the students are watching as another student is repeating — the students should not stare into space or distract the class.

B. Using syllable flash cards

- As you flip through them, have the entire class or selected students say the lower case and capitalized syllable flash cards for the new key word teaching lesson. Then drill each student until they know the new syllables well.

- As soon as they know the new syllables, mix in syllable cards from previous lessons, and drill each student individually.

- After the first primer is finished, you can cut back on using all the syllable cards from previous lessons. Drill only the ones taught in the more recent lessons. In addition, drill syllable cards which you have taught that look alike, such as ones containing 'u' and 'n,' 'm' and 'w,' 'b' and 'd.'

C. Using built word cards

- Hold up the built word flash card for the reading page you are about to teach. Say the entire word for the students and have them say it too.

- Point to the first syllable in the word and tell them what the syllable says. Use something like, "This part says [say the syllable]." Have the class say the syllable also by asking them, "What does this part say?" while you are pointing to the syllable.

- Continue through the word, syllable by syllable, having the class say each syllable after you have pointed to and said it.

- Then, point to the whole word again and say it at a natural speed. Have the students say it also.

- As an alternative to pointing to each syllable as you break the word down, you may wish to cover the word with a blank card and progressively reveal each syllable in turn.

D. Using blackboard drills

- Write the blackboard syllable charts neatly, lining up all syllables. Line up the syllables so that the letters that are the same in each syllable in the column (usually the vowels) are directly under one another.

TEACHING LITERACY & GETTING COMMUNITY INVOLVEMENT

- You could put the syllable chart on the blackboard prior to class[6] to save time, or you could write it as the class watches. If you do the latter, have the class watch and say the syllable you are writing.

- Drill the chart by having the students say the syllables as you point to each syllable with the pointer. You can have the entire class say it in unison as you point to each syllable, or you could have a sharper student read it for the class. Then you should listen to each student as they read the entire syllable chart.

- Always work left to right and top to bottom.

- When drilling the syllable chart, keep the drill moving. Encourage them to respond quickly as you move the pointer. Do not wait too long on any one syllable. If they don't know it, say it for them, have them repeat it, then move on.

- If a student says a syllable incorrectly, simply say it correctly, have them repeat it, then move on. Never repeat their mistake aloud, or dwell on it. Repeating the mistake would reinforce the wrong answer in the students' minds.

- In the beginning, you should drill all possible syllable formations. As the literacy course progresses, however, you will need to make choices about which syllables to put on the blackboard for drilling. Always drill the newest letter learned. The newest letter learned is usually put in the last row of the syllable chart. If you have letters that look or sound similar, such as "m" and "n," it is helpful to put them close together in the blackboard syllable chart so that the people can see and hear the difference. First, teach well those similar sounding or similar looking symbols in lessons that are not close together. Then, purposely drill them together so that the people understand the difference.

E. Teaching sight words

- A sight word is a word which contains parts that haven't been taught. We use sight words to make a sentence more natural and easier to read.

- Before the students start reading the page on which they will encounter a new sight word, write the sight word on the board. (Your lesson plan should give you a reminder to do this.)

- Never break a sight word down.

- Always teach it as a whole.

---

6. Have the students write blackboard syllable drills on the board before class as a way to start training potential teachers to write evenly and with good spacing.

- Do not use flash cards to teach the sight word.

- Don't use a sight word more often than is necessary, but do use it sufficiently if it is some- thing that needs to be used continually.

- Never let them struggle with a sight word, but tell them what it is as often as necessary until they know it.

- A sight word can be taught as a built word, but only after all its parts have been taught, and only if the students still don't know it.

F. Writing exercises

- Use the blackboard to teach them how to write a new letter or page number.

- For each lesson, the letter to be taught should have been included in your lesson plans. Arrows could be drawn to show how each letter is formed.

- Neatly write the new material on the blackboard by following the directions shown by the arrows in the lesson plans. Do not draw the arrows on the blackboard.

- Always draw the parts of the letter or number in the proper sequence. Draw it several times while the students watch you. (Be sure that you do not have them write a consonant without a vowel. We are teaching them to write syllables, not letters.)

- After they have watched you write it on the blackboard, have them write the same thing in their exercise books. Watch them to be sure they are doing it correctly. Initially, you may have to guide their hands.

G. Dictating exercises

- Learning to write is an essential part in becoming a fluent reader. By writing, the student is gaining sound/symbol recognition. This is why we have the students write dictation. Initially, you would dictate syllables, and then, words. Eventually you would start dictating sentences, and even short stories. What you dictate during any given lesson should be laid out clearly in your lesson plans.

- Dictate the first syllable, word, or sentence to them, as laid out in your lesson plans. Read it clearly. Read it several times.

- Tell them to write this syllable, word, or sentence. Walk around behind them and watch them write. Help them if they need help, but do not write it for them.

- After they have written the word or sentence, dictate the next. Again, speak clearly and read the word or sentence several times. Tell them to write the word or sentence on the next line.

- It may occasionally be necessary to write the word or sentence on the blackboard. This is not the normal process. Writing the dictated word or sentence on the blackboard is used mostly for special tutoring. It should not be used regularly in a classroom setting if you are going to keep the class moving. We do not want them to copy sentences from the blackboard, but to learn to think about the sounds and write them on their own.

- To provide variety in dictation, you may wish to give them a word and have each student make up a sentence of his own, using that word. This would work only after the students knew enough syllables to be able to think of a sentence they could write.

- Continue to watch them work and help them where they need it, but do not do the writing for them.

- When dictation is done, check the students' work, correct their mistakes[7]. Using red or blue pencil, show them the right way to write what was dictated. It is preferable to make corrections immediately so they will learn from their mistakes, but it is not always possible to do it in class. If the corrections cannot be done immediately, the teacher must do them outside of class time and return them to the students the next day. It is important that each student understands what has been corrected and why the correction was made.

- Every day go around the room and have each student read something they have written.

H. Dealing with capitals and punctuation during dictation

- Remind them that some sentences may wrap around, that is, fit on more than one line. Explain that capitals are placed at the beginning of sentences, but not at the beginning of each line.

- Initially, dictate not only the word, but also word breaks, punctuation, and capitalization. There is so much for them to learn at the beginning that you need to tell them when to put a space for a word break, when to use a capital letter, etc. Gradually you can taper off so you are just dictating the sentences.

---

7. Another option is for you as the literacy teacher to write the correct answers on the chalkboard and let them correct each other's writing. Of course, you would wait to start this practice until they have progressed to the point when they are able to make the corrections.

- Be sure they write capitals so the entire letter is sitting on the bottom line and is close to or touching the top line.

- Be sure that the lower case of 'y,' 'j,' 'g,' 'p' have the base of the letter sitting on the line, and the 'tail' below the line. The students will have a strong tendency to write these letters so the 'tails' are above the line.

I. Practice reading

- Encourage each student to become a good reader. A good reader is one who reads smoothly and up to speed. They will become good readers by learning to read words as a whole, without building them. Until they recognize whole words, however, they must build them by sounding out the syllables. Hopefully, as they get further on in the primers, they'll be reading words, and even phrases, at first glance.

- Oral reading helps to promote fluency. From the beginning, you as the teacher can read to them. Later, as they begin to read with speed and comprehension, individual students can read parts of pages while the rest of the students follow along in their primers. It helps for the students to follow along by pointing to what is being read. This helps them keep their place. They can use a clean twig, the eraser side of a pencil, or a toothpick. It is better if they do not use fingers because fingers tend to make the pages dirty or greasy.

- Randomly, call on students to read orally. This forces the class to pay attention and follow along in their books, so they will be at the right place when called upon to read. Caution them that they need to pay attention so they will know where to begin reading when you call on them. Most students want their turn to read aloud and so will learn to pay attention.

- Be aware that if slower readers are reading orally where the whole class can hear, and if they do poorly, they may be shamed. Try to avoid anything that would shame them. You can have them practice an assigned page or pages, but they need to be away from the rest of the class so they do not distract others. When they feel ready, they can read to you, without others listening in. Encourage them to practice reading outside of class time.

- As each primer is finished, it would be ideal for the students to practice reading in the graded reader that follows that primer. After they have practiced the reading book, the teacher should listen to them read it.

- The student should be able to read the final primer well before starting to read any of the post-literacy books.

TEACHING LITERACY & GETTING COMMUNITY INVOLVEMENT

At the end of the class[8]

- Collect all books, pencils, and erasers and stack them neatly.
- Tell the students when to return to practice or when the next class will be.
- Distribute any homework or extra materials which they are to do that day.
- Dismiss the class.
- Return all flash cards to their proper slot in the storage box.
- Erase the blackboard.

Teaching trade language literacy

After learning to read in the vernacular, the people with whom you are working may wish to learn to read in the trade language. They may feel that the trade language is more prestigious. Also, there is plenty of reading material in the trade language, such as newspapers and booklets, whereas there is probably limited reading material in the vernacular.

You can set up a program to teach the trade language to people who are literate in their mother tongue. This program would teach the sounds which occur in the trade language but which do not occur in the vernacular. Any other differences between the two languages would also have to be taught.

How easy or complex the transition will be is dependent on the differences between the vernacular language and the trade language. For more significant differences between the two languages, there will be greater problems and needs. If you are in a more complex situation, you may need to consider using trade language primer materials that are already available in the country, rather than spending your precious time writing a transitional trade language literacy course.

It is critical to keep in mind that the primary goal of the literacy program is to support the vernacular church planting and translation ministry. There may be some situations where it is an important part of those ministries for the believers to be literate in the trade language also, but at least initially, the vernacular literacy program is the priority and the trade language program is an "added extra" for later on.

---

8. Involve the students in these tasks.

8.19 Bible resources for the church

 OBJECTIVES OF THIS TUTORIAL

This tutorial gives an introduction to the area of providing Bible resources for the church. It introduces *Firm Foundations* - a series of foundational Bible teaching materials for both English-speaking settings and cross-cultural church planting and development.

Having access to His Word

We see overwhelming evidence all the way through God's Narrative that He desires people to have full access to His Word, and that because of His grace He takes it on Himself to provide a way for them to have that access. This also intersects with another essential part of God's character; He draws human beings into real partnerships with Himself in His purposes. As well as being the God who communicates, and the God of grace, He is also the God who *equips* and *sends*.

God's commitment to providing access to His revelation means that individuals, churches and communities should have access to the Bible in their language and also be able to read it. Along with a faithful, heart-language translation, the church needs to have access to a body of Bible teaching and study resources that will help them to correctly interpret and apply God's Word within their own cultural context; so they are equipped to encourage, to teach, to correct and to stand against error.

When God's Word is doing what He intends it to do among His people, we can expect to see people who know they are sent... a group who desires to reach out and who knows how to. We should see them sharing God's Word clearly and faithfully so that it is understood; presenting Truth so it engages with people's hearts at a worldview level; teaching so that God's Word is given its proper place and authority and sharing in such a way that people understand God's complete Narrative with Jesus Christ as its center. But in order for them to do that, they need to be equipped with the basic tools - reading and writing skills, a faithful Bible translation, and culturally relevant Bible teaching and study materials in their language.

Having the ability to use His Word

God's Truth - when it is communicated clearly and effectively - first establishes its own authority, then cultivates faith, develops correct understanding, and leads to valid applications. The Word itself equips God's people to engage with Truth and also to use it productively. Having understood it, believed it, submitted to it and begun to relate it more widely to their lives, they begin to learn how to ably *use* it as God's servants.

If they are accessing Truth at a worldview level, if the authority of God's Word has been established in their lives and if they're learning to make sense of each new part in light of the whole, then they are in a position of being able to find nourishment from the Word. They are able to make use of God's Word to feed themselves and to pass Truth on to others.

When Paul, under the Spirit's guidance, was encouraging Timothy in his ministry among the believers in Ephesus, he chose a term, which in modern English is often translated as "useful".

> **2 TIMOTHY 3:16,17 (NLT)** All Scripture is inspired by God and is useful to teach us what is true and to make us realize what is wrong in our lives. It corrects us when we are wrong and teaches us to do what is right.[17] God uses it to prepare and equip his people to do every good work.

He was telling his young friend to view God's Word as something that has very real, practical benefits. It works! It's not just theoretical truth, not just religious dogma, certainly not a set of confining rules. God's Word is a wonderful resource, a functioning toolbox that was available to Timothy and all believers - to parents, disciplers, teachers and church leaders.

A team approach to resource development

Encouraging other believers to be involved in Bible Resource development is often an important foundation for a healthy future leadership team. Other believers who are involved in resource development and are committed to the clear communication of God's Word to His people, will be more likely to feel a responsibility for ensuring that clear teaching continues into the future.

Care should be taken that the church perceives the initial resource development 'team' to be open, and not an exclusive in-group of the better informed. Eventually the idea of engiftment will be described from God's Word and will provide the rationale for a group with authority to lead the church. But for now the basis of engagement in developing Bible teaching and study materials should be a shared burden for ensuring that the things God wants to be communicated are indeed being passed on clearly to his children, and to their particular community as a group. This should be seen as not something borne exclusively by the church planters, but a common burden placed on those with the heart and ability to help and the deep local cultural and linguistic understanding to ensure clear communication.

Cross-cultural workers should make serious commitments to the believers about their intentions to help to equip them to reach out to others. The point cannot be made strongly enough - in word, attitude and action - that church planters truly see their new brothers and sisters in Christ as the co-workers and partners in ministry that they actually are. Providing them with adequate Bible resources and equipping speaks volumes about the fact that the 'team' really does include all those who have heard and accepted the Gospel.

One of the church planting team's goals should be that the church will eventually possess a 'Bible curriculum' that they embrace as their own, consisting of well-developed lesson notes for a systematic foundational teaching program beginning with evangelism, continuing on for the fledgling church and eventually for the mature church. It should also be a goal that the
local Body will include members who have the desire - and growing ability - to further contribute to the development of a Bible teaching and study materials for the church.

Foundational or Narrative Bible Teaching

Any Bible teaching that establishes the authority of the written Word must not only present it as logical, factual and historical but, above all, must portray the centrality of the person of Christ. This is done effectively by presenting a panoramic picture of God acting consistently at different stages of human history, with the purpose of ultimately revealing Himself to man through His incarnate Son.

A Foundational or Narrative approach to teaching the Bible, systematically dismantles a person's existing worldview and cultural assumptions and fills in the gaps of their understanding about who God is, what He has done, and what He is doing today. They will know what the basic message of the Bible is and how it all ties together, and they will understand the character of God from what God says about Himself and how He has related to people through history.

Before people can interpret isolated pieces of Truth and apply them to their lives, they first need to know who God is, how He has worked though history, why He sent His Son to earth, why Jesus had to die, on what basis we live in freedom, who the Church is and what God is doing today. The simple message of the Bible told as He has told it – through the history, events, and thoughts that are recorded in His Word - is the foundation on which a local church can be built, grow and reach out and then be able to confidently build a deeper understanding based on that solid foundation.

If you have engaged with Modules 1, 2 and 3 of the *AccessTruth* curriculum, you will already know that we are committed to Bible teaching that presents the Narrative foundations as a basis for a cohesive view of Biblical Truth.

The material presented in those three Modules is culturally contextualized Narrative Bible teaching. The material was written with the audience's culture, context and preferred methods of communication in mind. Decisions were made to provide access to the material in a variety of formats (digital, video, audio and text) to give people flexibility. The language used, length of the sessions, the questions asked, and the possible ways people would interact with the material (personal study, as group studies, classroom, etc.) were all considered carefully as a part of communication. The goal, as it is in any cultural setting, was to do everything possible when preparing the material and presenting it, so that the Truth has the best possible chance to engage people at a worldview level. In any context in which Bible teaching or church planting is done, the teachers or church planters will need to give serious thought and time into developing a culturally relevant and contextualized message that truly communicates to and engages their listeners.

The *Building on Firm Foundations* series of Bible teaching materials provides a comprehensive resource for teachers or church planters to use to develop a culturally relevant foundational teaching and study series for any cultural setting. It should not be considered as the only Bible resource that the church will ever have in a community, but it is helpful as a resource for church planters to provide a solid initial foundation of Truth for the church to use for outreach and to build on later as they develop resources for themselves.

Introducing the Firm Foundations materials

Foundational, chronological Bible teaching has been used successfully all over the world in many different cultural settings. God, in His Word, has progressively revealed Himself and His plan of redemption within the context of human history. Foundational, chronological Bible teaching follows this same pattern - *Firm Foundations* lessons start "in the beginning" to reveal truth, systematically and panoramically through the Old and New Testaments.

- Key Biblical themes that are crucial to a clear understanding of God's Word are highlighted.

- The Bible is seen as a whole - the panorama of God's working.
- Each lesson builds on the foundational truths laid in previous lessons.

It is a practical and proven approach for:

- Evangelism
- Grounding new believers
- Teaching maturing believers
- Planting churches

Trevor McIlwain developed Chronological Bible Teaching lessons as he worked cross-culturally with a people group in the Philippines. He saw the need to establish proper foundations, and that these foundations be Biblically laid. As he states, "...*the Scriptures were progressively revealed by God within the context and framework of history. Therefore, the best way to teach divine truth in any culture is God's way, within the chronological and historical framework of the Scriptures.*"

Trevor shared the basic outline that he had used with other missionaries who were also teaching cross-culturally. This outline eventually developed into detailed Bible lessons for evangelism and church planting. After effectively teaching the *Firm Foundations* Bible lessons, missionaries returned home with glowing testimonies. So enthusiastic were they about this method of teaching that pastors and other Bible teachers began to adapt the lessons originally written for cross-cultural evangelism and discipleship for use in churches and home Bible studies. Adaptations of the *Firm Foundations* materials have since been developed for many specific languages, cultural contexts, and age groups.

The original materials - called *Building on Firm Foundations* - have been used in many church and church planting contexts around the world, beginning in tribal church planting contexts. *Building on Firm Foundations* is the best version to use for developing materials for cross-cultural, church planting situations. The *Firm Foundations* material is a revision that has been designed for a modern, English-speaking context.

Building on Firm Foundations

These are the materials used by cross-cultural church planters as their guide for developing Bible lesson curriculums in local languages, and for equipping local Bible teachers.

This latest revised edition has been updated based on the lessons learned by using the original material in more than 200 different people groups. The following outlines the contents of the nine volumes of materials.

Building on Firm Foundations Vol. 1 - Guidelines for Evangelism and Teaching Believers

- Biblical and practical reasons for laying scriptural foundations for evangelism and church planting.
- Pre-Evangelism.
- Guidelines for Evangelism.
- Developing Lessons and Teaching.

Building on Firm Foundations Vol. 2 - Evangelism: Genesis to the Ascension

- The chronological Bible lessons for evangelism.

Building on Firm Foundations Vol. 3 - Teaching New Believers: Genesis to the Ascension

- The chronological Bible lessons for new believers in Christ.

Building on Firm Foundations Vol. 4 - Teaching New Believers: Acts

- The chronological Bible lessons for teaching new believers about the pattern and development of the church in Acts.

Building on Firm Foundations Vol. 5 - Teaching New Believers: Romans and Ephesians

- The chronological Bible lessons for new believers in Christ, exploring the books of Romans and Ephesians.

Building on Firm Foundations Vols. 6 - 9

- These volumes contain further chronological Bible lessons following on from Volume 5 and covering teaching for New Believers through to Revelation.
- They also contain teaching for Maturing Believers through Genesis to the Ascension, Acts and Romans to Revelation.

Firm Foundations materials

Firm Foundations: Creation to Christ
- Purpose: Evangelism - bringing people to repentance before God and faith in the Lord Jesus as their Saviour.
- Lessons cover: Genesis to the Ascension

Firm Foundations: Secure in Christ
- Purpose: Teaching new believers. Emphasising the new believer's position of security in Christ and laying foundations for teaching.
- Lessons cover: Genesis to the Ascension

Firm Foundations: Growing in Christ, Acts
- Purpose: Teaching new believers. Focus is the pattern and development of the church in Acts.
- Lessons cover: Acts

Firm Foundations: Growing in Christ, Romans
- Purpose: Teaching new believers. This course is an overview of the book of Romans - the basic body of theology that the Apostle Paul taught.
- Lessons cover: Romans

Firm Foundations: Growing in Christ, Ephesians
- Purpose: Teaching new believers. This course is an overview of the book of Ephesians.
- Lessons cover: Ephesians

Building on Firm Foundations and *Firm Foundations* materials can be purchased online in digital or print versions with supplementary materials at ntmbookstore.com

❓ DISCUSSION POINTS

1. Imagine that suddenly you have no translation of God's Word in your heart language and that you only have access to 25 short audio recordings of major Bible stories. In what specific ways do you think your spiritual life, activities, and thought life would be affected?

2. Think about the typical experience for a new believer in your cultural context:

- Would most new believers understand clearly how the Old Testament relates to the New, and how key Biblical themes are established there? (E.g., would they understand that God's character has not changed?)
- By what process would they eventually come to understand the 'big picture' themes of the Bible and see it as one integrated message with Christ at its center? (E.g., through personal study or reading, piecing together truth from messages they have heard, strategic teaching for new believers?)

➡ ACTIVITIES

1. Read *Firm Foundations Creation to Christ, Volume 1 - Part 1: Why the Bible Should Be Taught Chronologically - Chapters 1 - 2*. This reading activity has been included on the following pages.

(*Building on Firm Foundations Volume 1* is available for download at accesstruth.com. We recommend you take time to read this whole volume as it has helpful advice and foundational principles for anyone considering teaching God's Word.)

Tutorial 8.19 Reading Activity

This reading activity is from *Firm Foundations Creation to Christ, Volume 1 - Part 1: Why the Bible Should Be Taught Chronologically - Chapters 1 - 2*[1].

Chapter 1. The Master Builder's Plan

With a thunderous sound, the walls cracked and crumbled. Timbers splintered. The roof buckled, falling into pieces. Floor after floor crashed one upon another, crushing, trapping, killing the tenants. In a few moments, the high-rise apartments were reduced to rubble.

Investigation began to determine the cause of the disaster. Proof emerged, revealing that the builder had not followed proper specifications. Willing to gamble with the lives and the safety of human beings for the sake of money, he cut corners and economized.

The builder had disregarded the design specifications that the architect and engineers provided. He had followed his own way because it was easier and quicker and brought him greater profit.

The results? Sorrow! Destruction! Death!

It's just an example, but it speaks of what is happening all over the world when it comes to building the Church. Whether in evangelism or preaching and teaching of the Word of God, we often carelessly disregard our Master Builder's plans for building His Church. We are so engrossed in our own ideas, schemes and passions that we don't stop to consider if we are working according to God's divine directions or whether our work will pass His final scrutiny.

God's work of building His Church

God is the builder of His Church (Matthew 16:18). But He has chosen His earthly children to be partners together with Him (1 Corinthians 3:9).

The Christian's work in building the Church is similar to that of a building contractor. Just as a contractor is responsible to follow exactly the plans given to him by the architect, so we are responsible to follow God's plans for building His Church.

---

1. Used by permission from Trevor McIlwain.

God is the true builder of all things. "For every house is built by someone, but He who built all things is God"(Hebrews 3:4).

God builds everything according to His eternal plans. He will not change. He will never accommodate man's ideas or modify His plans to go along with current trends. He will never permit any change in the specifications which He has laid down for all He has planned to do in what we call time. His work always has adequate foundations; He builds carefully, patiently and precisely. He refuses to take shortcuts in anything He does, and He never uses inferior materials or methods which are contrary to His holy and perfect nature.

The first account in Scripture of God's building work is when He created the heavens and the earth. "By the word of the LORD the heavens were made, And all the host of them by the breath of His mouth ... For He spoke, and it was done; He commanded, and it stood fast" (Psalm 33:6, 9). God was the Creator – builder of all things, seen and unseen. He created everything according to His perfect plan, and He declared that it was all good (Genesis 1:31).

Later in the Scriptures we have the account of God's command to Noah to build an ark. After commanding him to build the ark, God did not leave Noah to formulate his own plans. God told Noah exactly what must be done. Noah, God's faithful workman, did everything just as the Lord commanded him (Genesis 6:22).

When God chose to dwell with Israel, He commanded Moses to build the tabernacle. And how was Moses to build it? "For He said, 'See that you make all things according to the pattern shown you on the mountain'" (Hebrews 8:5). Every detail, from the silver sockets which were the foundations for the boards of the tabernacle to the outer coverings of badger skins, was to be made exactly according to the divine pattern shown to Moses on Mount Sinai. Moses faithfully followed these instructions. (Hebrews 3:2).

God's work of building the heavens and the earth was done by the power of His Word. Noah and Moses followed the words of God in all that they built. Likewise, God's present work of building His Church is also being accomplished through His mighty Word. "For it is the God who commanded light to shine out of darkness, who has shone in our hearts to give the light of the knowledge of the glory of God in the face of Jesus Christ" (2 Corinthians 4:6).

The building of the universe was the work of God alone. He did not use any angelic or human agent. But the great work of building the Church, like the work of building the ark and the tabernacle, has been committed to His children. "We have this treasure in earthen vessels" (2 Corinthians 4:7). "We are ambassadors for Christ" (2 Corinthians 5:20). "You shall be witnesses to Me … to the end of the earth" (Acts 1:8). God has chosen to bring His Church to completion through the teaching of His Word by the members of the Church.

If the ark and the tabernacle had to be built exactly according to God's plan, should not the Church also be built according to His plan? Surely the Bride of Christ is of even greater importance than the ark or the tabernacle. The use for the ark came to an end, and the tabernacle was superseded by the temple, but the Church is to last for eternity. Therefore, "If anyone defiles the temple of God, God will destroy him. For the temple of God is holy, which temple you are" (1 Corinthians 3:17). Every man's work, in relationship to the building of the Church, is going to be tried by fire. It will all come under the scrutinizing gaze of the great Master Builder whose servants and co-laborers we are.

Whether we are seminary professors, pastors, missionaries, Bible class leaders, Sunday school teachers, youth workers, or concerned parents wishing to see our children taught the Word of God, "We are God's fellow workers." We must therefore be wise, taking careful note to make sure we are doing our work in the way He commanded (1 Corinthians 3:9-23).

Building as a wise master builder

Paul refers to himself as a wise master builder (1 Corinthians 3:10). He laid the foundations of the Gospel on which the Corinthians' faith and hope were built, and he warned the Bible teachers in Corinth to be careful how they built on those biblical foundations which he had laid (1 Corinthians 15:1-4).

When I began my ministry on the mission field, I realized that I had a similar responsibility to that which Paul had. I was responsible to lay the foundations of the Gospel and then build up the individual members of the Body of Christ in a remote island of the Philippines. I desired to be a wise master builder like Paul, but I wasn't sure how to be wise and careful as I built. I prayed for answers as the following questions gripped my mind and guided my search:

By what standard did Paul judge his building methods and work and thus conclude that he was a wise master builder?

- How can all subsequent builders be sure that they are proceeding in the correct way and that their work will meet with divine approval?

- Has God only told us what to teach in His Word, or has He also shown us how to teach?

- Which is the clearest, most simple, and yet most comprehensive method of teaching the Word of God to prepare people for the Gospel, and to teach them God's way of salvation?

- How can we be sure that the foundations we lay, on which others are to rest their faith, will see them safely into Heaven and stand firm in the great day of testing?

- How should we teach in order to build up God's children and lead them into the knowledge of the whole counsel of God?

- What checklist should we use to determine if we are making headway, and whether the building is being brought to completion in accordance with the divine plan?

Years passed before I understood the answers to these questions. Why did it take so long? Because traditional Bible teaching methods influenced my thinking. I found the answers I needed when I finally looked to God's Word alone

The effectiveness of Biblical principles

After the Lord had shown me the biblical teaching principles that I present later in this book, He then opened opportunities for me to share these principles with others who were also searching. In 1980, I taught a seminar for missionaries in the Philippines. These biblical teaching principles excited and gripped the hearts of my co-workers who were struggling with problems identical to those I had faced in evangelism and in planting and guiding the development of churches to spiritual maturity. These missionaries returned to their work with fresh enthusiasm, for they now had clearer guidelines and precise goals for their teaching ministry.

Seminars were also held in Bolivia, Indonesia, Papua New Guinea, Senegal, Thailand and the USA. These initial seminars provided biblical guidelines for evangelism. The missionaries went back to their ministries and laid down firm foundations for saving faith in Christ by teaching a chronological overview of the Bible story, beginning in Genesis and concluding with the ascension of Christ.

The results were immediate and lasting. Many people from various tribal groups have come to a clear understanding of God's nature and character, their own sinfulness, helplessness and hopelessness, and Christ's all-sufficient saving work through His death, burial and resurrection. Their understanding of God's plan of salvation and the certainty of their faith far surpassed that of many others who had professed conversion previously. Furthermore, through chronological teaching, many of those sincere tribal people came to realize that they had misunderstood the missionaries' message when they were first taught. They are now trusting in a message which they clearly understand.

One of the first reports of great blessing came from Bob Kennell and George Walker. They had followed these scriptural methods when teaching the story of the Bible to the primitive, and previously unevangelized, Bisorio tribe in the Sepik region of Papua New Guinea. The Bisorio people responded to a message which they clearly understood from the Scriptures. Theirs is no blind faith, based merely on what the foreigner said. Instead, it is based on a clear understanding of the God of the Bible and the history of redemption.

Confusion about laying foundations

Christ and His Gospel are the only foundations which God has ordained as a basis for the faith of guilty sinners (1 Corinthians 3:11; 15:1-2). Nevertheless, there is great confusion, even among Christians, regarding these foundations and the correct way to establish them through preaching God's Word.

In the construction of any building, the foundations are the first part of the structure to be prepared. The majority of Gospel preaching, however, is usually done with very little foundational preparation. This lack has contributed to a multitude of false professions and the uncertainty of many new Christians about the foundations of their faith.

Another mistake Bible teachers tend to make is failing to teach the Bible consistently as one book, just as God has prepared it for us through progressive revelation. Teachers of the Word carefully devise and prepare outlines, but few stop to consider that the Bible has an inbuilt teaching outline, which, if followed, will give a clear, uncomplicated, comprehensive coverage of the entire Word of God.

Many teachers approach the Bible as if it were a treasure chest full of beautiful, precious gems. We assume that these jewels have not been given a definite pattern or design. We think that the responsibility is ours to arrange the jewels in some order which will enhance their beauty and cause them to be better appreciated. While recognizing the value of the Scriptures, many Bible teachers fail to see that there is a definite, divinely-given teaching outline which runs through the entire Word of God. We therefore proceed to arrange the Scriptures into what we consider to be comprehensive and lucid outlines. This is a basic mistake. Admittedly, good Bible teaching outlines are helpful; but too much time is spent developing methods and theories for Bible teaching, and insufficient time is given to simply teaching the Scriptures as they have been written.

The majority of Christian teaching emphasizes individual doctrines of the Bible rather than presenting the Bible as one complete, interdependent revelation of God. Heresies, misinterpretation, overemphasis of certain Scriptures, and denominationalism can, in most cases, be traced to this lack of chronological and panoramic Bible teaching.

After many years of listening to nonsequential, topical, doctrinal sermons, most of which are based on isolated texts, many church members still do not know the Bible as one book. Often-repeated verses and some doctrines may be known; but the Scriptures, according to their divinely given historical structure, are seldom understood.

This is equally true in Sunday school programs. Children are usually taught stories from the Bible out of chronological order, and large portions of God's Word are never taught to them at all. Even a faithful Sunday school pupil is unlikely to graduate with an overall knowledge of the Bible.

The approach when teaching the Scriptures in other lands to people without previous Bible knowledge has been similar. Few changes are made to the methods used in the homeland. Insufficient time is generally given to teach the Old Testament background and foundations for the Gospel. Syncretism of heathen and Christian beliefs is often the sad result. Many in foreign lands who have professed Christianity do not understand the Gospel, nor do they understand the Scriptures as one book.

Many missionaries are so eager to preach the Gospel that they feel it is an unnecessary waste of time to teach people too much of the historical portions of the Old Testament Scriptures. Nevertheless, these Old Testament historical sections form the basis for a clear understanding of the coming of Christ and the necessity of His death, burial and resurrection. The Old Testament Scriptures, correctly taught, will prepare the heart of the believing sinner to receive the Gospel in true repentance and faith.

Objective and overview

The following chapters record my frustrations, my search, and also my joy at discovering divine teaching principles and guidelines in the Word of God. Additional volumes of Firm Foundations: Creation to Christ contain clear, simple, yet comprehensive lessons for the unsaved and the children of God which follow the flow of biblical history.

Through my own experiences, but more importantly, on the basis of the truth of God's Word, I will endeavor to show that the Scriptures were progressively revealed by God within the context and framework of history. Therefore, the best way to teach divine truth in any culture is God's way, within the chronological and historical framework of the Scriptures.

Chapter 2. Check the Foundations

The Palawano tribe, living on the island of Palawan in the southwestern region of the Philippines, was downtrodden for centuries.

The proud, fierce Moros who lived on the smaller islands lying off the coast of Palawan oppressed these timid, fearful jungle people for many years. Numerous stories, now part of Palawano folklore, tell of the massacres and molestations of the Palawano tribal people by these marauding Muslim sea warriors.

Yet another oppression for the Palawanos came from Filipino settlers who migrated from other islands of the Philippines. They came seeking land for rice fields and coconut plantations, and for timber from the virgin forests for export. Many of these settlers took advantage of the native people of Palawan. They easily intimidated these unassuming, uneducated jungle people. Through fear of these aggressive settlers, many Palawanos left their ancestral lands and coconut plantations close to the sea for the less hospitable foothills and mountains of the island's interior.

Then came a time of even greater sadness and tragedy. Their island home was invaded by the Japanese. This was a fearful era in the Palawanos' history. Women were molested, and children were brutally murdered. Livestock was stolen and killed. Rice, their basic food, was often deliberately and maliciously scattered by the invaders as they knocked down the Palawanos' granaries. The suffering of these years surpassed all other segments of their inglorious history.

Then came an unexpected reprieve from their fear and degradation. The US liberation forces landed in Palawan. In all my years with the Palawano people, I heard only praise and admiration for these soldiers, never one word of reproach. While I was visiting in the homes of the tribal people, many of the older Palawano men asked me if I knew some particular officer by whom they had been befriended. They spoke of them with great affection. They obviously enjoyed remembering incidents when the "Amirikans" had warned the national Filipinos not to ill-treat the Americans' little Palawano brothers. The Palawanos saw it as a sad day when the US forces withdrew from Palawan, and their future became uncertain once again.

Years passed, and then, quite unexpectedly for the Palawanos, another American came to their part of the island. He was even more generous than all the other Americans they had known. Meanness and anger are frowned on in Palawano society. This missionary displayed love and kindness. Through his ministry and that of the missionaries who followed him, several thousand Palawanos professed conversion to Christianity, but not understanding what it meant. They were baptized, and organized into indigenous churches.

When we arrived years later, we questioned the Palawanos as to why they had so readily submitted to baptism. One man answered, "We would have done anything for that first missionary. If he had asked us to cut our fingers off, we would have gladly done it for him."

The danger always exists that previously rejected and exploited people will respond to the Christian missionary's message, not because they see their real need as sinners and understand the Gospel, but because of genuine appreciation for the missionary and a longstanding desire to escape their difficult and degraded sociological conditions. This was the major reason for the people movement to Christianity, which took place almost immediately when the first New Tribes missionary preached to the Palawanos.

Confusion regarding the Gospel

Following this, more missionaries arrived to assist in the work. They faithfully taught the duties of believers to those who had professed conversion. Unknown to the missionaries, the majority of the Palawano church members interpreted the responsibilities of believers in the only way that they could as unsaved people. They thought the duties of the believer were the things they must do so they could continue to be "in God."

"In God" was the term the Palawanos usually used to describe their conversion to Christianity. They had come into God by their acceptance of Christ through faith, baptism, church attendance, singing, prayer, not stealing, and not committing adultery. The truly dedicated also thought that abstinence from alcohol, betel nut, and tobacco were necessary to guarantee their continued position "in God."

During their church meetings, they sometimes spoke of Christ and His death. More frequently, however, they testified of their faithfulness to the Lord by abstaining from sinful works and by church attendance. Obviously missing was praise to God for their salvation by Christ through His unmerited favor alone. Even though salvation by faith through grace alone had been taught, the majority had not clearly understood. They were trusting in a mixture of grace and works.

In spite of the emphasis on Christian living, many failed to live according to biblical standards. Divorce, remarriage and drunkenness were normal in the Palawanos' old way of life, and they continued to be major problems in all of the churches. The missionaries and the church elders were very concerned. They constantly exhorted the people to lay aside these old ways and follow the new way in Christ. The wayward church members would repent and function outwardly as Christians for a while; but often, they would fall back into their old ways until they were once again challenged and revived, starting the cycle all over again.

There were faithful individuals who were true believers among the Palawano people. However, the Palawano church as a whole was like a building that lacked the correct foundations. Large cracks appeared continually in the upper walls. The missionaries and church leaders spent their time running from church to church, trying to patch up the gaping holes. The problem was the people's basic foundational understanding of the Gospel.

Because most had turned to Christ for deliverance from their difficult lives and had never seen their own personal sinfulness and inability to please God, they had not realized that their only hope was to trust in God's provision for all sinners through the death, burial and resurrection of Christ. If they had trusted only in Him for God's acceptance, then their faith would have produced godliness and obedience to the commands of Scripture, not in order to obtain salvation, but as the fruit of true saving faith.

In 1965, my wife and I, along with our two children, began our work as missionaries with New Tribes Mission in the Philippines. We worked with the Palawano tribe over a period of 10 years. My responsibility was to see the elders and the churches brought to maturity through further instruction from the Scriptures.

Extensive hiking over the trails with the more zealous church elders was the only way I could reach and teach the more than 40 small churches scattered among the mountains and jungle. Through these visits to the Palawano churches, it soon became evident that the majority of the professing believers were confused and uncertain about the basic foundations of the Christian faith. They agreed with the necessity of Christ's death for man's salvation. However, most thought that Christ's death only secured a part of their salvation and that they were responsible to obtain the remainder of their salvation by obeying God.

The true spiritual condition of the people became apparent as I began to question them concerning their basis for salvation. I usually began by asking, "What must a person do to be saved?"

They were often reluctant to answer, but after some encouragement and direct questioning of individuals, they would begin to respond. Some answered, "Trust in God," and some said, "Believe on Christ."

To these answers, I replied, "What if a person truly believes and puts his faith in Christ as his Savior, but he does not attend church? Could he truly be saved?" Many answered emphatically, "No!"

Others said, "Yes, if a person truly believes, he is saved, even if he does not attend church."

"But," I added, "what if that person is not baptized?"

Only a few thought that a person could be saved without baptism.

I then added what seemed, to many, to be the deciding point, "But what if that person who truly trusts in Christ were to get drunk or commit adultery? Could he really be saved?" Only a few in each congregation believed that such a person could be saved, and even they had grave doubts.

In addition to questioning, I found another method to be effective in determining what the Palawano church elders and Bible teachers believed. I would first teach them the truth and then contradict the truth by teaching error. In the Palawano culture, it is improper to contradict a teacher, because this could cause the teacher to lose face and become embarrassed. This, in turn, would cause the person who had contradicted the teacher to also be embarrassed. Even so, these church leaders needed to be taught to stand for God's Word, regardless of the cultural discomposure caused by confronting a teacher with the truth. False cults were increasing on the island, and these Palawano church leaders were faced with the endeavors of these false teachers to lead them and their congregations into error. I needed to be sure that these Bible teachers really understood the Gospel, that they were personally trusting only in Christ, and that they would be able to stand firm against false teachers. Of course, I only used this method after months of teaching these men. This method would not have been effective if used in the beginning of my association with the Palawano leadership. They would have verbally agreed with me in spite of what they actually believed in their hearts.

On one occasion, approximately one hundred Palawano elders and teachers had gathered for our monthly conference. I had taught for many hours from the Scriptures on salvation by grace through faith alone. Then, without warning or explanation, I began to teach faith plus works as the way of salvation. Then I paused abruptly and pointed to one of the men and asked him, "Is what I have just said correct? Is it true that sinners are saved, not only by faith, but by their good works?"

The tribal teacher hesitated and then finally answered, "No, it is wrong. We are saved by faith alone."

Feigning surprise, I continued to question him, "Do you mean to say you are telling me, the missionary, that I am wrong?"

Hesitatingly, he said, "Yes, you are wrong."

Still not giving them any clue to my real thoughts, I turned to another man and said, "He says that what I said was wrong. Do you agree or disagree?"

He answered, "What you said was wrong."

I then asked him, "How long have you been a Christian?" His answer indicated he was a much younger Christian than I.

"Oh!" I said, "I have been a Christian for many years. I have also been to Bible college. Do you still think I could be wrong?"

Again, he answered that I was wrong.

Even then, I did not show agreement or disagreement but turned to a third man and asked him what he thought. Much to my surprise, he said, "You are right!"

Thinking he had misunderstood, I repeated what I had said previously, stating that we are saved not only by faith but also by our good works.

Again, he said that my statements were correct.

I then asked him, according to my usual procedure, to give scriptural proof for his statement. To my even greater surprise, he turned to Ephesians 2:8-9. Hoping he would understand his mistake once he read these verses, I asked him to read them to all present. He did so and concluded by saying, "There it is. We are saved, not only by faith, but by our good works also."

Many of the men listening were now smiling, but I was looking to the Lord for wisdom in what to say to avoid embarrassing him.

I asked Perfecto, for that was his name, to read Ephesians 2:8-9 once again. He did but still maintained that these verses were teaching salvation through faith plus good works. I knew to simply tell him he was wrong would not establish the truth in his mind. It was important that he see for himself what these verses actually teach.

I said to Perfecto, "Those verses do not seem to be saying what you claim they do. Read them once again very slowly to yourself so you will understand what they really mean."

While we waited, Perfecto read the verses through slowly. Finally, he looked up at me with a look of great surprise and said, "No, I am wrong! We are not saved by faith and works, but by faith alone through God's grace."

The Palawano situation which I have described is not an isolated one. Multitudes throughout the world are members of evangelical churches but have no firm biblical foundations on which they build their hope for eternal life. Illustrations could be given from many areas of the world, including our own home churches, where confusion and syncretism have occurred through the sincere but unwise or careless ministry of Christian workers.

From South America, Dave Brown wrote in 1988 about the Guajibo churches in Colombia:

> "The Guajibos have a long history of missionary activity. As early as 1650, the Jesuits made missionary trips into this territory which covers almost the entire eastern plains of Colombia. They were particularly interested in the Guajibo tribe, as it was the largest in this area (today numbering about 15,000). When the Jesuits entered the area, the Guajibos were still nomadic; but with the progress of time, they have now settled in small permanent villages. About 1958, news of a new religion called the 'Evangelical Way' began to trickle into this area. It immediately

attracted widespread attention; and before long, with the arrival of more information, many began to accept this new way of life. Today, almost 30 years later, this new influence from the outside world has made its mark on the Guajibo tribe. Many native-style, thatched-roof churches can be found throughout the region with religious meetings being held regularly.

"In each locality, a semi-annual evangelical conference is held. The first one I visited was attended by 700 Indians, some having traveled as far as a three days' walk. We were the first white missionaries to visit the area; and yet, here were 700 people gathered together to sing and preach to each other. Was there really any need for us as missionaries? Was this not a New Testament church in action? It was only the assurance that God had led us here that kept us.

"With the passing of time, serious problems have come to the surface in the Guajibo church. We are finding that they never really understood the message in the first place. Even those who seem keenest have hangups in the fundamentals of salvation. They quote catechismal answers to questions but do not understand the substitutionary work of Christ. 'Having a form of godliness, but denying the power thereof ...' (2 Timothy 3:5). And so, we have been forced to look back at the mistakes and failures of the past to try to determine where we are now, and to look to God for divine direction for the future."

How is it possible that people who attend church and have been taught the Gospel still do not understand that salvation is by the grace of God alone? Are we missing something in our preaching?

Shepherds should know their flock

While it is true that the Gospel can be understood and refused, there are other reasons why people can be part of evangelical churches but not be truly saved. One is because many pastors, youth leaders, missionaries, and Christian workers do not check the spiritual foundations of those whom they are teaching. Even when Christian workers do make the effort to find out what people are really understanding and trusting in for their salvation, few are willing to confront people with their true condition before God.

It was only through persistent questioning that I found out that some of the Palawano church elders and many members were ignorant of basic biblical truths and had misunderstood the way of salvation. The majority of the people had been trusting in a false message for more than 10 years, but the missionaries who had taught them were unaware of the misunderstanding in the people's minds. Certainly, we must be wise in questioning people; but many Christian teachers are so cautious not to offend that they rarely, if ever, find out the truth about their congregations.

Some Christian teachers think that knowing a person's spiritual condition is not their responsibility. They believe it is something which should be totally between a person and the Lord alone. But the Lord has given His people not only the responsibility to preach the Gospel to the unsaved but also the responsibility to be shepherds of the flock of God. How can we protect, strengthen, and feed them if we do not even know who are the sheep and who are the goats?

I freely admit, as one who is a Bible teacher and has served as a missionary and a pastor, that it is much more comfortable to teach from the pulpit than to face people on an individual basis in order to meet their real needs. Nevertheless, if we are to have an effective ministry and follow in the steps of the Chief Shepherd, we must have one-to-one contact with the flock.

The Gospels contain many accounts of our Lord Jesus' personal contacts and ministry with individuals. Three well-known encounters are Nicodemus (John 3:1-12), the Samaritan woman (John 4:1-26), and the rich young ruler (Matthew 19:16-22). In each of these encounters, Jesus made clear their true spiritual condition, and then He applied the correct spiritual remedy from the Word of God. The Apostle Paul's ministry also involved personal contact and exhortation (Acts 20:20, 31; Colossians 1:28).

Throughout the mission fields which I have visited, I have found a great reluctance on the part of many missionaries to seriously undertake this important task of knowing the true spiritual condition of each person under their care. Yet, it is unwise to instruct people in Christian living, merely hoping they have been born again. If we allow mere professors to act like God's children, even though they have no genuine faith in Christ, the result will be their everlasting damnation. This was the case in the Palawano churches. The great majority of professing Palawanos did not understand the Gospel. They had been instructed to live like Christians, but many were not children of God. Had they not been alerted to their grave danger, they would have gone on in this condition to an eternity without Christ.

One Sunday morning, after I had been teaching the Word of God in an evangelical church in Sydney, Australia, an elderly man said to me, "I am in deep trouble. I need to speak with you." Not knowing him personally, I did not understand what type of trouble he was referring to. The next day, I visited him in his home. As I sat talking with him, he said, "Your preaching has disturbed me. I have been a member of the church for 40 years, but I do not know the Savior." Later, I learned that, even though some fellow church members had wondered if he was saved, they had never questioned him. Most presumed he was a child of God. How sad if he had not finally faced up to his true condition before God!

An elderly Palawano man who had attended meetings for months came down to visit us from his little hut on the side of the hill. As we sat talking, I asked him, "Grandfather, what are you trusting in for your acceptance by God? What is your hope?"

He replied, "Grandchild, haven't I been coming to the meetings? When you pray, I close my eyes. I try to pray. I can't read, but I try to sing." And truly he did. He used to sit right at my feet and stare up into my face as I taught God's Word. He tried to do everything as I did it. But this old man had not understood the Gospel. He thought the things done in the meeting were a ceremony or ritual to please God in order to be accepted by Him.

I said to him, "Grandfather, if that is your hope, if you are trusting in what you are doing, then God will not accept you. When you die, you will go to Hell. God will not receive you because of these things." We continued to talk for some time about these matters before he returned home. Later, some of the people came and told me that Grandfather was angry and he was not going to come to any more meetings.

I thought, "That's good. That's a beginning. At least he now knows that attending meetings will not save him."

I began visiting Grandfather in order to teach the foundational truths of the Gospel to him personally. He listened attentively, and he did eventually begin once more to attend the meetings. But even when my wife and I moved from that area to live and teach in another place without any Gospel witness, he still had not made a clear profession of faith in Christ.

Sometime later, we returned to visit the church in the area where this old man lived. Stepping out of the Mission plane, I asked the tribal people who had run down to the airstrip to welcome us, "Is Grandfather still living?"

They said, "Yes, he is. But he is blind and crippled."

Immediately, I made my way up the hill to his little old, rickety hut and sat down with him. He was pleased that I'd come. After visiting with him for a while, I said to him, "Grandfather, you are going to leave this world very soon. What is your hope? In what are you trusting for your acceptance by God?"

He answered, "Grandchild, it is like this. When I stand before God, I am not going to say to Him that I am not a sinner. God knows that I am."

I thought, "Well, praise the Lord! He has been taught that much of God."

He continued, "I am going to say this to God, 'God, You see Your Son there at Your right hand? He died for me!'" And then turning to me, he said, "Grandchild, won't God accept me because of Him?"

I answered, "Grandfather, He certainly will!"

Cultures and people differ. Not all cultures respond to questioning, regardless of our persistence. Nevertheless, it is important to find out what they understand and believe. If there is a more appropriate and cultural way to get this information than by questioning, it should be followed. But, regardless of our methods, we must ascertain the true spiritual condition of the people, for only then will we know the correct spiritual medicine they need from the Word of God.

What is the Gospel?

Another reason why some people in evangelical churches remain unsaved is the way in which the Gospel is presented. Many dedicated Christians present the Gospel in such a way that unsaved, unprepared people do not understand that they deserve only God's judgment, that salvation is completely God's work, and that sinners are unable to contribute anything towards their own salvation.

Romans 1:3 tells us that the Gospel is God's good news "concerning His Son Jesus Christ our Lord." It is God's assurance "that Christ died for our sins according to the Scriptures, and that He was buried, and that He rose again the third day according to the Scriptures" (1 Corinthians 15:3-4).

The Gospel is first and foremost about Christ. It is the message of the finished, historical work of God in Christ. The Gospel is a work of the Godhead alone. Christ was "smitten by God" (Isaiah 53:4). "It pleased the LORD to bruise Him; He has put Him to grief." The Lord made "His soul an offering for sin" (Isaiah 53:10).

Many confuse the Gospel, God's work FOR us in Christ, with God's work IN us by the Holy Spirit. The Gospel is entirely objective. The Gospel is completely outside of ourselves. The Gospel is not about the change which needs to be made in us, and it does not take place within us. It was completed in Christ, quite apart from us, almost two thousand years ago. The Gospel is not dependent on man in any way. It is distorted when we turn people's eyes to what is to be accomplished in them. We were not and cannot be involved in any part of Christ's historical, finished, redemptive work. The sinner must be taught to look completely away from himself and trust only in Christ and His work of salvation.

The following is a portion of an article written by missionaries who are truly saved and very sincere, but the way they presented the Gospel is incorrect. In this article, they are giving an account of a conversation which they had with a tribal lady. They wrote, "Every Wednesday night, we visit Biaz' parents. We read a portion from Genesis and talk about it and ask questions. One night, Biaz said, 'I am so scared because the bad is in me, and I don't want God to throw me into the fire.' "

It is clear from this quote that Biaz was a soul prepared for the Gospel. There was an acknowledgement of personal sin and a fear of God's judgment.

But what was the answer of the missionaries? They told Biaz, "If you ask Jesus to throw the bad out of your liver and give you His Spirit, then you belong to Him and you don't need to be frightened anymore, and you will go to Him." Instead of the missionaries telling Biaz the historical, objective message of the Gospel as God's complete provision for her sin and God's coming judgment, they turned Biaz' attention to what needed to be accomplished within. What they taught Biaz was not the Gospel.

Unscriptural terminology

We distort and confuse the Gospel in people's understanding when we try to present the Gospel using terminology which turns people's attention to what they must DO rather than outward to what God has DONE on their behalf in Christ. We should use terminology which directs repentant sinners to trust in what has been done FOR them through Christ, rather than directing their attention to what must be done IN them.

Some common terminology is, "Accept Jesus into your heart." "Give your heart to Jesus." "Give your life to Jesus." "Open the door of your heart to the Lord." "Ask Jesus to wash away your sins." "Make your decision for Christ." "Ask Jesus to give you eternal life." "Ask God to save you." These commonly-used phrases confuse people's understanding of the Gospel.

As we prepare people for the Gospel, we must bring them to the point where they realize they can do nothing. But even when people do understand their inability to do anything, many evangelists, missionaries, and preachers tell enquirers things such as, "Now, you must give your heart to Jesus." Having told them they are unable to do anything, they then tell them what they must do. What is the result? Confusion about the Gospel! People turn inward to their own experience, instead of outward to trust only in Christ's death, burial and resurrection on their behalf.

Methods and terminology used in evangelism all over the world have so distorted the Gospel that Christians need to be taught afresh the basic fundamentals of God's saving work in Christ, so their presentation of the Gospel will be according to the Word of God. Even though many people have been saved under present evangelistic methods, many others have not clearly understood the Gospel. The message they heard so emphasized man's part in conversion that God's perfect finished work and complete provision for helpless sinners in Christ was not understood and believed.

If people's attention is directed inward to their own doing, even those who are truly saved will often lack assurance of salvation. The question will constantly arise within their hearts, "Was I sincere enough? Did I do it correctly? Did I truly receive Christ? Did I really give my heart to Jesus?"

I have taught students in Bible College who were concerned and confused over these issues. One day, a student came to me deeply troubled. She talked with me about her conversion. She was concerned, "Did I do it in the right way? Was I really sincere? Did I really accept Jesus into my heart?" These questions plagued her. She had finally decided that, just in case she had not done it in the correct way, she would check with me to see what she should do.

At her conversion, she had realized she could do nothing to save herself. But the evangelist told her she must ask Jesus into her heart and give her life to Christ. From that time on, she was constantly concerned as to whether or not she had done all that she should have done. As I talked with her, I explained that it wasn't a matter of whether SHE had done it correctly or not, but whether the LORD JESUS CHRIST had done everything correctly on her behalf. Did He satisfy God? If so, was she trusting, not in her own doing, but in Christ's finished work on her behalf?

The Gospel is not man accepting Jesus as his Savior, but that God accepted the Lord Jesus as the perfect and only Savior two thousand years ago. The Gospel is not man giving his heart or his life to Jesus, but that Christ gave His life, His whole being, in the place of sinners. The Gospel is not man receiving Christ into his heart, but that God received the Lord Jesus into Heaven as the mediator of sinners. The Gospel is not Christ enthroned in the human heart, but that God enthroned the Lord Jesus at His right hand in Heaven.

Do we see the great distinction between these two messages? One is subjective and puts the emphasis on what man must do. The other is objective and puts the emphasis on what Christ has already done. The sinner is only to trust in what has already been done on his behalf. The Lord Jesus cried, "It is finished." He did it all. He took upon Himself the load of sin, the full responsibility for the sin of mankind. Because Christ paid the complete debt, God raised Him from the dead and accepted Him into Heaven. The resurrection was God's sign to all that He accepted the Lord Jesus Christ forever as the perfect Savior. God is satisfied. Is the convicted sinner? Will he rest the whole weight of his soul's salvation on Christ's acceptance by God as the perfect Savior? Will the sinner cease, once and for all, trying to do anything to save himself? Will he trust only in God's Son for salvation?

Some would call this type of Gospel presentation "Easy Believism." When they present the Gospel, they consider it is necessary to place before sinners the need to take up the cross and follow Jesus and the necessity of crowning Jesus Lord of their lives. Some preachers believe that, by insisting on this, they prevent people from making false professions. The answer to false professions, however, is not found in adding to the Gospel by requiring the sinner to promise to follow, obey, and suffer for Christ. There aren't any strings attached to the Gospel. The answer to true conversion lies in the correct preparation of the sinner's mind and heart for the Gospel. The Holy Spirit accomplishes this as the sinner hears and understands from the Scriptures that he is lost, helpless and hopeless, and stands condemned before God, who is his righteous, holy Creator and Judge.

Dependence on external, observable actions

This confusion regarding the presentation of the Gospel has another serious consequence. Multitudes, whose salvation is doubtful, assure themselves of their acceptance by God because, sometime in their life, they did what the preacher told them to do. They made their decision. They went forward and did what was required of them. Even though their lives have not been changed by the power of Christ and their way of life reveals an unconverted spirit, they still take refuge in what they did. They are trusting in what they did and not in what Christ has done. Multitudes of mere professors are resting their acceptance by God on their action of going forward or praying a prayer in response to the appeal.

Because much evangelistic preaching is subjective and experience-oriented, the attention of the hearers is placed on themselves and their personal response to the preaching. Christians excitedly report the salvation of little children, teenagers, and adults, taking it for granted that they have understood the Gospel and are truly converted, simply because they have displayed an outward decision for Christ.

In most evangelical circles, it is the norm to require people to publicly indicate their decision for Christ by raising their hand, standing, or walking to the front of the building, and praying a prayer of acceptance of Christ. The majority of Gospel preachers and Christians place so much emphasis on the invitation and people's outward response that many Christians are now convinced that it is an integral and vital part of the ministry of the Church. On one occasion, when a relative of mine clearly preached the Gospel but did not give a closing appeal, a Christian lady when leaving the meeting expressed her disapproval by the remark, "He didn't even give people the opportunity to be saved!" The danger is not that people are given the opportunity to publicly express their faith in Christ. The danger is the emphasis before and after the invitation which causes people to rest their salvation on their own personal actions in response to God, rather than on the actions of Christ which are declared in the Gospel.

When addressing this subject during a seminar with missionaries in the Philippines, I made the statement that I had never led any of the Palawano believers to the Lord, and I carefully explained what I meant. I had not asked the Palawanos to pray and to verbally accept Christ in my presence, nor did I tell them that they needed to pray a prayer of acceptance in order to be saved. I simply preached the Gospel and then exhorted the Palawanos to place their faith completely in Christ and the Gospel. Where, how, and what they actually did at the time of their conversion was not the important thing.

One missionary in the seminar strongly disagreed with my statement, "A person does not need to pray in order to be saved." When she objected, I replied, "Then I have led many people astray. I told the Palawanos that if they simply believed the Gospel and trusted in Christ, they would be saved. But I did not tell them that they must pray. According to what you are saying, I must now ask the Palawano believers if they prayed when they believed. If they did not, then I must tell them that unless they do, they will be lost."

Some people use Romans 10:9-10 to substantiate their claim that a person must make a verbal acceptance if he is to be saved. But this would then mean that mute people or those on their deathbeds who are beyond speaking would be unable to be saved. In addition, it would mean that unless a person was with someone else to whom he could confess with his mouth the Lord Jesus, he, too, would not be able to be born again. The first section of Mark 16:16 says, "He who believes and is baptized will be saved." Does this mean that baptism is necessary for someone to be saved? Of course not! The first part of Mark 16:16 must be interpreted in the light of the rest of the verse, "but he who does not believe will be condemned." All such Scriptures must be interpreted in the light of the unmistakable emphasis of the whole Bible – salvation in Christ is received through faith alone and is not dependent on any action of man.

On one occasion, during a conversation with another missionary, he told me how, many years earlier, he had come to assurance of salvation. His assurance came unexpectedly at the close of a meeting when the preacher asked everyone who was saved to raise his hand. Since, at that time, the man did not know if he was truly saved, he tried desperately to keep his hand down, but it was forced up by a power outside of himself. He related that, because of this experience, he never again doubted his salvation. Yet another Christian told me how she was assured of salvation through an unusual experience. When confronted by a wild, vicious bird, poised to attack her, she looked it in the eyes and said, "You can't touch me for I am a child of God." Because the bird did not peck her, she felt certain from that time that she was indeed in the family of God.

Experiences, regardless of their vivid and startling nature, should never be the grounds for believing that one is saved. The Word of God alone must be the foundation for assurance of salvation. John says of his Gospel, "But these are written that you may believe that Jesus is the Christ, the Son of God, and that believing you may have life in His name" (John 20:31). Each Christian is responsible to make certain that his preaching and evangelistic methods focus on Christ and His death, burial and resurrection as the only firm foundation for his hearers' assurance of salvation. Just as the physical eye does not behold itself but sees only the object on which it is focused, so true faith looks only to Christ. We should never accept any outward act of a professed convert as the basis for acceptance as a born-again person. The only scriptural basis for receiving a person's claim to salvation is his understanding and faith in the foundational truths of the Gospel.

In Palawan, a wizened, almost toothless old Palawano lady, who had been sitting for more than an hour on the front porch of our house, finally got around to her reason for visiting. Smiling, she said, "Grandchild, I am trusting in Jesus."

Even before she spoke, it was evident that she had something to tell me because she had patiently waited until all of our other visitors had gone home.

Even though I had guessed that her news was related to her faith in Christ, it did not lessen my excitement and joy when she declared her dependence on the Savior. My natural reaction was to reach out and hug her, but Palawano decorum and culture, as well as a fear that such an action would seal her in a sincere but unfounded faith, restrained me. To immediately accept her testimony, without carefully questioning her, would not have been judicious. She might have been following the other members of her family who had already come in the preceding days to express their dependence on Christ and His redemptive work. For her own sake and for the fledgling church in that area of Palawan, I had to do whatever I could to ensure that her faith was resting on the foundations of Scripture which I had endeavored to lay down.

"Grandmother," I answered her, "It gives me great joy to hear that you are trusting in the Lord Jesus as your Savior. But why did you trust in Him? Why do you need the Lord Jesus?"

"I am a sinner," was her immediate answer.

"But Grandmother, why do you say that? You love your family. You are kind and a very hard worker."

"Yes, but I am a sinner before God," she insisted.

"But Grandmother, even though you are a sinner, why is it that you need the Lord Jesus? Why did you trust in Him? What has He done for you?"

"Ah, Grandchild, He was the One who died for me. He died for my sins."

Tears of joy filled my eyes as I replied, "Grandmother, I am so very glad to hear what you have said, for God's Word says that all those who trust only in the Lord Jesus as their

Savior, believing that He died for them and then rose again, have all their sins forgiven by God and will never go to Hell. They have eternal life and will be received by God into Heaven."

How different was the testimony of this illiterate tribal woman compared to that of my wife's aunt, who went forward in response to an altar call at an evangelistic meeting in Australia. We were excited to think that this may be the first of Fran's relatives, outside of her immediate family, to be converted. So, while visiting with her, Fran began to question her regarding her profession. It soon became obvious that her aunt was taken up with her own personal feelings and experience rather than the historical accomplishments of Christ on her behalf. In an endeavor to determine her aunt's real grounds for assurance, Fran asked her, "Aunty, why did you go forward to the invitation of the preacher? Was it because you realized that you are a sinner?"

"Sinner? I'm not a sinner!" she exclaimed.

In spite of her lack of understanding of even the basic truths of Scripture, Christians had accepted her as having been saved simply because she had responded to the invitation.

Regardless of how careful we may be in questioning professing converts, there will always be those, as portrayed in the Parable of the Sower, who will appear to be Christians but will fall away after a time. Being fully aware of this danger is all the more reason why we should do everything we can to retain the purity, simplicity, and objectivity of the Gospel message, so that people will rest in the rightness of Christ's actions, and not their own.

8.20 Developing Bible resources

> ✓ **OBJECTIVES OF THIS TUTORIAL**
>
> This tutorial outlines a process to use when developing contextualized Foundational Bible teaching sessions and studies in a cross-cultural church-planting context. It also includes a personal testimony of developing Bible teaching resources in a real context.

Introduction

This Tutorial covers material from *Building on Firm Foundations, Book 1, Chapter 12 - Bible Lesson Preparation Process*. The Building on Firm Foundations lessons were originally written for church planting teams in tribal areas, which is reflected in these lesson development notes. However, these same lessons have been used in many different contexts around the world; not only in tribal areas, and you will find this lesson preparation process helpful to you whatever context you are working in.

Bible Lesson Preparation Process

Use this lesson preparation process when following the *"Building on Firm Foundations"* teaching plan.

A. Initial Study and Preparation

Ask the Lord for help, believing that it is His message that you are trying to communicate.

John 14:14; 1 Corinthians 3:7; Luke 1:37

Read Volume 1 of Building on Firm Foundations (BOFF).

Even if you have read Volume 1 previously, read it again before actually beginning lesson preparation. It is vitally important that you understand and are convinced that the underlying reasons for teaching chronologically are based on biblical principles. Only then will you be able to teach with conviction and persist when the teaching process may appear long and tedious.

Read the introductory chapters to the BOFF phase you are planning to teach.
Note the teaching goals for this particular phase so you can refer back to them when you are actually preparing the lessons.

Read and study the larger volume of material of which this lesson is a part.
Read all the BOFF lessons for the phase or the book of scripture you are preparing to teach and also read in both the vernacular and your mother-tongue the scripture portions which will be covered in the lessons.

B. Understand individual BOFF lessons

Read the BOFF lesson and the Scripture portions for the lesson.
Read the Scriptures in your own mother tongue, the vernacular and the national language.

Read through the lesson at least two times and more if necessary. Read several lessons ahead of the one you are preparing to teach so that you are aware of what is coming up in the future lessons.

Identify and think about the goals and themes for the lesson as taught in BOFF.
Note the goals and themes. Refer to them constantly as you prepare your lesson.

After studying each lesson, teach it in your mother tongue.
If you have no other opportunity, teach the lesson as daily devotions with your wife, children, or colleagues. If your fellow missionaries are also involved in the lesson preparation process, then take turns teaching lessons to each other.

C. Contextualize the lessons in the language and culture

Keep your target audience in mind.
Be conscious of the level of education, capacity for listening to monologue and degree of biblical background of your future audience.

You may need to adjust the amount of information to be included in each lesson. Divide lessons if they are too long for the intended group or for the length of the sessions. However, be conscious that each lesson was written as a unit. If changing the length of a lesson is necessary, then consider carefully if the lesson themes have been adequately covered. Also consider if the section you have covered can stand alone as one narrative unit.

Identify and mark in the lessons those points which could clash with the religious, cultural or world view of the people you are planning to teach. Write these in the lessons at the point where it would be necessary or most appropriate to address the particular barrier.

Prepare a lesson outline in the vernacular with lesson development notes.
This lesson outline should include the main content of the lesson, with all the major heading points in the vernacular. Include notes to yourself regarding illustrations, barriers, teacher's notes and teaching aides such as dramas, pictures, maps, charts, etc, that will be necessary for teaching the finished lesson. Check to see all that has been suggested in the BOFF lesson.

Write a word-for-word Bible lesson in the vernacular as a preliminary draft.
Your language ability and cultural understanding should be to a level where you can write a full lesson draft on your own. Although BOFF lessons are not for word-for word translation, they have been prepared with translation in mind. Check each point and the content of your lesson alongside the BOFF lesson to make sure you have included all the pertinent doctrinal themes, emphasis, illustrations and other suggested teaching aides.

Put a teacher's note following the cultural illustrations in the lesson which instructs the native teacher to think of other suitable cultural illustrations that will speak very clearly to their people.

D. Format the lessons

Keep the tribal teachers in mind when formatting the lessons.
Lessons should be prepared as though the tribal teacher is going to be the one teaching. All teacher's notes, cultural examples, etc., should be printed in a finished form suitable for the tribal teacher to follow. Decisions about formatting should be made in cooperation with tribal teachers as much as possible, considering what they prefer and what is easiest for them to use.

The BOFF lessons have been formatted with tribal ministries in mind. In addition, examples of lessons already formatted by other missionaries may be available.

Make decisions early so that all the lessons are consistently formatted.
Consider the following points during preparation of initial lessons so that a consistent lesson template is available for all following lessons:

Use of icons: Be consistent with icons. Put teacher's notes in separate boxes. Mark review question headings with a large question mark. Use a book icon to indicate when it is time to read Scripture. Use an eyeball icon to indicate when the teacher has to show a picture or use a prop. Include a list of materials the teacher will need at the beginning of the lesson.

Breaking up the text: Use bold headings for each point. Don't have large areas of plain text.

Table of Contents: In a volume with a large number of lessons, the table of contents may not only include the title of each lesson but also a brief summary of what each lesson is about.

Lesson Outline: It is helpful to have a lesson outline, including major headings, at the beginning of each lesson.

Headers and Footers: Include on each page the lesson number, the title of the lesson, and the page number.

Other issues to consider: You will need to decide whether or not to add pictures (full or in thumbnail) to help the teachers.
It is recommended that you use numbers and not English alphabet letters (a,b,c) for lists or outline points.
Some lesson writers have developed a 'teacher's page' to lay out what needs to be done in preparation for teaching the lessons, such as gathering teaching aides.

E. Check the lesson with mother tongue speakers

Explain the purpose of the comprehension check to your helpers.
The mother tongue speaker's role (ensuring naturalness and clarity of communication), and your role (the authority for scriptural truth or biblical content) should be clearly explained. A relationship of trust and openness should be developed between you, the lesson writer, and the checkers.

Give your helpers a general overview of what the lesson is about.
Explain the general topic and tell the story, giving them an initial overview of the material.

Teach each point. Don't read. Teach.
Teach each point carefully, allowing them time to understand and think about the subject so they don't become lost in too large an amount of material.

Do a comprehension check.
Prepare comprehension questions about each point in the lesson and then ask them of the helpers.

Some lesson writers ask the mother tongue speaker to repeat the points back to them while they record them for future reference. If you do this, remember that your helper may not yet understand the overall theme or scriptural principles being expounded.

Identify any communication problems.
Consider possible reasons for any difficulties in communication; is it because of world view issues, grammar problems, discourse features not being used correctly, poor illustrations?

Discuss ways to improve communication clarity.
Ask for better ways to say, explain, or illustrate the problem areas you have identified.

F. Prepare the lesson for teaching

Complete the first draft.
This first draft is your preliminary draft including the changes you have made after checking it with mother tongue speakers.

Share the lesson with your tribal co-workers.
After you have taught more phases, you will be able to check this original first draft with more people. This should include reading or teaching the lesson and then asking what they understood. Adjustments to the lesson should then be made based on their comprehension and suggestions.

Back-translate the required number of lessons for your consultant check.
Ask the church planting consultant which lessons to back-translate. If this is the first back-translation you have done, ask the consultant for guidance on how literal to be and how to handle proper nouns, etc. Send the back-translations to the consultant for content check and arrange for a translation and comprehension check.

Practice teaching the lesson.
Teach the lesson to your partner, or at least teach through the whole lesson on your own as practice before teaching it to the whole group.

Revise the lesson after teaching.

Almost inevitably, some changes will be necessary after you teach each lesson to the people in the vernacular. Because of the burden of the work at this point, it is very easy to miss out on this step.

Have a plan for this first revision. Have a partner, spouse and literate tribal listeners (particularly those from the lesson checking team) take notes while you are teaching. They should note any mistakes in the lessons or areas which did not clearly communicate the thought you intended. Later, you will have to decide the reason(s) for this lack of communication and decide whether it necessitates a change in the text of the lesson. Consider also the various aspects of your oral delivery.

Make decisions about printing, distributing and publishing the curriculum.

Include the people as much as possible in the work of printing and publishing the lesson materials.

The first edition may be stapled loose leaf sheets. After lessons have been taught a few times and other necessary changes made, they can be printed in a more finished form. Initially, Phase 1 and the lessons for the other phases will probably be in small booklets. Later, phase lessons may be published in one or several volumes for easy storage and portability. Single lessons can be half-foolscap size and larger volumes could be A4 size. You should check to see what is most convenient for the teachers.

When there is a local church, then a good model is to pass on the lessons to the Bible teachers and maybe to others when they are first taught the material. It then immediately becomes theirs, and it is their responsibility to teach it to others. But outreach to others should be with accountability to the church and not left up to the individual to decide when, where and who he will teach.

G. Extra materials

Consider translating or preparing introductory materials from Volume 1 and the introductions to each book of the BOFF series as discipleship tools for the tribal Bible teachers.

Always keep in mind whether or not anything you, as the initial church planting team, have used is reproducible or accessible by the local tribal church for future outreaches. Any extra materials that you use to teach (props for dramas videos, pictures, maps, or others materials) should either be provided by you for future tribal church planting teams or be easily reproducible by the tribal teachers.

Bible resources for the Tugutil

In the following story John Sharpe, a former church planter, shares about how the Bible resources were developed for the Tugutil people in Indonesia.

A personal testimony from John Sharpe[1]

In thinking back to my own experience of being involved in curriculum development, we were one of many church planting teams who were firmly committed to using Trevor McIlwain's *Building on Firm Foundations (BOFF)* lessons as the model for evangelism. At that time the early edition of *BOFF* books had just been released and wonderful reports were coming in of the fruit being seen from those works using the approach for Church planting.

In developing the initial lessons for the Tugutil work, I had the great privilege of working with an amazing young man who though illiterate and monolingual, had a wonderful hunger to learn and better understand the world beyond where he lived. He also had an amazing capacity to learn new things and a wonderful memory.

In preparing lessons I would first study the English lessons from the *BOFF* book and while doing that I was also teaching them to our 9-year-old twin daughters. Obviously that required them being contextualised for 9 year olds but I would also be constantly thinking about how that truth could then be contextualised for the tribal people so that it would really connected with them at a worldview level. This is the reason why it's vital to first gain an understanding of their worldview; sadly something that isn't always done with many who are working to cross-culturally communicate God's Word. Once I had the lesson contextualised and ready in English, I would then translate it to the best of my ability into the tribal language.

Then with both in hand I would sit down with Habiana and read the newly translated Scripture portions through to him several times, for that particular lesson. I would then explain enough of the bigger story to ensure that he understood the overall context. My co-workers were also hard at work translating the Scripture portions required for each lesson. Habiana and I would then work on improving my translation of the lesson and I would read and reread those portion of the lessons until we were both satisfied that it was communicating correctly. We would also prepare comprehension questions for each lesson and Habiana's answers would give me a good appreciation of whether our lessons were on track.

---

1. For John and Betty Sharpe's full story see their book, *The Tugutil - The true story of God's life changing work among the Tugutil people of Indonesia*

The next step with Habiana was to then read to him smaller portions and get him to paraphrase them back to me in his own words. This was to ensure that the lessons flowed naturally in the language. We would then go through the entire lesson and once he felt it was communicating well, we would record Habiana on tape. I would then take that recording to my wife Betty who would transcribe it. Then I would meet with the other two teachers on our team and go through the lesson thoroughly checking it out for content, key terms and illustrations and consider the possibility of using drama if it really fitted the particular lesson we wanted to teach.

Something that we didn't do that we should have, was to have Habiana sit in those meeting and then run those changes past him and get his final approval of the lesson as it was about to be delivered to the people.

We would then record whoever was teaching that lesson on to a cassette tape and make copies that would be distributed out along with Global Recordings hand wind tape players. Many would also come to our houses at night and listen to the recorded lessons over and over.

At that time we were teaching, our consultants required that we had a minimum of 20 lessons fully prepared before we commenced teaching, just to ensure that continuity in delivery of God's Story would not be interrupted by unforeseen delays - of which we had many. Over time as the believers grew in their understanding, those lessons were revised and much improved by the believers themselves.

In all my life I have never experienced anything as thrilling as seeing God's Narrative progressively unfolded to people who previously knew nothing of it and then witnessing their lives being transformed before our very eyes. It's certainly an experience that I hope you also, one day get to enjoy.

TUTORIAL 8.20

❓ DISCUSSION POINTS

1. In what specific ways were John, Betty and Habiana equipped (specific skills, abilities, understanding, etc.) for their particular roles in Bible curriculum development for the Tugutil church?

2. As you engaged with the lesson development process outlined in this tutorial, did you feel that it is a process that would produce faithful initial teaching lessons for the church? Is there any part of the process you might add to or change? Why or why not?

➡ ACTIVITIES

1. Read *Building on Firm Foundations Volume 1, Part 2 - Chapter 10, Developing and Teaching Phase 1 Lessons* and *Chapter 11, Lesson Layout*.

(*Building on Firm Foundations Volume 1* is available for download at accesstruth.com)

8.21 Ata Bible resources 1

 OBJECTIVES OF THIS TUTORIAL

This tutorial is taught by Kaikou Maisu and Mike Griffis and outlines the Bible resources available to the Ata church, Papua New Guinea.

Introduction

In the next three tutorials we will be hearing about Bible Resources from a local church elder, Kaikou Maisu, who is from the Ata people group in Papua New Guinea. The Gospel was first shared there by missionaries in 1992. If you'd like to see more about God's work there, you can watch the video on the AccessTruth website - *The Ata: God's Narrative Continues*.

Kaikou has been a believer since 1992. He has been involved in many outreaches in the Ata area, moving with his family to teach the Gospel in unreached villages. He was also co-translator for the Ata New Testament translation, which was published in the year 2000. He has been a faithful teacher and overseer in the Ata church as well as visiting and serving other local fellowships in various locations in Papua New Guinea.

Joining Kaikou to share about Bible Resources, is Mike Griffis. He and his family were invited in 2005 to move to an Ata village, where they learned the language and culture. Mike became part of an Ata village church leadership team for the five years they lived there, and was involved in teaching and discipleship as well as helping the Ata to adapt to cultural and technological changes. Mike served the Ata by helping them to be better equipped to partner with other churches and with the wider Body of Christ.

In this first tutorial, Kaikou and Mike will begin by sharing about some of the Resources that are available to the church.

The following content is a transcript from the video for Tutorial 8.21.

KAIKOU -

Today we are going to explain the kinds of materials we have to help to support the life of the church and to help in the growth of the church, and also to give the believers assurance that they are truly God's children. These 'tools' that we are about to describe and show here, all have one substantial foundation. All of these materials are based on what is in God's Word itself. Because we know that God's Word - that has been translated into the language of the people here and is now in their own language - is actually God Himself speaking to us, and God Himself who has revealed His will, and who has clearly communicated His plan for human beings. And so through His Word, we can understand His will, His plan, and His thinking. So having His Word in our language is not an insignificant thing, or an inconsequential thing. It is extremely important. Because it is through His Word that He is revealed or communicated to us. It is God Himself, in His Word.

So the first 'tool' that people need to help them understand God, is this book we call 'Highway'. But before we get into the material in 'Highway', there something helpful we share with people first that is in the form of an analogy to help them evaluate their existing beliefs. I'll share the analogy with you now.

The analogy talks about an old string bag and a new string bag. The old string bag represents the existing beliefs of the people, and all the things they were trusting in, like rituals, spirits, ancestor worship. And the new string bag represents the Word of God. Because God's Word is something new that they are about to hear. This analogy helps people to begin to understand, that the Word of God they are about to hear is something entirely new.

Then we begin to use the material in 'Highway' which clearly lays out God's desire and His overall plan from His Word. When people hear all of that, they understand the reason people exist, and what their real standing before God is. They hear God's Word clearly in a way that helps them to really understand it. Their eyes are opened and they understand how God really sees them. This first course of teaching from Genesis to Christ, reveals for them what their real need actually is. The teaching in 'Highway' gradually builds a foundation of truth in the lives of those who are hearing it, so they come to clearly see what their real need is. Which of course is that their trust should be in the Lord Jesus Christ.

So then after they become God's children, then what should we teach them? Should we go straight to the Epistles? No. Instead we build slowly on the foundation they have, and we use another resource we call 'Branch Road'. Because once people have heard God's Word taught clearly from the beginning, and they have become His children, then the material in this 'tool' helps them to understand their true position, 'inside' the Grace of God, and the love of God, and that the basis of their new life is only Christ Himself. This material here helps them to understand their position, and that they can truly find "rest" in their new life of faith. As we have already said, we share the material in 'Branch road' with people, so that they will understand their position, and know that they are safe in Christ. It's true they still live in this world of sin, but they know they are 'in Him', and that God loves them and is pleased with them, because His Son is perfect and without sin. And because of that they know that there is nothing that can ever take them out of the position of acceptance they have with God because of Christ.

MIKE -

So as we are describing the way in which resources are developed for the church, we are mentioning here in the first series of resources that are developed, how those resources focus on the way in which the people who are listening, are first understanding the foundations of God's Word being taught. So therefore they are hearing the story of God's character as it is established, for example, in the book of Genesis; God clearly at work amongst the people who existed at that time; God showing forth His character in the way in which He handled His relationship with human beings from the beginning. They are seeing the way in which the book of Genesis moves forward and God develops a chronology of that narrative as He continues, in different stages and in different ways, to work with human beings to help them to clearly understand the moving forward to Christ, and they way in which their sin has created a barrier between them and God in that process.

So that first narrative that is being taught is the establishment of God's character and the person of the Lord Jesus Christ as well, in the way in which God moves from His character, up in to Christ. So then when we reach the life of Christ, not only have we established the clear flow of the narrative and not only have we established the need of people for salvation, but we have also begun to build significant foundations through the series of lessons, such that it points forward towards a firm place where this new church that is going to exist, can develop to maturity - looking forward into the future.

KAIKOU -

The next thing we teach is the Acts of the Apostles. But why would we teach people the Acts of the Apostles next? Well, it's because people can see that today there are many different churches, but they can see the true foundation of that work in Acts and how God Himself planted that first church in Jerusalem. They can see that whoever believed in Christ, became His gathering, or His Body on the earth. And they understand the work of the Holy Spirit as they see His power demonstrated through the live of the Apostles. And they also learn that in their new lives, as the Holy Spirit now lives in them, that His work is to guide and lead God's children today also. So, as we teach people through the book of Acts, they begin to truly understand the foundation of new life that they now have.

But they also hear about the responsibility and the work that the Lord Jesus gave to the Apostles to take His Word out to other communities. God sent them out to do that. So people come to see that same responsibility is now theirs today. God has given that responsibility to His Church and they are the way for His Word to get to all the people who have not yet heard. So we teach from the Acts of the Apostles so that they understand they are part of His Body.

After teaching from Acts, we go to another resource that teaches from Romans. The reason we now begin to teach people from Romans is because we know that Romans lays out all of the foundational truths for their new lives. When new believers hear what God teaches in His Word in Romans, they hear how they should now walk, and how they should now live. And they hear where the strength comes from for them to continue in their new walk. They learn that it is faith in God and that it is His strength that they have to live in each day. Each day they get their strength to walk with God from the Holy Spirit. So the teaching from Romans is a wonderful resource. It really provides a solid foundation for the new walk of faith for God's children.

After we have taught from the book of Romans, we can continue to build on that foundation with the other Epistles. We move on to teaching from Ephesians, because by this point God's children have already heard what the foundations are for their walk of faith, and now they need to hear what the basis for their growth is. Ephesians describes all the good things God has given us for our spiritual growth. And it clearly teaches that the basis for all of those things is faith. Faith in the work of Christ is the basis for all the good things God does in our spiritual lives.

As well as that, the believers come to understand their part in the Body. There are many groups of believers and they live in different places and cultures, but the reality is that they are all one. Because of their shared faith, God sees them all as one, and He has given them all His Holy Spirit.

They also get foundational help in the area of marriage. God teaches them about marriage by using an analogy, so that husbands understand how to really look after their wives and children, and wives know their role in the family and in supporting their husbands in the best way. In order to explain that clearly, the analogy of the

Church of Christ is used, specifically the relationship between the Church, and Christ as the Head of the Church. The believers get a huge amount of help from that.

MIKE -

So as you hear us articulating the foundations of the church, I assume you are getting a sense that we are describing a process and a view toward the maturity of the church that is a long and extensive process. That's why these resources are here before us.

As Kaikou mentioned, in the establishment of these new believers in Christ, they as individuals are hearing about their sin and about the salvific purposes of the Lord Jesus Christ, and they are understanding that the Lord wants them to have a new identity in Him. So they as individuals are being established one by one in the person of the Lord Jesus Christ, in His righteousness. And yet at the same time we want them to understand the way in which their new life in Christ as individuals connects back to the early foundations of the Church as well. And so for that reason, as Kaikou mentioned, we go into the book of Acts next, so that the historical setting of the Church is clear. So that we have a very clear understanding of the way in which, whatever churches emerge after the fact, have connected clearly back to the way in which the Apostles worked in the book of Acts. Not only that these Apostles existed in some sort of a theoretical way, but that it was in real life settings that they were ministering. They had heard the truth taught, and they were ministering themselves in their very real historical context.

So as we are teaching the book of Acts, [we need to be] establishing those historical contexts and establishing the people - the personalities of those authors - very clearly. And establishing the locations in maps, showing how they worked, where they travelled, what they endured, how the Gospel changed their individual identities. And not only on an individual basis, because we want then to show how these churches were emerging through the work of personalities like Paul and Peter. How these churches, these congregations of believers were gathering, and explaining that historical context in such a way that in the places where we are planting churches today - that individuals are making decisions to connect their identities to the person of Jesus Christ. That they are also understanding the way in which He is bringing them together as new groups of believers with a corporate identity that connects back to those early Apostles in the book of Acts. And that they way they suffer or endure hardship today is a reflection of the roots of the faith that are seen and represented by those personalities in the early days of the Church.

So as that corporate identity is growing in the book of Acts, we need to explain the person of the Holy Spirit. We know that early on in Acts it is described clearly how the Spirit came and gave gifts to the Church. It is an early foundation for leadership development in the church - the Holy Spirit being the source of strength and power that they will depend on into the future as they together, as a body of believers, move forward in their growth to maturity.

? DISCUSSION POINTS

1. What would you say are two or three of the top considerations for Kaikou as he thinks about the particular Bible teaching the believers under his care should hear?

2. Summarize, in point form, any specific things mentioned by Kaikou and Mike that believers can come to understand through the book of Acts.

8.22 Ata Bible resources 2

 OBJECTIVES OF THIS TUTORIAL

This tutorial is taught by Kaikou Maisu and Mike Griffis and outlines the Bible resources available to the Ata church, Papua New Guinea.

Introduction

In this second tutorial from Kaikou and Mike, they discuss the important Narrative and Foundational Bible resources available to the Ata church, as well as the place for topical Bible teaching, and Mike describes the importance of building an underlying framework to provide a Biblical theology for the church.

The following is a transcript from the video for Tutorial 8.22.

KAIKOU -

Now we are going to talk about the teaching from Corinthians. Because we know that within the church, there are still things like tensions between families, and that other similar issues still exist. So as we teach from 1 Corinthians, it helps the believers to understand that the reality is that they are all one in the Body of Christ. It also helps those who are teachers and leaders in the church, to be able to build on the foundation of the believers' faith in Christ, and their understanding of God's grace, so that when they stand up to teach God's Word, or work with people, then it will all be based on the grace of God. And they will also know that there is no other foundation for growth in peoples' lives - it is just the grace of God.

People believe in God; in the power of God and in the wisdom of God, and that He is the One who helps them each day in their lives. They know that whatever it is that they are doing to help the Body of Christ, that it isn't because any person, or any law, is forcing them to do it, but it is the work of the Holy Spirit within that motivates them. They know that God is already pleased with them, and it is the love of Christ that motivates them in their work. Also as we look into this particular book, it helps us to know that even though we exist here on earth, that we can truly know God and understand Him. Because we can look at the life of Christ and see a picture of who God is. We look at the work of Christ; how he was nailed to the cross, and His blood sealed the new agreement, and we also know the work of the Holy Spirit within us. So this book helps us because when sin does happen, then the people of God will not just overlook it, because they know that if sin is left to develop within a church, it can seriously hamper growth and damage the testimony of the church. But there is a way to deal with it. There are steps to take to correct the situation, which include removing that person from the fellowship so that they learn to understand what God's desire is for His people as they live together.

Next we begin to teach from 1 Thessalonians and 2 Thessalonians, where we learn more about God's overall plan. Because many people don't understand God's plan for the people of the earth. So we go to these books where God clearly articulates His plan. He lays out His plan for His people who have died and for those still living, and for those who have died who don't belong to Him. God's plan for them is also clear. That is why we then begin to teach from Thessalonians.

I'll give you an example… When this material was first taught to us, we also heard some rumours and talk about the 'end times'. And those rumours produced fear in the hearts of God's children. They were afraid when they heard about the end times and Antichrist. Because if people don't clearly understand God's plan, then that kind of talk makes them very fearful. So we teach from this part of God's Word so His plan becomes clear to them. His children then understand that everything is part of God's plan, and that God sees them and knows each one of them. Then they are no longer fearful when they hear talk about these things, when people talk about 666, or Amageddon, or Antichrist, they are no longer afraid, but they have peace and joy. They are secure in their lives in Christ and in God's plan. They know that God has not forgotten them and He hasn't overlooked them.

They can also remember all of the foundational truth that they have heard. It strengthens their faith as they see God working out His plan to save Man. The story of Noah, for example, gives them peace because God protected His people from what would happen later. And in the story of Lot, God destroyed the two towns of Sodom and Gomorrah, but he protected Lot and his children from the destruction. So in this teaching here, God's children find encouragement and assurance that God has them in a place of safety.

MIKE -

OK, so as Kaikou is describing the progression of teaching, and we are describing how we have moved from the book of Acts into this group of Epistles, we are describing a process which isn't random. I trust that is being clearly understood. And moving into Romans, Ephesians, 1 Corinthians, 1 and 2 Thessalonians, there are various themes that we are trying to establish that are dependent on the way that this new group of believers who have come about through hearing the Gospel presented clearly, who are understanding their individual identities in Christ, who are understanding the corporate identity that connects back to the Church. They are then beginning to see the way in which those Apostles that we communicated about, that we described in the book of Acts, are the ones responsible for sharing their perspective of faith that the Lord Jesus Christ Himself has been revealing to them. They are sharing their perspective on the faith and the needs that these churches have - at the time and in specific settings. And yet, as believers today, we know that those principles of the growth of the church are universally applied. And so selecting the book of Romans for example, to describe the basis of that grace of God that we have established as being revealed in the person of the Holy Spirit as He teaches our hearts. And He is continuing to teach us today as believers. He is continuing to teach about His grace, continuing to teach about the way in which we are dependent on His grace. Then in the book of Ephesians and the book of 1 Corinthians, we are given a snapshot of a church that was undergoing difficulties in these areas of not living up to the identities that they had in the Lord Jesus Christ and in which Paul engages with them and describes their shortcomings. And he describes the opportunities that they have to grow to represent that identity in grace that is based on all the things that we have been teaching to this point.

So we are trying to reiterate the opportunity that the believers have to see the way in which God's grace is worked out in day-to-day situations in their lives as they grow to understand more and more clearly that identity as applied to their real life situations today. And as we see, there is a time element that is really significant here. We're not, in an instant, dumping a load of works-related life on them. We are not trying to create an identity of them in their own efforts, in their own strengths, trying to work their way to the identity that God has for them - either as individuals or as a body of believers. But through the progression of carefully teaching line upon line, and precept upon precept, we are giving them the opportunity to gradually see the Holy Spirit to be at work in their hearts to bring them towards that clear identity that He has for them - that they have seen a picture of, that progresses along through the teaching.

Then we come to a point where we want to, for example, in the area that was mentioned in 1 and 2 Thessalonians and that really ties back to the way in which we as human beings who are sinners die. We died spiritually before we became believers, and then as we become believers we take on the life of Christ, and we put to death the deeds of the flesh. Then in Thessalonians there is the mention again of death in the natural sense that our bodies are dying, and the question comes up, 'What does that mean for us as believers?' Then we have an opportunity to come back to a topic like death, for example, and to carefully describe or sum up what we know about that topic, based on a real need in that community. A need, because people are dying as a natural process, in the community where we may be working, and we are wanting them to understand clearly how to apply the flow of the narrative that they have heard to that point. Beginning all the way back to the character of God, but continuing on through the Epistles, we are wanting them to understand, and in a summary way, to apply all the points that they have been taught to a topic that is really significant to their life. Many of these types of topical lessons develop based on a need that arises at the time, but being carefully to base that material on what has been clearly taught to that stage. Not going ahead and trying to find areas ahead of where we are actually teaching at this stage, to continue to teach clearly about those kinds of topics that are significant to the church.

Another example of that are lessons about the topic of marriage, which obviously is very important to the church. A set of lessons that is, in a sense, topical, but it is not a stand alone set of materials or tools because it ties and connects back into those things that have been clearly established in the foundations that have been taught to that point.

So Kaikou is going to continue on with another area relating to some of the other Epistles that move us forward.

KAIKOU -

Like we have been saying, the church of our Lord has already been born, and the Lord is beginning to raise up leaders from within that group. So at this time we begin to look at 1 Timothy and Titus. Because that helps the believers to recognize those God is raising up and to understand the role that the Lord has for them in the church. And this part of God's Word gives specific help to those who are beginning to work in the church to understand their roles. They are encouraged to know that God Himself has raised them up for this work. Also believers begin to understand a new basis of authority for their leaders, and they see it is the Holy Spirit who is guiding these leaders to look after them. They trust and respect them before God because they are able to see that God Himself has raised them up to take care of His people, so in their hearts they are able to respect and appreciate their leaders. And the leaders fulfill their roles humbly and with reverence, when they think about the fact that it is God's work they are doing.

Then we move into the book of Revelation, which, as we know, talks of things that will happen in the future. But even today a lot talk comes from unbelievers, and they spread rumours about things that they say will happen later on. So this book encourages God's children by helping them to understand His plan. They also heard some of these same things in Thessalonians, that are now covered again in Revelation, so they are reminded of those things. The two books complement and support one another, and God's children get a clear picture of God's plan, and they find peace and encouragement in that and it strengthens their faith.

As we have already said, we have all of these resources that explain God's Word. We give praise to God because we see the life and growth of the church, based on the new birth that they also received from Him. And it is God who guided those who produced all of these helpful resources. They help to strengthen the faith of God's people, and help them to continue to grow in the new life they have received. It's true that we are part of the Church and of groups of believers, but the things of the world still exist too. So when we think about what teaching the people of God might need, we think about what would help them most to grow in their understanding of the grace of God. We trust that God is going to lead and guide us as we decide which portion of God's Word we should teach at which time. For example, we had been taught all the books that we have already mentioned, but then what portion should we hear next?

Well, next we went into lessons from Galatians, which was a huge help to us at that time. Because this particular part of God's Word, helps God's children to evaluate the foundations of their previous worldview. It also helps them to correctly assess teaching they had heard in the past and the motivation of those people who had taught it. Now a complete change has taken place and they are living a new life. Galatians helps them to understand the grace of God more clearly, and it also helps them to be able to correctly judge or evaluate their legalism from the past, and to clearly separate that from God's grace. So they are able to stand firm on the foundation of grace, and to defend the heart of the Gospel itself. And they have the assurance that comes from trusting in God alone.

This Epistle also helps the believers to be able to correctly assess anyone who comes in to teach God's Word. Because as we know there are many teachers of God's Word, and they say things like, "We are all one", or "We all have one God". But there is help from Galatians because they can clearly see that there are those who are truly part of their fellowship, and they have heard their teaching and trust that God has raised them up to teach, and their teaching is based on the grace of God.

There are a lot of other Epistles represented here, and in each of those parts of God's Word we can see beneficial teaching to help the church and believers to grow. I'll use the example of Philippians here. We know that this portion of God's Word is very helpful for believers, because it talks about their personal responsibility for sharing God's Word. God specifically guides certain people to stand up and teach His Word, and it is also His plan that they will plant churches in other communities. But the believers in the sending church must also know their role in God's work. It's enlightening to read about the time the Apostle Paul was in prison in Rome, and how the Philippian believers gathered their resources to help him. And not just that time, but they helped on his other missionary journeys too. They supported and encouraged him in his work. So that really opens the eyes of God's children, to realize they have an important role to play in the outreach of the church, as they support and encourage the work of reaching out.

MIKE -

OK, you have explained all of these Epistles here, and the specific help each one is to the believers, but could you now tell us about 1 John and how that met a need in the church?

KAIKOU -

At the time 1 John was first taught it greatly helped the believers lives. Because when they heard that portion there, it helped them to really grasp the new life that they had in Christ. And another important thing that they realized, was that they still live in a world of sin, and that the root of sin still exists within them, so they still sin. But this Epistle really helped them to submit to God, and to truly listen to what God says and respect that. Because no matter what sin they fall into, the way to God is open, so there is no excuse for them not being open and honest with God. So whatever happens, whatever they do, they can immediately share it with God, and then real life change can begin. That's the thing the believers understood. That real change happens, only when someone understands that yes, they do sin, but they can openly share that with God and apologize to Him and He will help. Because they know God is there and He wants a relationship with them, and to help them with the things they are struggling with in life.

Another important point here relates to their understanding of Christ. He came to earth as a man, but they must know He wasn't just a man. They need to respect Him for who He truly is. He came to earth as a man, and had a body, but actually He was

God. And they need to understand what He came to do; to die on the cross. And that He died in order to pay their debt for their sin. And that is the reason they love and respect Him, because of what He did. They are awed by that. Even though He was God, He gave up His life to pay for their debt of sin.

MIKE -

Yes, it's amazing, thank you. So I know that you went into the book of Philemon, can you tell us anything about that, and how it helped the believers?

KAIKOU -

Yes, they found a lot of help in there for them as a church. Because there are certain men who lead the work of God, and some who have other roles in it. And they considered how they demonstrate affection for the believers. They were given a great example here in Philemon. Because Paul demonstrated his true affection by sharing God's Word clearly, so that Philemon truly understood and was brought to life. It helps too, because there was sin that had come between them, or something that had come between Philemon and Onesimus. But we can see that even though something had happened there, that Paul reminds Philemon that what he believed, is the same thing that his brother also believed. So that unifies them. So whatever it was that had come between them, he shouldn't think of that any more. Because they are one in belief and are brothers in the faith, and can love one another because of that. So that is a huge help to believers in their lives.

MIKE -

Yes, that's good. So tell us about James, I know you are teaching that right now.

KAIKOU -

Yes, we are very thankful to God, because we didn't just jump into James before some of the other teaching, a lot of other teaching came before, and now we are hearing James, and that is helpful because there is already a strong foundation of grace. And we know the teaching from James is heavy, and it talks about how the fruit of our lives will be obvious. It is very helpful right now for us, because of course we want our lives to produce fruit, but it has to grow out of the foundation of grace. So we find a great deal of help in James. The other teaching we have heard helps many other areas of life, but James specifically helps us as we talk to other people. It helps us to think carefully about the things we say, so whatever we say is helping the people of God in some way.

MIKE -

So you have talked about all these Epistles from the New Testament, and these resources that cover all the books in there, but what about this one from the Old Testament that covers the story of Ruth? I know that all of the books in God's Word are helpful, but what can you tell us about this particular Old Testament book?

KAIKOU -

Yes, well, the story of Ruth from the Old Testament is a great example for us to help us to really understand the grace of God and also the plan of God. So in the story of Ruth, the believers are able to see God's plan, because they can see that even though Ruth was a Gentile woman, she was able to truly know God. He was the God of the Israelites, the One that they feared and respected, and their obvious reverence for God attracted Ruth. She saw that and was convinced that the God of Israel was the true living God. She saw that and then went and joined with the Israelites. So that example really helps the believers, because they can see this part of God's plan to send the Deliverer, and this part of God's Word describes His actual family line, and how it came about that Ruth came from outside and joined the Israelites, and became a woman of God and a part of God's plan to send the Deliverer.

MIKE -

In this time of discussion, we have tried to establish the rationale for the ways in which we make resources accessible to the church. We have attempted to communicate of course the foundational basis of the Word of God, obviously, as our primary resource. Our desire then is to give access to the Word of God through a process of carefully narrating the Word of God as it is unfolding through the ages. It ties all the way back to the character of God in Genesis. The way that He worked amongst His people, the way that the nation of Israel came about and was a light to the world, and the way that God, in His wisdom, had the mystery of the church hidden in the plan that He had in mind and that was seen in the work of the Apostles and of course through the life of Jesus Christ.

So we are attempting to establish the rationale for that underlying framework of God's overarching narrative plan. And then we have moved forward and described the rationale for different letters that form the basis of our New Testament, and even into our Old Testament; understanding the person of Christ as the key to seeing clearly what God has been about throughout the centuries. And yet, not leaving behind this carefully developed process of narrating our way through the story that God has for us in the Scriptures. We want that framework to be clearly established. In the process of narrating our way through the story of what God has been about over the centuries we are very intentionally creating a Biblical theology upon which any other organizational scheme of theology may be built. Also then, we are giving access to a narrative establishment of an underlying hermeneutic as well by which we can understand clearly, when we come to a new portion of Scripture, we can clearly understand, as we engage with that, the way in which that part of Scripture connects to God's broad story of redemptive history. And in turn, the way in which we carefully and correctly apply that portion of Scripture to our lives today as members of the growing Body of Christ, which He intended from the beginning as part of the unfolding of His great plan for our lives.

? DISCUSSION POINTS

1. Sum up what you hear Kaikou and Mike saying about the role of topical teaching (on marriage, death, etc.) within the wider flow of Narrative teaching.

2. Kaikou is a first-generation believer from a previously unreached people group. Do you think this fact affects his view of God and His Word? If so, in what ways?

8.23 Ata Bible resources 3

> ✓ **OBJECTIVES OF THIS TUTORIAL**
>
> This tutorial is taught by Kaikou Maisu and Mike Griffis and outlines the process of discipleship for local believers as they took on the responsibility of developing Bible resources for the Ata church, Papua New Guinea.

Introduction

In this last tutorial from Kaikou and Mike, they talk about the process of resource development, specifically the discipleship process for the Ata men as they began to take on the roles of Bible teaching, leading and developing teaching resources. They also discuss the importance of written resources in safeguarding the truth.

The following is a transcript from the video for Tutorial 8.23.

MIKE -

We have previously described the theoretical or the philosophical basis, or the rationale for the way in which resources are developed for the church, and we have described God's Word, obviously, as a foundation for that. Now we would like to move to more of a discussion of the shared responsibility and process for the resources that we see here before us and that are important tools for the work of the church.

So now we would like to change topics a little bit and talk about the way in which the church, and the church planters who are in that situation, have shared ownership of the process of developing resources; the shared responsibility that represents. And the way in which our desire is to see the church feel fully equipped for taking full ownership for the ongoing development of the resources that the church requires as they move ahead in their growth to maturity. So, we hope to insert some 'snapshots' along the process of all of these resources having been developed, such that we can see the way in which that balance of shared responsibility changes over the course of time.

In order to be able to do that, as we see and assume lots and lots of written texts before us, we have to return to the very foundational idea of not only God's Word being made available as the primary resource, but also people being able to read and write that. Read and write in their own languages, read and write material that will help them as they move forward in the tools being developed.

And so Kaikou is going to begin to share that process of learning to read and write and then going on into the development of the resources themselves as the church moved forward in maturity.

KAIKOU -

Like Mike said, we are going to talk about something foundational to the life of the church. The local language literacy school has a very important role, because people need to learn how to read and write. If people gain the skill of reading, then it helps them because they are able to read God's Word for themselves. It's true that they are able to hear it from those who stand up and teach it, but it is much more helpful to them if they can read it for themselves as well. Then if they are in their homes, or wherever they are, they can read. Whatever issues they are facing in life, they can go and read. So the work of teaching literacy is very important, because it allows people to learn to read and write in their own language.

As I already said, being able to read and write in their own language is a huge help to the believers. We have some resources here to help those who teach literacy, to guide them in the best way to help their students, as they teach them to read fluently and to write well. These literacy resources help them to do their work well. And there are other resources like this that are specifically for students that give them exercises and practice in both reading and writing.

I'd like to give an example to explain the relationship between the work of developing Bible teaching resources, and the work of teaching people to read and write. The fact is that literacy teaching, and the teaching of the Word of God, must go together, they can't be separated. Because if you just have Bible teaching without literacy, it's helpful of course, but people need to be able to read God's Word so He can speak directly to them. Because without that, then the foundations just won't be very strong. But if a person is able to read, they know that God is speaking directly to them.

So what can I say about the work of teaching people to read… imagine, for example, a bird trying to fly with only one wing. It wouldn't be able to fly to another place.

It couldn't even fly into a tree. But having two wings allows that bird to fly. It's the same with this tool that helps the believers in the church if they are able to read and write well. They are able to gain and learn so much more from God's Word, and have a much greater ability to take it to other communities that don't yet have any access to God's Word.

Once people are able to read and write in their own language, then that gives them the ability and the confidence to become teachers of God's Word. In the beginning, those that first began God's work here carried the full responsibility for it. They prepared the teaching material, and they stood up and taught God's Word. Then local men began to take part and to share in that work. They were able to do that because they had confidence in their ability. They were confident firstly because of their literacy skills, and also because of all the Bible teaching they had heard. Those two things really helped them to begin to share the work. They knew that they had a level of literacy to be able to teach.

So in the beginning it really was only the work of those who started the work, they did it and were responsible for it, because they were the only ones able to do it then. But then quite quickly local people leaned to read, and they understood the Word because they had heard it taught clearly. Then they felt equipped to be able to teach others as well.

They were discipled and equipped gradually. At first just sharing a short portion from the early Bible teaching material. Because at the time that material from 'Highway' was first being taught, the people listening always knew they had the opportunity to stand up and share their praise and joy with others about what they were hearing. And that time provided a great opportunity for people to stand up and begin to share with others who were hearing God's Word. Then as time passed, their understanding deepened, as they were hearing more and more of God's Word. And as they studied too God helped them grow in their understanding. And so they felt more and more equipped to take on the responsibility for teaching and sharing God's Word as part of the work.

They were hearing the Bible teaching in the village meeting, then as they were back in their own homes, they saw it as an opportunity, to discuss and share with one another the truth that they "owned" as their own. So in their homes they discussed together this new truth they were hearing, because they were so amazed by God's Word. Also there were resources to help believers who wanted to teach, like recordings that were made of the teaching, which helped new teachers as they talked about what had been taught. And they could discuss with each other what was being taught. Then eventually the local teachers were able to teach longer portions, or ask questions about what had been taught.

So the responsibility for the work began to change hands from the beginning. Because people were being equipped with literacy skills, and they were being equipped by God through His Word as they heard it. Because they felt equipped they were confident to teach even though it was something entirely new for them. And it was a wonderful thing for them and for those listening.

MIKE -

So Kaikou has described up until now, the earliest stage, or snapshot of the way in which the resource of God's Word has been used and the tools that accompany that in teaching. We wanted to mention also, in conjunction with that, that we are seeing, and trying literally and very definitely, to find opportunities for those who are participants in hearing the Word of God taught, to be included as much as possible in the process of they, themselves, being responsible to share God's Word with others around them.

So we are hearing the way in which, very early on in the progression of being taught - even for the first time - that the attempt is made to give over responsibility in certain areas of teaching to those who are hearing and them being included as participants in the work. Because the recognition is that they need to begin to take responsibility for as much as they can. And yet, at the same time, we are wanting to give care to the way in which that responsibility is handed over. Not only because we want to see God creating a clear identity for them in their engiftment through the Holy Spirit enlivening their hearts and giving gifts to them - perhaps as teachers, for example. So those we identify who might have the gift to teach, we want that gift to begin to be used, or implemented in the way that they are working together with church planters in those settings.

Not only that, but also very significantly they are exhibiting a desire to apply the truth that they have heard, that they have received. Even in the early stages, of demonstrating a faithful desire, a faithful hunger, for the Word of God to truly apply to their lives so that a growing sense of humility in their place in God's plan is accompanying that engiftment that we see exhibited. So just the caution of taking care in the early stages to cultivate a process of discipleship that accounts for both engiftment, and accounts for a genuine desire to apply God's Word to our lives as we move forward, growing as His disciples and look forward to the leadership roles that God might have for each one in the church.

So as God's Word is being taught for the first time, there is a group of hearers who have taken in God's Word, have applied it to their lives, who have become believers, some who have begun to take on certain areas of responsibility in the re-communication of God's Word. As that body of truth grows and is understood, as the momentum in the desire for God's Word being shared with others around them and in other communities - as that momentum and that hunger grows, and the recognition that the church that has been formed is sharing responsibility for sharing God's Word out to others - comes into existence, then we see the resources that have been applied by that group of growing believers in a new setting. Those resources can then be shared outward again to others. And at this time we see opportunities for these ones who have been growing in their understanding of how to teach those resources through various means that Kaikou is describing, they begin to reach out to others and to actually carry the primary responsibility for being the teachers in those new settings where they are going to share God's Word.

KAIKOU -

As he said, the resources are a help to those people who are beginning to teach God's Word, and who are beginning to take it to people who haven't yet heard. All of these resources are a support and help to new teachers, who feel it is their responsibility to share God's Word with others. These resources give them the ability to take God's Word out and to share the Word with those who haven't heard.

Often that means they will suffer and face many challenges as they do that. But they are dedicated to that work because they want people to believe. And they know that whatever suffering they go through, it will only deepen their resolve to continue to do their work. They are convinced that their work of taking God's Word to new communities, is their God-given responsibility, and they represent their local fellowships also. And when are out living and working in other communities, they know they find support and encouragement from their local churches, and also further teaching from God's Word. All of these resources that have been provided to help them, are a great encouragement to them as they go out to teach those who haven't heard as well as those within the church.

We have been talking about the work of taking God's Word to new communities, and an important part of that is how they will continue to grow. They won't be able to grow unless they are hearing more teaching from God's Word, and they also need resources for teaching and discipleship. Those who are going to teach them have access to good resources, and can get further teaching and lesson material, to help them in their work. So when they are working in a new community, they can work with the people in that community, and teach God's Word in a clear and systematic way, so that it provides a good model for the people there.

They should carefully build the foundations of truth so the people can grow in their spiritual understanding. And if they are going to help existing churches, where the truth of God's Word has been planted before, then they shouldn't just teach whatever they feel like teaching. They should think about the overall progression of God's work there, and teach the specific material that is needed for healthy growth. So one church might need teaching at a specific point, and another church might be at a different point. So different teachers might be using different resources, depending on which community they are teaching. The important consideration is to carefully build the foundation of truth, which is what God desires for each particular group of His children. To be fed so that they grow in a healthy way, from the part of God's Word that will help them most in that growth.

MIKE -

So as Kaikou is describing the way in which we make use of God's Word and specifically make use of these written resources that are tools for outreach to other communities, and we all together as believers in these situations stand on the common basis of our understanding of what has been carefully recorded, both in God's Word, and what has been provided in resources that help us to understand a common process for sharing God's Word with others.

We want to highlight that that creates a safeguard, even in situations where people groups would be described by some perhaps as 'oral cultures' or that 'orality' would be the primary basis for the ways in which they relate to one another. And yet we are introducing a written system, or a way to provide parameters or boundaries, such that as God's Word is communicated, from one set of communicators - leaders perhaps - to the next, that we all understand the mutual boundaries and basis for that. Then as you can imagine, as God's Word gets extended farther and farther beyond that point of origin, that we all together have a comfort level and are understanding the way in which God's Word is going to be understood and the way in which God's Word is going to be applied to each individual life as those hearers take that in, and then form communities of believers, form churches for themselves.

So that shared identity in God's written Word and in the resources that are written down and passed down from one group to another, are really significant in that process.

To this point we have described the introductory ways in which that balance of shared responsibility - between those who are being taught for the first time God's

Word, and those who are the initial teachers of God's Word - how that responsibility is balanced and shared. Our ultimate goal and desire is for those new believers who are growing in maturity to eventually take full ownership of this set of curricula that is being developed for the benefit of the church. So we have described these first steps of their going out with this resource that has been developed to new areas, new teaching opportunities, and they themselves taking responsibility for teaching that new material.

As we progress then through what we would describe as the foundational framework of the Epistles, that we have talked about, we continue to find ways to engage the growing disciples and growing teachers in the process of the development of this curriculum. Perhaps in opportunities of application, of God's Word to their lives, as we develop these lessons. Or in areas of the ways in which their own cultural background understanding comes to bear on what is being taught from God's Word, or supporting resources and texts that they have heard already from other parts of the Scripture prior to this point, that they bring those in to the way in which we write lessons.

As we move forward, we are moving towards a time when those who are demonstrating responsible application of God's Word to their own lives and demonstrating the kind of aptitude that we see in those we want to see as leaders in the church. As we are teaching forward we come to the time when we are teaching in Timothy and Titus and we are clearly explicating the qualifications for those leaders, the qualifications that we want those leaders to have, and we see those who are applying that standard to their lives. There comes a time when we indeed appoint leaders in the church who take on the eldership role and responsibility for those bodies of believers.

So as we come to that point then, we sense the opportunity again for another kind of a shift in responsibility and ownership of this curriculum development process that's ongoing for the church. And Kaikou is going to talk a little bit about some of the steps that occur as this growing group of leaders who have demonstrated competency in applying God's standard for their lives, that as they move forward in development of curriculum, some of the kinds of steps that they might be involved in.

KAIKOU -

We are going to talk about the church developing teaching resources, so that they can continue to grow. The task of developing teaching material is the responsibility of the elders of the church. But when did they take on that responsibility?

When we first heard the teaching from Revelation, there were no fully developed Bible lessons given to us for that. The lessons were taught clearly and fully to us, but the actual written lessons were not put in the hands of the church. That was going to be the work of the teachers and elders to develop those written lessons themselves. They began by writing the points that they would later use to teach from. These points were written when they heard the lessons being taught. This marked quite a change in the work of lesson development, as it became the work of the believers, or the leaders. The new lesson material was still taught to us, but the writing of lessons was done by the church leaders. They would hear the lesson taught, they would write down points, then they would develop lessons and teach them to the churches.

Then we moved on to Philippians. There was another development as we prepared Philippians lessons. There were no lessons, because it was the responsibility of the leaders to read it and to discuss how it should be taught to the believers. We read through the whole book and talked about it, using our understanding and the foundation of truth that we had, to decide how it should be presented to the believers. We began by writing down all of the important headings, then we worked together to flesh out the lessons fully using those headings. The Holy Spirit helped us in our work and we finished all the lessons.

Then we took those lessons and taught them to some of the believers. We wanted to check their comprehension. And those believers helped us to make changes to the flow of the lessons, or to make some of the examples communicate more clearly, and generally to give input on how the lessons communicated. Once that comprehension check was done, we taught those lessons to the whole group of Bible teachers. These are the steps we went through in learning to develop lessons. We taught the lessons to all the Bible teachers, so then they could go out and teach them in the churches where they work.

MIKE -

So as Kaikou has described some of the progressions that we see in opportunities for those who are leaders and who are growing in maturity in the church, to engage with this process of curriculum development - the development of resources for the church. What we are trying to illustrate is not so much the specific prescription of opportunity, as much as the kinds of opportunities that we want to encourage. We are trying to foster a genuine growth in confidence based on a common understanding of the Scriptures in the various places where we are teaching.

As we have established that underlying framework - in the beginning that we remember, that started with Genesis and moved its way through Acts and into the

Epistles, establishing the life of the church, their understanding of their growing life in the Lord Jesus Christ in His grace, moving into the future era of God's culmination of all events in the end times that we see in Revelation - we have established that underlying framework, both as a narrative progression but also as a Biblical theological progression. So on the basis of that underlying narrative framework, then we feel confident as we encourage the process and progress of these steps of involvement, that there is a substantial safeguard basis for these teachers to continue to develop lessons that would be of benefit to the church, based on God's Word that they have previously received.

I think about two different aspects of what we would describe as a further along place of ownership and responsibility for teachers in lesson development. One is this continuing growth in the opportunities for learning in technological helps that may or may not be available to them. For example, in their early days, of literally doing notes in notebooks and using a blackboard to write the lessons out, and it was quite a tedious and lengthy process. Then having opportunity later to introduce computer technology and to allow those who have the aptitude to learn to type to be the ones to help to input those lessons so they can be sent away to be printed - either printed locally, or printed in another place where printing is available. But nonetheless, the idea that many times there is an accompanying technological development that really facilitates the growth in the ability of the teachers practically to produce the lessons or the curriculum that they are working on.

In addition then, to see the team coming to a point where their ownership of the process is as extensive as them being able to read together books of the Scriptures, books of the New Testament or perhaps some books of the Old Testament, and together to read that book sufficiently well - to use the translation that has been developed and to use the outline that is available in the translation itself - to outline the logical flow of the teaching material. And together to actually create a teaching outline for the flow of that book of the Bible, and then together to be able to flesh out, not only the narrative or the expositional content of the book, but also to feel very confident in that expositional flow to insert culturally relevant applications. To insert supporting texts that would now include a large part of the New Testament and some of the Old Testament as well and then to be able to apply those lessons that they are developing to people's lives in the community around them in the way that they feel very confident that the parameters that have been established over the course of quite a long period of time, of learning to apply God's Word to their lives in a very personal way and of growing in confidence in the exposition of God's Word, and teaching God's Word. A solid foundation has been established, giving them confidence that they can really take on the whole process from start to finish of reading God's Word for themselves, having resources that have been developed, being able to gather as a team to develop new teaching material, to put it into a form where they call all collectively access it and then to teach it to the church and to feel confident that at the end of the process they have taught God's Word faithfully and clearly in a culturally relevant way to the communities in which they are living.

❓ DISCUSSION POINTS

1. Summarize in point form what Kaikou and Mike say about the role of literacy.

2. Think about the process of discipleship described here - as it relates to the development of resources - and summarize in point form the process of the shift in responsibility from the church planters to the local leaders and believers.

ACCESSTRUTH

Training Resources for Making Truth *Accessible*.

RESOURCES FOR

- Discipleship
- Evangelism
- Church Planting
- Language Learning
- Bible Translation
- Cross-cultural work

Equipping God's people to be more effective as they serve in cross-cultural contexts, either locally or globally.

accesstruth.com

www.ingramcontent.com/pod-product-compliance
Lightning Source LLC
Chambersburg PA
CBHW080408300426
44113CB00015B/2443